THE AUTHOR Richard Tames read history at Cambridge and took his Master's Degree at the University of London. He has been a speaker for the Japanese Embassy for twenty years and was formerly Head of External Services at the School of Oriental and African Studies. He is the author of *Encounters with Japan* and *Servant of the Shogun*, a biography of William Adams and also of *A Traveller's History of London* in this series.

SERIES EDITOR Professor Denis Judd is a Fellow of the Royal Historical Society and Professor of History at the University of North London. He has published over 20 books including biographies of Joseph Chamberlain, Prince Philip, George VI and Alison Uttley, historical and military subjects, stories for children and two novels. He has reviewed extensively in the national press and in journals, and has written several radio programmes.

The front cover shows a detail from a Yokahama print ca. 1870, showing the first railway in Japan which ran between Tokyo and Yokohama.

Other Titles in the Series

A Traveller's History of Japan

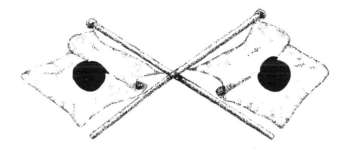

A Traveller's History of Japan

Second Edition

RICHARD TAMES

Series Editor DENIS JUDD
Line drawings SCOTT HALL

INTERLINK BOOKS
An Imprint of Interlink Publishing Group, Inc.
NEW YORK

Updated edition 1997

First American edition published 1997 by

INTERLINK BOOKS
An imprint of Interlink Publishing Group, Inc.
99 Seventh Avenue
Brooklyn, New York 11215

Published simultaneously in Great Britain by The Windrush Press

Library of Congress Cataloging-in-Publication Data

Tames, Richard.
    A traveller's history of Japan / Richard Tames.
        p.   cm. — (Traveller's history)
    Includes bibliographical references and index.
    ISBN 1–56656–260–0
    1. Japan—History.   I. Title.   II. Series.
DS835.T3243   1993
952—dc20   93–8074
                                                               CIP

Printed and bound in Canada

This book is dedicated to the memory of
Professor Keith Thurley – a friend of Japan

Contents

Preface

In 1902 Britain signed a limited treaty of alliance with the rising world power of Japan. This was done mainly, it must be said, in order to gain a competent military friend in East Asia who would keep a watchful eye on an expansionist Russia and a moribund China, and who would thus, by proxy, contribute to the security of the British Empire's brightest jewel, India. To many Britons, the step was a sign of weakness, and King Edward VII privately bemoaned the necessity of an alliance with 'little yellow men' simply to protect the Indian Empire. To others, the Japanese were an inscrutable and impossibly remote people, who had recently been ruthlessly mocked in Gilbert and Sullivan's *Mikado*. As so often, it needed Kipling to produce a reassuring image:

> East is East, and West is West, and never the twain shall meet,
> 'Til two strong men stand face to face before thy judgement seat.

Within two decades, however, the Anglo-Japanese alliance had been scrapped, and after 1941 Japan proceeded to rip the heart out of Britain's Far Eastern Empire and to threaten the territorial integrity of both India and Australia.

Today it is not, thankfully, Japanese militarism that poses a threat to Western security and self-esteem, but Japan's extraordinary capacity to produce a range of high-tech consumer goods of such outstanding quality, reliability and value that they swamp and outsell most of their European and American equivalents. Bismarck once ruminated that the twenty-first century would belong to Canada; but, as the twentieth century draws to a close, Japan looks infinitely the better bet.

Since it is no longer possible comfortingly to dismiss the Japanese as a far-off and fundamentally inconsequential people, we desperately need to understand them. Richard Tames' book will go far to satisfy that need. It is written with great authority, clarity and scholarly balance. It provides, in addition, a comprehensive history that is lively, detailed and immensely readable. Despite the Western caricature of the Japanese tourist, polite and bedecked with cameras (made in Japan, naturally), the Japanese are as yet not great travellers to other people's countries. But increasing numbers of foreigners go on holidays to Japan, and I can think of no better introduction to the complexities of Japanese society and to the richness and variety of the Japanese past than this accessible and well constructed book.

As Richard Tames points out, the Japanese are an astoundingly homogenous people:

> To be Japanese is to be a Japanese citizen, born in Japan, living there and speaking Japanese. State, people and language coincide to a degree altogether remarkable in the modern world. Ninety-nine per cent of all the Japanese in the world live in Japanese itself... Japan has no minority greater than one per cent which is different by virtue of religion or ethnicity.

The early European travellers to Japan were impressed by a people who seemed: 'tractable, civil, wittie, courteous, without deceit, in virtue and honest conversation exceeding all other nations lately discovered'. But there was something else. On their first, accidental, landfall some Portuguese shot at duck while waiting for their ship to be repaired. Although the Japanese had never seen a gun before, they took note, and within six months had learned how to manufacture them. Thus, some four hundred and fifty years ago, the Japanese gave early warning of their potential as rivals to Europe's global technological and industrial supremacy.

Denis Judd

The Past in the Present

'In Japan, more than in any Western country, it is necessary to take some trouble in order to master ... preliminary information ... He ... who should essay to travel without having learnt a word concerning Japan's past, would run the risk of forming opinions ludicrously erroneous...'

This advice, from Murray's *Handbook for Travellers in Japan*, published over a century ago, still holds good.

A generation later the poet Edmund Blunden, who taught English literature at Tokyo University, warned newcomers that 'Japan does not disappoint the stranger; she corrects his fancies, perhaps a little grimly and then begins to enrich him with her truths.'

The Japanese

The Japanese see themselves largely as Westerners see them – polite, loyal, hard-working, conformist and not profoundly inventive. They also see national characteristics that foreigners often overlook – their high average level of education, their profound sensitivity to nature. And they reverse some commonly-held prejudices, regarding themselves as warm, impulsive and sentimental and Westerners as cold, calculating and unfathomable.

Writing a century ago Basil Hall Chamberlain, doyen of early 'Japanologists', observed that the most characteristic virtues of the Japanese were cleanliness, kindliness and a refined aesthetic sense, while their shortcomings included a disregard for the intrinsic value of truth and an inability to appreciate abstract ideas. Acutely aware of how prone Western visitors were to pass snap-judgments on Japan and its people, he reminded his Western readers that cultural contact was a two-way process and Japanese, though they were usually too tactful to articulate them, made judgments of their own:

> ... the travelled Japanese consider our three most prominent characteristics to be dirt, laziness and superstition ... Europe and America make a far less favourable impression on the Japanese visitor than seems to be generally expected. Be he statesman or be he valet, he is apt to return to his native land more patriotic than he left it.

Japanese take pride in the orderliness of their society and the antiquity of their culture. Above all they take pride, diffidently, perhaps, but nonetheless fervently, in the fact that they are Japanese – and no one else is. This is not entirely true, but Japanese nationals largely ignore the extent to which it is not. The residents of Japanese descent in California, Hawaii, Brazil and Peru are not, in a sense, 'really' Japanese. To be Japanese is to be a Japanese citizen, born in Japan, living there and speaking Japanese. State, people and language coincide to a degree altogether remarkable in the modern world. Ninety-nine per cent of all the Japanese in the world live in Japan itself. No other nation with a population over 100,000,000 exhibits such homogeneity. Despite the persistence of dialect forms, all Japanese can speak the national standard version of their language – which no other country in the world speaks. Although they have a strong attachment to their rural roots, the average urban Japanese would find the sort of regionalism that animates a Catalan or an Ulsterman difficult to grasp. Japan has no minority greater than 1 per cent which is different by virtue of religion or ethnicity. There are about a million Christians. There are some 600,000 Koreans, though many of these have become culturally assimilated to the extent of not even speaking Korean any longer. There are some tens of thousands of Ainu, the descendants of the aboriginal inhabitants of the Japanese archipelago. Other nations of comparable size, whether they consider themselves mosaics or melting-pots, are striking in their diversities of race, religion and language.

A WORLD APART?

Japanese identity is seldom challenged by the effects of alien contact. Whatever impression they might give, the Japanese are not yet among the world's great tourist nations. The annual number of Japanese travelling abroad passed the 10,000,000 mark for the first time in 1990; even so this represented only 8 per cent of the population. (During the same year 50 per cent of Britain's population travelled abroad.) Little wonder, perhaps, when a 1988 poll revealed that 80 per cent of Japanese who like to travel abroad admit to being afraid of getting into trouble or having an accident.

Largely innocent of foreign contact overseas, the Japanese are unlikely to be troubled by foreigners at home. There are more Arabs or Americans in the London region than there are Westerners of all nationalities in the whole of Japan. Tokyo's most cosmopolitan area has a population which is just under 95 per cent Japanese. Little wonder that the Japanese for foreigner – *gaijin* – literally means 'outside person'.

NIHONJINRON

The distinctiveness of Japan has given rise to a distinctive genre of writing – *Nihonjinron* – books about the notion or condition of 'Japaneseness'. There has been a constant stream of such books for over a century and often they find their way onto the bestseller lists. They tackle the matter from every possible perspective – from linguistics to psychiatry, from brain-hemisphere functions to child-rearing practices. Barriers which allegedly arise from a perception of profound cultural differences between Japan and other peoples have a demonstrable basis in fact. But are the Japanese really unique? Certainly many of them like to think so.

KEEPING IN STEP

The Japanese must be the world's greatest natural team. Surveys reveal that 90 per cent consider themselves middle-class, 87 per cent say they like to look like everyone else and 84 per cent confess themselves unable to turn down requests from other people. Ninety-nine per cent of homes have a colour TV and a washing-machine; 98 per cent have a refrigerator and a vacuum-cleaner. The same percentage of households still makes New Year offerings to the gods. Over 90 per cent of girls at senior high school possess a piggy-bank, a stuffed toy, a brush-pen, an English–Japanese dictionary and more than forty-six cassette tapes. Eighty-five per cent of couples are still married in a Shinto ceremony. Over 80 per cent of families own a *kotatsu* (traditional-style heater), a *futon* (floor-mattress), a sake-server and an abacus. (Modernisation does not = Westernisation!) If you want to be different in Japan join the 2 per cent or less who have a yacht, a BMW, a home help or a law-nmower; play chess, bridge or billiards; go in for body-building, judo, karate or kendo; oppose the emperor or belong to the Communist party; are divorced or admit to having an affair; have naturally very curly hair; or eat croissants for breakfast.

How did the Japanese get to be like this?

Read on.

CHAPTER ONE

Myths and Mysteries, Prehistory to AD 500

Land of the Gods?

Modern Japan seems an unlikely setting for one of the world's most advanced industrial cultures – four-fifths mountainous, poorly endowed with minerals and energy supplies, periodically battered by typhoons, earthquakes and volcanic eruptions, lacking even a great navigable waterway like the Rhine or the Danube. But, in the light of a long history and the requirements of pre-modern technologies, nature was not unkind to the ancestors of the Japanese. If occasionally violent, it was also generous. The climate, if humid in the south and frigid in the far north, avoids the extremes in which for millennia many other peoples have battled for mere survival. Rainfall is abundant, the flora varied, afforestation dense and the surrounding seas rich in fish, still the major source of dietary protein.

W.G.Aston, one of the pioneers of ancient Japanese history, noted that the earliest forms of Japanese religion were grounded in a reverence for nature which reflected gratitude and delight, rather than fear. Perhaps surprisingly there was no powerful myth of a terrible earthquake god and even the storm god was conceived as benign. The Japanese saw divinity all around them – in the awe-inspiring sun and moon, in useful springs and berry-bearing bushes and also in things that struck them as simply beautiful, like flowers and even rocks. If, as seems likely, their ancestral homeland was the bleak Siberian plain or the arid mountains of northern China and Korea, Japan may indeed have seemed a demi-paradise of fruitfulness in comparison. Certainly the names they gave it seem to confirm this, 'Land of Abundant Reed Plains' or 'Land of Fresh Rice Ears of a Thousand Autumns'.

For most of its recorded history, Japan was large in relation to its population. Small by comparison with China or the USA (Japan is pretty much the same size as California) it is nevertheless larger than Italy, Poland, Germany or Britain. For the first thousand years of its statehood it was a 'frontier society', extending its boundary ever northward by conquest and settlement.

A WORLD APART?

Above all, Japan has had the blessing of isolation and thus freedom from the constant invasions which have so dramatically shaped the history of its Asian neighbours. The adoption of foreign ways has been a formative element in the evolution of the national culture, but the process has usually been voluntary, selective and gradual. It has also been conscious. Foreign visitors and goods have never, since Japan began to achieve statehood around the fourth century AD, silently penetrated across frontiers undetected but arrived a few at a time and visibly, by ship. The habitual tendency of the Japanese to distinguish between 'foreign' and 'native' aspects of the culture (even if the latter now includes baseball and *curri-raisu* – curry and rice) has very ancient roots. Paradoxically the very willingness of the Japanese to acknowledge how much they have borrowed has led many to dismiss them as a copycat nation, incapable of originating their own culture. A moment's reflection on the uniqueness of Shinto, the distinctiveness of the Japanese language, the individuality of the Japanese aesthetic and the sheer number of untranslatable Japanese words for specific modes of perception and feeling, should suffice to dismiss such inanity.

Kind or unkind, the peculiarities of Japan's natural endowments have had a marked effect on the cultural patterns which have evolved within her clearly marked boundaries. The distinct transitions which mark the passage of the seasons have had the most profound and enduring impact on generations of Japanese poets and painters. No less significant has been the convoluted legacy of a corrugated landscape. According to Emeritus Professor Sakamoto Taro, a leading

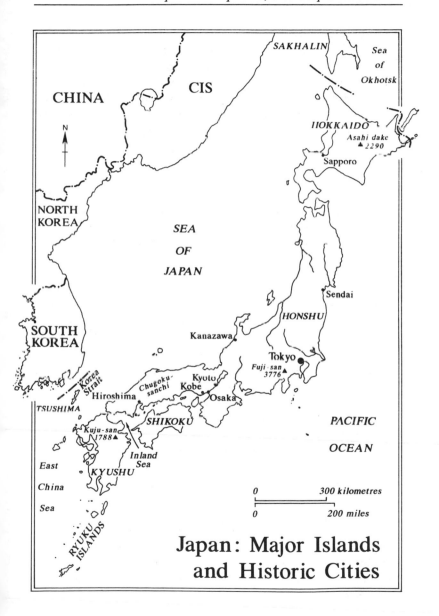

Japan: Major Islands
and Historic Cities

expert on the ancient period, the country's 'mountainous, confined topography' must bear much responsibility for 'the lack of mighty vistas in the spiritual life of the people, their strongly exclusivist, sectional attitude, and the tendency to give birth to small, regional governments'. In Japan's subsequent history these traits have found expression in the cult of *kami* (guardian spirits of specific localities), in sentimental attachment to one's *furusato* (home village) and in dedicated loyalty to a feudal clan or, in modern times, one's company.

Gods of the Land?

The Japanese are intensely interested in themselves. Consequently they are interested in who they were and where they came from. The notions of ancestry and identity are closely interlinked. Consider, for example, the line taken by the same distinguished Professor Sakamoto, writing in 1971 in a semi-official publication intended for foreign teachers and students:

> Who, then, were the men (*sic*) who settled on this Japanese archipelago and were responsible for unfolding the history of Japan? One thing certain is that they are a distinct people, resembling in their physical features neighbouring peoples such as the Koreans, Manchurians and Mongolians, but not necessarily identical. It is also certain that the same people has been in residence consistently from the Stone Age up to the present day, with no transfers on the way due to migration or conquest ... the backbone of the Japanese people consists of a group of the primitive Ural-Altaic linguistic stock that came from northern Asia via Karafuto and Hokkaido.... The main stock received certain additions from the Ainu, who came from the north, from Koreans ... and also, in the southern part of Kyushu, from Indonesia. This racial intermingling continued on into historical times, but was at no stage sufficient to effect a general change in the nature of the basic stock.... While not rejecting other stock, they seem to have absorbed it without in any way sacrificing their own integrity or special characteristics.

Beneath the bland academic prose and carefully qualified statements lies an implied claim to a special sort of national identity, though the actual words 'racial purity' are never used. The *Encyclopaedia Britannica*, by contrast, notes with brusque scepticism:

> The present Japanese people were produced by an admixture of certain strains from the Asian continent and from the South Pacific.... Nothing can yet be proved concerning their relationship with the people of the Pre-Ceramic period, but it cannot be asserted that they were entirely unrelated.

Sir George Sansom, writing over sixty years ago, when there was as yet little firm archaeological evidence to underpin the debate about ethnic origins, summarised the position with judicious tentativeness in language of characteristic elegance:

> The archaeological evidence proves only that there was a fairly uniform civilisation in Japan prior to the Christian era. The ethnical fusion which produced the Japanese race goes back to a remoter antiquity, of which we have no knowledge, and the most that we can safely say is that the Japanese from the end of the Stone Age onward exhibit a blend of many ethnic features.

Sansom goes on to offer an intriguing analogy between the settlement of the British Isles and that of the Japanese archipelago:

> Behind each is a great and variously peopled continent, beyond each is an immense stretch of ocean. Each was a pocket, in which immigrants driven by the pressure of hunger and fear, or perhaps by the plain desire for change, might assemble, and where, because they could not go farther, they must fuse or perish.

Uncovering the Past

Japan's archaeological record is now believed to be much longer than was thought when Sansom was writing; but modern scientific archaeology is less than a century old. Its founding father was the American E.S.Morse (1838–1925), first Professor of Zoology at Tokyo University (1877–9) who excavated a 'shell mound' at Omori, near Tokyo, thus throwing the first light on the daily life (and more particularly the daily diet) of Stone Age Japanese. Although Japanese scholars eagerly followed Morse's lead in conducting excavations they became increasingly hampered by right-wing political pressures when it came to publication. Discoveries that inconveniently contradicted the officially approved account of Japan's national origins – which traced the descent of the current emperor back to the accession to the throne in 660 BC of Jimmu, descendant of the Sun Goddess – could not only cost the luckless scholar his job but also land him in prison. The past was to be revered rather than investigated.

Post-war democratisation has lifted the intellectual shutters and the post-war construction boom has inadvertently uncovered a wealth of sites to be systematically recorded and analysed. (Tombs thought to be royal, however, are still under the watchful control of the Royal Household Agency; access to them is strictly limited and many remain untouched.) More than 15,000 archaeological sites have now been excavated, at least 2,000 of which date from the Paleolithic (Old Stone Age) period. It now seems certain that Japan has been inhabited, not for 3,000 years as was thought at the beginning of this century, but for 30,000, and perhaps even as much as 50,000.

PEOPLE BEFORE POTS

The very first inhabitants of Japan were a hunting-gathering people who used stone tools and weapons but were ignorant of pottery and weaving. They came via land-bridges which, until about 20,000 years ago, linked what is now the Japanese archipelago with the Asian mainland, with Hokkaido being joined to Siberia and western Honshu with Korea. What is now the Sea of Japan, dividing Japan from Korea, was then an immense lake.

THE JOMON CULTURE

Global warming around 10,000 BC appears to have had the benevolent effect of enriching plant and animal life and thus enlarging the margin for survival. The inhabitants of Japan mastered a technique of firing coiled clay to make pots. The culture of this period is known as Jomon (cord-marked) from the distinctive decorative style of its ceramics. The pots were used to cook, to store food and water and for burial purposes. With the passage of time decorative motifs became increasingly lux-uriant, progressing from simple herring-bone patterns to snake's-head designs. Jomon pottery is the oldest pottery in the world to which a definite date can be assigned and, in its variety of design, remains unsurpassed by that of any other stone-age culture.

Jomon people also made baskets of wicker and wore robes made from the bark of mulberry trees. Rubbish-tip remains suggest a diet of bear, boar and deer; fish and shell-fish; yams, wild grapes, walnuts, chestnuts and acorns. There may have been occasional trade between highland and coastal regions, exchanging obsidian for salt. Stylised clay figurines, known as *dogu*, have been found in quantity; they may have been used in rituals associated with healing or birth. Jomon people also wore jewellery of bone or shell and filed or pulled out their teeth. What became the Japanese language, a distant relative of Korean and an even more distant relative of Mongolian and Turkish, also probably developed in this period.

The ancestors of the Japanese shared their land with the Ainu, a north Asian Caucasoid people, distinguishable from the Japanese by appearance, language and culture. The eventual fate of the Ainu was to be driven ever further into the inhospitable north. Japanese, referring to them as Ezo or Emishi, came to regard them as barbarians. Eventually they were confined to the island of Hokkaido where their descendants number only some tens of thousands. Anthropologists and tourists, in their very different ways, have contributed to preserving the vestiges of their highly distinctive culture (*see pp. 137, 269*).

YAYOI CULTURE

A new cultural phase began *ca* 300 BC and over the next five centuries Japanese life changed profoundly with the introduction of wet rice cultivation in paddy-fields and the revolutionary technologies of weaving and metal-working. Most societies have proceeded from a period in which bronze was the main metal to one in which iron superseded it. In Japan bronze and iron metallurgy arrived from China together. Nevertheless, despite the significant advances in warfare and agriculture which mastery of metals made possible, this era is also named after a pottery type, unearthed at Yayoicho in Tokyo in 1884. Jomon culture was not, however, suddenly displaced and the two ways of life co-existed for some time before Yayoi culture emerged as dominant.

An extensively-excavated and partially-reconstructed Yayoi-period site can be seen at Toro, Shizuoka. The village had thatched-roof houses, raised storehouses (on rat-proof collared posts) and complex irrigation and drainage systems. The regularity of paddy-field palings and the planks used to build storehouses suggest the ready availability of iron-bladed tools, though stone reaping-knives were also still in use. Basic Yayoi artefacts, such as the hoe, the pestle and *geta* (wooden clogs), are recognisably the forerunners of traditional Japanese household goods.

Yayoi burials containing grave goods such as beads, figurines and bronze mirrors imply a society with marked distinctions of social rank. It seems likely that these distinctions were signified by facial tattooes or body-painting. Mounds set apart from more general burial sites point to the existence of petty kings or chieftains. Some metal objects, such as weapons, bells and mirrors are so delicate that they were almost certainly made as ritual objects or status symbols rather than for actual use. Their sacred character is attested by their discovery in caves and on hilltops rather than among the remains of regular settlements.

The religious beliefs of this period involved a form of shamanism and focused on fertility, purity and fear of the dead but it is hazardous to be more precise than that.

THE KOFUN PERIOD

The last stage of Japan's prehistory begins in the fourth century AD and is known as the *Kofun* ('old tomb') period from burial mounds, round, square or combined in a 'keyhole' (*zenpokoen* – 'square front and round back') shape which is unique among mound-building cultures. More than ten thousand *kofun* have been discovered. The earliest and most numerous are in the Yamato region, south of Kyoto. From this region the royal house of Japan takes its name and from its early rulers claims descent. The largest *kofun*, associated with the legendary Emperor Nintoku, lies on the Osaka Plain; it covers eighty acres, is almost 500 metres long and surrounded by three moats. In terms of the labour required for its construction Nintoku's mausoleum easily rivals the pyramids of Egypt and must be reckoned one of the great monuments of the world.

The slopes of many *kofun* were profusely planted with earthenware *haniwa* ('rings of clay') in the shape of priests, dancers, mourners, ani-

The tumulus of the Emperor Nintoku in Osaka. Constructed in the fifth
century it is 475 metres in length

mals, ships, houses and other objects, though most were simple
cylinders. They were probably functional (to stabilise the earth) as well
as decorative and provide detailed evidence of a martial and aristocratic
society dominated by mounted warriors who wore tailored, quilted
clothing or armour of overlapping plates. The sheer numbers of surviving *haniwa* imply mass-production by specialised craftsmen.

By the fifth or sixth century a single kingly line seems to have been
asserting its pre-eminence in the Yamato region and claiming descent
from the Sun Goddess. The distribution of Yamato-made ritual goods,
such as bronze mirrors and iron swords, well beyond this core area,
suggests acknowledgment of suzerainty and vassalage by lesser *uji* (clans)
and their chieftains, who appear to have been awarded such titles as
'Leaders of Provinces' or 'Attendant Families'. Great importance seems
to have been attached to these titles, which recognised both rank and
lineage, so much so that later sources ascribe to Yamato rulers the
promulgation of decrees against false claims and forgeries. A preoccupation with titles has therefore been a significant cultural trait in
Japan since the very emergence of its statehood.

The richer treasures found in later *kofun*, such as crowns or shoes of gold and silver, suggest both increasing concentrations of power and wealth and greater contact with the far more advanced civilisation of China and its Korean off-shoot. The 'curved jewels' (*magatama*) found in tombs of this period are identical with those found among the regalia of the Korean kingdom of Silla. Some of these *magatama* were made of materials, such as jade, which are not to be found in Japan but originate in central Asia. Almost all of the largest *kofun* contain mirrors, swords and jewels as marks of the highest rank. At the coronation of the current Japanese emperor he, like his ancestors, was invested with the 'Three Sacred Treasures' as symbols of his exalted position – a mirror, a sword and a jewel.

YAMATO AND YAMATAI

Throughout the Yayoi and Kofun periods there were contacts between Japan and the peoples of China and Korea. Professor Egami Namio has suggested that the *haniwa* horsemen and the increased presence of horse-related grave-goods, such as saddles and stirrups, indirectly chronicle a dramatic invasion by Central Asian conquistadores on horseback in the fourth century, a knock-on from the steppe nomad incursions which shook China and Korea at that time. Certainly the technological achievements of the period imply the presence of mainland teachers or at least models. There is, however, no documentary support for the invasion theory. But there is evidence to suggest that Japanese rulers pursued a 'forward policy', meddling in the politics of the Korean peninsula, and held what might even be regarded as a small colony at its southern tip. Korean historians, not surprisingly, play down the significance of all this and certainly the predominance of influences was from Korea and China to Japan, rather than vice versa. The fact that immigrant groups served as the first scribes and chroniclers in Japan, when the Japanese language had no form of writing, leaves little room for doubt about the relative sophistication of Japanese culture *vis-à-vis* that of its mainland neighbours.

While the extent and nature of the contacts between Japan and the rest of Asia remain a subject for further research, it is certain that the earliest written accounts of Japan are Chinese. The *Wei Chronicle*, dating from the third century, covers 'Yamatai' among its 'accounts of

A sixth- to seventh-century *Haniwa* figure

the eastern barbarians'. Japan as a whole is the 'Land of Wa' (Wa in this reading signifying dwarf), divided into many petty states. The most powerful ruler was identified as a cloistered sorceress, Himiko ('Sun Daughter'), who was eventually buried with a hundred of her slaves. The inhabitants of 'Yamatai' exhibit a number of characteristics very recognisable as Japanese, combining stoicism with sentimentality and a propensity for drunkenness with a strict regard for propriety. Law-abiding men, with faithful and uncomplaining wives, they already appear to have acquired a deep dread of foreign travel. Was 'Yamatai' Yamato? Possibly. But it also might have been in northern Kyushu.

The debate among Japanese scholars started in the eleventh century. It has not yet been resolved.

SO FAR – NOT VERY FAR

For a summary of Japan's progress on the eve of its impassioned embrace of Chinese culture it is difficult to improve on Sir Hugh Cortazzi for bluntness:

> ... Japan was a primitive agricultural society with at best a rudimentary system of government. Its religious practices amounted to little more than an animist fertility cult without coherent philosophy or ethical system. Its traditions were little more than blood-thirsty and crude myths. It had no written language and no literature, although some poetic songs were preserved in the oral memory of a few.... Art was limited to the making of unglazed and simple pottery, the modelling of pottery figures and the making of increasingly complex metal items.... Japan before the arrival of Chinese influence ... had no real claim to a civilisation of its own.

Perhaps one might modify that slightly – Japanese culture? Yes. Japanese civilisation? Not yet.

But the larger point to bear in mind is that, despite the huge gulf between the two countries in terms of size and level of cultural development, Japan went on to absorb Chinese achievements – not to be absorbed by China.

CHAPTER TWO

Chinese Shadows,
500–800

Buddhism

Tradition holds that in 552 (though it may well have been in 538) the Korean state of Paekche presented to the Yamato court an image of the Buddha, together with a collection of scriptures expounding his teaching. Shortly afterwards this was followed by the despatch of experts versed in the Chinese classics, in medicine, in music, in calendric calculation and in divination. Although some conservatives opposed the new religion it attracted the patronage of the ambitious Soga family, who had risen to prominence through their skill as managers of royal estates. The conservatives were led by the Nakatomi clan, guardians of traditional ritual, and the Mononobe clan, whose special expertise lay in defence and security. In 587 the Soga emerged from a brief but bloody struggle over the imperial succession as the most dominant faction at court. By the end of the century Buddhism was firmly established as the cult of the power élite.

As Sansom observes sardonically:

> There is a somewhat ironical interest in the fact that this gospel of gentleness was recommended to the Japanese by a hard-pressed monarch begging for the loan of troops, and owed its adoption by them in a great measure to the bitter jealousy of political rivals.

Just as Christianity in the same period served as a vehicle for the transfer of Mediterrranean sophistication to northern Europe so Buddhism was accompanied by the importation of the high culture of China. The leaders of Japanese society initiated a new phase in their relations with the mainland – a deliberate, organised and sustained attempt to acquire and transplant both its practical and intellectual achievements. The time was especially propitious . In 589 the Sui had reunited China after more than three centuries of division and in 618 the T'ang established one of its most brilliant and durable dynasties. Japan was fortunate to have as its mentor the most powerful and advanced country in the world.

SHOTOKU

The Soga hegemony was confirmed by the accession to the throne in 593 of a Soga empress, Suiko, with real power placed in the hands of a regent, her nephew, Prince Shotoku (574–622) who was also part Soga himself. Taking China as their pattern Shotoku and his Soga patrons proceeded to revolutionise the institutions of their native country. In 603 he began to introduce Chinese methods of bureaucratic rule, matching rank to office and favouring promotion (if not initial selec-

Prince Shotoku, courtly sponsor of Chinese culture

tion) on grounds of merit. By the middle of the eighth century all posts were to be assigned within a clearly-defined hierarchy of twenty-eight grades, ranging from 'Senior First Rank' to 'Junior Eighth Rank Lower Grade'. These titles were to continue in use until the modernisation of the state on Western lines over a thousand years later (*see Chapter 7*).

Shotoku's 'Seventeen Article Constitution', issued in 604, set out the basic parameters of a new political landscape. It was less a constitution in the modern sense than a list of moral maxims but it still deserves its original name, which literally means 'splendid decree'. Rather than first among equals, the ruler was henceforth to be indisputably supreme and referred to as *Tenno* – 'Heavenly Sovereign'. All citizens, including therefore the great clan leaders, were his subjects and owed him obedience. Governmental powers, hitherto diffused, were to be centralised. In the religious sphere Buddhism should be revered and in the moral, the teachings of the Chinese sage Confucius (*ca* 551–478BC). Loyalty, diligence and self-control were praised as supreme personal virtues because they all contributed to harmony, the supreme social virtue. In the same year, 604, the Chinese calendar was also adopted.

In 607 Shotoku despatched a large diplomatic mission to China; another was sent in 608 and another in 614. The official letter to the Chinese emperor, sent with the mission of 607, referred to Japan, for the first time in history, as the 'Land of the Rising Sun'; and, by addressing the Chinese ruler as sovereign of the 'Land of the Setting Sun', implied parity of status between the two states, rather than a tributary relationship. Missions several hundred strong continued to be sent for the next two and a quarter centuries despite their great expense and the danger involved in a sea voyage of five hundred miles through stormy waters and often in the teeth of Korean hostility. The nominal leadership of these expeditions may have lain with their courtly figureheads but their significance derived from the efforts of the monks, scholars, painters and musicians who made up their entourage, and the emigrants – from concubines to craftsmen – who accompanied their return.

Shotoku appears to have been not only pious but learned, composing his own commentaries on the Buddhist sutras, as well as supporting the foundation of monasteries. By the time of his death Japan was said to have forty-six Buddhist temples and 1,345 monks and nuns. By the end of the century the number of Buddhist temples had increased more than tenfold. Shotoku became the focus of a cult as early as the eighth century, some of his devotees regarding him as an incarnation of the Buddha himself. He is conventionally styled *Shotoku Taishi* – 'Crown Prince Virtuous Sage' – and remains one of Japan's most revered culture-heroes. His likeness still adorns the modern 10,000 yen banknote. The Asuka river valley, where he held court, has yielded the remains of more than fifty temples, palaces and burial mounds.

The Taika Reforms

Soga dominance degenerated into despotism after Shotoku's death (his own son was assassinated in 643). The Soga were overthrown by an imperial *coup d'état* in 645. The name chosen for the new era was Taika – 'Great Change'. Led by the successful conspirators, the Emperor Tenji and his henchman Nakatomi no Kamatari (614–69) (*see p. 35*), the government embarked on a second wave of Chinese-style reforms, eagerly supported by Sinophiles from the previous embassies. Five more major diplomatic missions were sent between 653 and 669. Enthusiasm for reform as a means of strengthening the state may have been further stimulated by the disastrous defeat of a Japanese armada at the hands of a mixed Chinese–Korean force in 663. This ended a century of Japanese efforts to hang on to the foothold on the Korean peninsula. The major features of the Taika programme included:

– establishing a capital, with Chinese-style buildings
– creating central government ministries
– attempting to reduce provincial administration to a uniform pattern
– building roads and horse-stations to improve communications
– instituting a centralised system of taxation
– carrying out a census
– drawing-up systematic codes of law.

In practice the reformers had to compromise with vested interests and the limits of their resources. These resources were, however, enlarged by the incorporation of southern Kyushu into the state and the gradual conquest of northern Honshu from its Ainu inhabitants. Japanese adoption of Chinese practice was by no means slavish and wherever the need was felt Chinese procedures were either modified or ignored. The Chinese method of ascertaining bureaucratic merit through rigorous competitive examinations, for example, was never introduced; the hereditary principle was already far too strong in Japan for it to be swept aside. Many 'appointments' were therefore little more than confirmations of familial succession. Although court ceremonies and amusements, such as music (*gagaku*) and dances, were also drawn from China the existing imperial rituals associated with Shinto were dutifully maintained. This underlined an enduring and fundamental distinction between the Chinese and Japanese emperors. Chinese political philosophy envisaged the possibility of a lapse in imperial virtue and capability, leading to the withdrawal of the 'mandate of heaven'. Japanese tradition recognised no transferable mandate. It had been conferred on the Yamato line not by virtue of its military prowess nor as a result of its political skill but simply on account of its divine descent. The mandate was therefore for all time. Emperors might be vigorous and decisive men or mere infants subject to factional manipulation. Their legitimacy remained unimpaired. The ritual duties required of them were in essence simple. To this day, for example, the emperor continues to plant out rice in the spring and cut it in the autumn in a specially-reserved plot tucked away in a corner of the grounds of the Imperial Palace.

The new system of government was eventually embodied in the *Taiho* ('Great Treasure') penal (*ritsu*) and administrative (*ryo*) code of 702. The principles underlying the *ritsuryo*, Japan's first formal legal code, remained the basis of the legal system until the nineteenth century, although the specific laws were revised in 718 and 757.

Provinces were to be supervised by centrally-appointed governors. All rice lands were in theory state property, to be divided equally among its peasant cultivators in return for taxes paid in produce, cloth and labour, including military service. Lacking powerful foreign enemies, however, the court neglected to develop a standing army beyond the scale of a palace guard, which remained the preserve ·of the aristocracy. Coins were minted for circulation on a number of occasions but the economy, far less developed than that of China, continued to function mainly through barter. The oppressiveness of the land-holding and taxation system caused many farmers to desert their land. The government soon departed from the fundamental principle of the *ritsuryo* system of state ownership to recognise rights of private property in land newly brought under cultivation. Much new territory was reclaimed but, as only aristocrats and wealthy monasteries could afford the expense of large-scale reclamation, in the long run this innovation had the effect of re-establishing the very evil which the Taika Reform had been intended to destroy – the creation of autonomous, non-tax-paying estates (*shoen*) in the hands of potentially 'overmighty subjects'.

Nara

In 710 the capital was fixed permanently at Heijo, later known as Nara. Previously it had been customary to abandon the royal palace on the demise of an emperor, presumably to avoid the pollution associated with death. With the proliferation of government offices around the supreme ruler this practice became increasingly expensive and disruptive. The century after the foundation of Nara represents the high point of Chinese cultural influence in Japan. The grid-pattern layout of Nara was modelled on that of the T'ang metropolis, Ch'ang-an, though it was much smaller – three miles by two and two-thirds as opposed to the Chinese city's six miles by five. Even this proved far too ambitious and the envisaged western half of the master-plan never materialised. Even so it may have had a population of 200,000 by the middle of the eighth century. The peaceful state of the country at large is attested by the fact that its capital had neither defensive walls nor an encircling moat.

After the transition to Kyoto (*see pp. 32–3*) the entire settlement virtually withered away. Modern Nara is, in effect, a secondary growth with a population of 300,000 and attracts over a million visitors a year. Its most spectacular celebration is the Grass Burning (*Yama Yaki*) Festival, held on Wakakusayama Hill every 15 January, when huge fires are lit to 'purify' the city's Buddhist temples.

An Aesthetic Revolution

The Japanese responded with greater alacrity to serene and splendid Buddha images than to abstruse Buddhist texts. Not only did they quickly learn to produce exquisite sculpture of their own, they also constructed elegant buildings in the Chinese style to accommodate them. The monastic complex founded by Shotoku between 601 and 607 at Horyuji on the western edge of the Nara plain is almost certainly the most outstanding example of T'ang period architecture in the world and the pagoda of its western temple is the oldest extant wooden building to have been definitively authenticated. Its Golden Hall not only contains images dating from the seventh century but also displayed, until 1949 (when they were virtually destroyed by fire), frescoes in the style of Indian cave-temple paintings. The Todaiji (Great Eastern Temple) in Nara enjoyed the special patronage of the imperial family, who looked to its devotions for spiritual protection for themselves and the nation as a whole. The original buildings covered no less than five city blocks but were razed to the ground by Minamoto no Yoritomo in 1180 (*see p. 50*) and badly damaged again in 1567. The Great Hall housing its main Buddha image (*see p. 267*) remains the largest wooden building in the world. Around 770 the court ordered the production of a million Buddhist charms; those that survive remain among the world's earliest examples of the printer's art.

EMPEROR SHOMU

The most enthusiastic patron of Buddhism was Emperor Shomu (reigned 724–49) who ordered the establishment of a monastery and a nunnery in each province of his realm and in 749 became the first Japanese emperor to renounce the throne in favour of a monk's tonsure. In 752 he came out of retirement to dedicate a bronze image of the Vairocana Buddha (Daibutsu) at Todaiji temple in the presence of 10,000 Buddhist monks and foreign dignitaries. Standing 53 feet high, it is said to have absorbed 500 tons of copper in its main structure and the entire national output of precious metals in its embellishment; much repaired, it continues to impress by its size, if not as a great work of art, being the largest bronze sculpture in the

world. Todaiji today also houses some 140 designated national
treasures.

Shomu's personal belongings survive nearby in an impressive
wooden storehouse, the Shosoin, which is one of the world's most
extraordinary time-capsules. Its contents run to some 9,000 items
including many luxuries brought along the Central Asian 'silk route'
from as far away as Persia. Many of these treasures were used in the
ceremonies which accompanied the dedication of the Daibutsu. A
selection is displayed each October in the Nara National Museum.

Buddhist influence reached a further high-point during the reign of
Shomu's successor, the Empress Koken (749–58 and 764–70), who fell
in thrall to the priest Dokyo (d. 772). His ambitions towards the throne
led to his exile and the scrupulous avoidance of female rule until almost
a thousand years later when the occupants of the throne had been
reduced to virtual ciphers.

During the Nara period Buddhism remained largely confined to the
capital and the ruling class. Its spread to the provinces and the common
folk came later, as a consequence of its Japanisation at the hands of
inspired teachers (see Chapter 3). One of the earliest of these was Gyoki
(668–749), an itinerant holy man who raised funds for the building of
Todaiji and encouraged charitable works such as the construction of
dykes, bridges, roads and village clinics. Common people venerated
him as a saint and he has also been hailed as 'Japan's first civil engineer'.
Indicators of the spread of Buddhist influence throughout state and
society include the substitution of banishment for execution and of
cremation for burial and a growing prejudice against the eating of meat.
At first Buddhism was perceived largely as a powerful form of magic, a
means of propitiating ghosts, fending off misfortune or securing
worldly benefits. Appreciation of its spiritual depth came only gradually.

A Craftsman Reflects

Master-carpenter Nishioka Tsunekazu spent twenty years of his
working life on the restoration of Horyuji. The experience left him
with a new respect for the men who built it – and a new distaste for the

The Horyuji Pagoda

standards of his own times. Nishioka is insistent that '. . . the ancients did not blindly imitate foreign styles. . . . They created new techniques based on a deep understanding both of foreign techniques and of the local geography and climate.' Buildings were restyled with much deeper eaves to allow for Japan's rainier weather. Instead of setting key pillars on stone bases they were sunk deep into the ground to help them resist typhoon winds and earthquakes. Above all, Nishioka concludes, the craftsmen of the seventh century showed a deep and detailed knowledge of their materials – 'I learned that Horyuji is great not because it is old but because it blends human wisdom with the life of the wood.' The 'reverse-engineering' involved in dismantling the ancient structure uncovered for Nishioka the scientific rationale underlying the folk-wisdom of his craft, which decreed that timbers from trees that grew on the southern slope of a mountain are to be used on the southern side of a building, timbers from trees that grew on the northern side are to be used on the northern side – 'In other words, buy not the trees but the mountain.'

The restorationist found that this principle is carefully followed at Horyuji. Trees that grow on sunny, southern slopes are prolific in branches, and therefore knots, which make them strong. At Horyuji all the timbers on the southern side of the main Buddha-hall are knotty, southern timbers, while those on the north side have none. A similar dichotomy applies to valley and mountain-top growths, with valley trees growing straight but weak, 'like people who grow up in a protected environment, surrounded by family and servants.... Trees, like people, only grow strong if they mature by standing up to hardship.' Weaker timbers are not useless but have to be combined with stronger ones in the right way:

> Today strong and weak timbers alike are cut into uniform lengths and combined any old way. But the (ancient) builders.... carefully combined timbers that twisted in different directions to produce a stable, solid structure.... The pieces were combined to maintain a balance of strength. If a soft piece of wood was used below, a hard piece would be used above.... That is why a building could last 1,300 years.

Nishioka's comparisons between Horyuji and later structures are not flattering. Neglecting to respect 'the life of the wood', the seventeenth-century builders of the Toshogu shrine complex at Nikko (*see p. 74*) produced only 'decorative candy boxes' of limited durability. Horyuji's unornamented beauty derives from the simple grandeur of its structure – '. . . like a sumo grand champion. Clad only in a simple loin-cloth, he overwhelms simply by virtue of his awesome physique.'

Toshogu, by contrast, is like an over-dressed geisha who, weighted down with ornament, would 'topple at a touch'.

Nishioka's comparison leads him to a majestic dismissal of five centuries of the built heritage: 'The Muromachi period in the fourteenth–sixteenth centuries (*see Chapter 4*) marks the transition from a structural to an ornamental emphasis in Japanese architecture. In my opinion, all architecture since Muromachi is decadent.'

As for the standards of the late twentieth century:

> No one thinks at all about the life of a house.... Wood houses built according to today's Building Standard Law last only twenty-five years.... But it takes sixty years for a cypress sapling to grow large enough to make a single temple pillar. If people discard wood after only twenty-five years of use, the earth will become a wasteland. This is the kind of stupidity that Japan.... a nation that calls itself a cultural state, actually mandates. The root of this evil is the notion that money can buy anything, that money gives people the freedom to do whatever they want.

A Literary Revolution

With Chinese culture came the Chinese system of writing. It was not a straightforward transfer, partly for linguistic reasons, partly for social ones. The Japanese and Chinese languages belong to entirely different groups, with marked differences in both grammar and phonics. Chinese, for example, is a tonal language; changes in pitch register changes in meaning. Japanese is not tonal. Chinese words tend to consist of single syllables while Japanese words are often compounds of many syllables. Adapting Chinese orthography to render Japanese meanings was no easy task. Chinese characters were sometimes used to represent their pictographic meanings (i.e. a stylised drawing of a mountain represents a mountain) and sometimes for their phonetic value (i.e. to represent a specific sound). Eventually two phonetic syllabaries (codes which symbolise syllables, not, like alphabets, single sounds) were evolved to supplement the use of Chinese characters (*kanji*). The cursive *hiragana* is largely used for grammatical functions while the more angular *katakana* is mostly employed for the writing of words borrowed from foreign languages.

The social barriers to the spread of literacy relate to the purposes for which it was used. Knowledge of writing, probably through Korean scribes, came to Japan in the fifth and sixth centuries when the élite was preoccupied with internal conflicts and schemes for overseas conquests. Writing was largely needed for routine administrative chores such as compiling accounts and registers and drafting occasional items of diplomatic correspondence. Perhaps a modern analogy might be the employment of computer experts. As Sansom has suggested:

> ... the nobles perhaps felt that, as they could purchase the service of specialists, there was no reason why they should suffer the drudgery of learning to read and write Chinese. So long as writing appeared as a mere mechanical accomplishment, a craft not much different from, say, weaving or painting, it might be left to clerks. It was when it was seen to be the vehicle for a new religion and a new political philosophy that it first became essential to the ruling classes.

No less significant than the acquisition of literacy, therefore, was the acquisition of a conviction of what literacy was for. Scriptures were to be studied for the sake of spiritual advantage, albeit crudely conceived. Official chronicles were to be compiled for the glorification of the ruling dynasty and the guidance of governors. Poetry was to be composed to authenticate the claim of the literate man to be a person of breeding and sensitivity. Such compositions were to be recorded in calligraphy whose elegance was also a crucial indicator of cultural sophistication. (The manufacture of brushes and ink for calligraphy remains an important local craft in Nara.)

THE BIRTH OF JAPANESE LITERATURE

The most important literary compilations of the Nara period are the chronicles known as the *Record of Ancient Matters* (*Kojiki*) of 712, the *History of Japan* (*Nihon Shoki*) of 720 and the poetry anthology entitled *Collection of Myriad Leaves* (*Man'yoshu*) (*ca* 760). The two chronicles meld together (often contradictory) myths and traditions to fabricate a record of antiquity intended to compare favourably to that of China in terms of length and splendour. Most of the 4,516 poems in the *Man'yoshu* are *tanka* of 31 syllables (arranged 5-7-5-7-7) which typically link a scene from nature with a particular human emotion or mood, e.g.

> When spring comes
> the melting ice
> disappears completely;
> If only your heart
> Would melt like that to me.

Shinto

Buddhism did not displace the native religion of Japan but it did provoke it into self-awareness. The nameless cult of sacred places and beings (*kami*), devoid of scriptures and expressed in the simplest of rituals, came to define itself as Shinto – the Way of the Gods. The compilation of the *Kojiki* and *Nihon Shoki* signalise the determination of the ruling dynasty to preserve and reconcile Shinto with the Way of Buddha (*Butsudo*). Shinto deities were matched with their Buddhist counterparts and arranged into an orderly hierarchy (*honji suijaku*). The creation myth recounted in the *Kojiki* and *Nihongi* links the ancestry of the Yamato house with the Sun Goddess Amaterasu Omikami, asserts the heavenly origin of the 'three sacred treasures' and thus bathes their possessor in a halo of divinity. The great shrine complex at Ise was already centuries old when these chronicles were compiled. Its inner sanctum is devoted to the Sun Goddess, its outer part to the presiding deity of rice and harvests. Representing the ritual purity which lies at the heart of Shinto it has been dismantled and rebuilt in the same 'grain-storehouse' style with fresh timbers of untreated cypress every twenty years for thirteen centuries.

More modest constructions will be encountered throughout Japan, usually in places where *kami* are believed to be manifest and often surrounded by groves of trees. Simply built of uncarved wood and with a thatched roof, a Shinto shrine is approached through a plain arch of two uprights with two cross-bars (*torii*). The visitor customarily performs an act of ritual lustration, rinsing the mouth and hands with clear water, before approaching the shrine itself. More elaborate acts of purification (*harai*) may involve immersion in a pool (*misogi*) or beneath a waterfall or involve the services of a priest who symbolically 'sprinkles' water by waving a wand of white paper strips (*gohei*). The practice of such rituals to the present day implies a persisting Japanese dread of defilement or pollution – which should not be confused with sin. Generations of Christian missionaries were to be variously appalled or bemused by the apparent absence among the Japanese of a sense of guilt. Guilt is not a characteristic feature of the Japanese moral universe – but shame is. Nowadays, as in the past, Shinto tends to be associated with the positive aspects of creation – with planting and harvesting, with marriage and the blessing of infants. Shrines still do a brisk business in talismans and amulets. The American journalist John Gunther once remarked acerbically that 'Japan has never been sweet sixteen'. Perhaps, but the survival of Shinto, so unarticulated, so persistent, suggests that, in a curious way, it has never lost its innocence either.

CHAPTER THREE

The World of the Shining Prince,
800–1185

A Golden Age?

The four centuries between the shift of the capital to Kyoto (794) and the foundation of warrior government in Kamakura (1185/92) constitute a period in which the imperial court patronised the development of a refined culture whose legacy in literature, sculpture, architecture and religion forms one of the richest strands of Japan's national heritage. It is, moreover, a living legacy. Kyoto remains the nation's premier destination for visitors. The Byodo-in temple is treasured as a jewel of craftsmanship. The Tendai, Shingon and Pure Land sects of Buddhism, dating from this period, even now command the widest followings. *The Tale of Genji* and *The Pillow Book of Sei Shonagon* are still read and savoured by student and savant alike. And the Japanisation of Chinese culture, which quickened after the ending of official contacts between Japan and China in 894, gave birth to the *kana* scripts in use today (*see p. 219*).

But, if this period is in one sense a golden age, it is also one spattered with blood and disfigured by misery. The vast bulk of the population endured hardships unimagined by the 'cloud-dwellers' of the capital as huge areas were periodically ravaged by bands of renegade warriors or pirates. The imperial response to such disasters was usually indifference or impotence, as might be guessed from entries in official chronicles which record as significant events that 'Red sparrows collected on the roof of a palace building and did not leave for ten days' and 'The

Emperor gave a winding water banquet and caused scholars to compose verses'. (This effete entertainment involved a sort of picnic during which refreshments were floated past guests in little boat-trays on the streams criss-crossing the palace grounds.)

Court life, of course, had terrors of its own, for treachery and assassination remained part of the normal currency of politics. Nowhere was this more evident than in the sordid annals of the accomplished and ruthless Fujiwara family. And none, high or low, was spared from the horrors of periodic visitations of the plague. The colourful street procession which accompanies Kyoto's celebrated Gion festival originated in a fearsome epidemic which prompted the people of the stricken city to parade every holy image they could assemble in the hope of divine intercession to end their suffering. Similarly the Pure Land sect owed its rapid growth to the widespread belief that the world was passing through its pre-ordained 'last days'. The rise of samurai rule, brutal but effective, may have been regretted by the aesthete but many no doubt had reason to be grateful for it. And the enduring triumph of the aesthetes was that even as the provincial military elbowed them aside they remained in awe of their culture.

The Capital of Peace and Tranquillity

In 784 Emperor Kammu decided to move the imperial capital to enable him to escape from the overbearing influence and squabbles of the Buddhist hierarchy of Nara. Ironically the city he eventually settled in now has 1,600 Buddhist temples, plus 400 Shinto shrines and ninety Christian churches.

The initial site located by Kammu's favourite, Fujiwara no Tanet-sugu, at Nagaoka, was bedevilled by natural disasters and, a year after work began, the loyal but luckless courtier was murdered by the emperor's younger brother, Prince Sawara, who was intriguing for the succession. Taking these hints as omens, Kammu abandoned the project on the eve of its completion, despite the fact that it had absorbed at least an entire year's national revenue and inflicted almost a decade of wretchedness on 300,000 half-starved conscript labourers. A new location was fixed five miles away between the Katsura and Kamo rivers and work was recommenced. Sawara, meanwhile, was starved to death and his fellow conspirators killed or exiled. (Interestingly enough the prolonged illness of the true heir-apparent and sudden death of his mother was attributed to Sawara's vengeful spirit which was placated by posthumous promotion to emperor and re-interment in an imperial mausoleum with dedicated temple *en suite*.)

A PLANNED CITY

'Heian-kyo' 'capital of peace and tranquillity' – now known as Kyoto (Capital City), was to be Japan's official capital (apart from a break of six months in 1180) from its first occupation in 794 until the 'Meiji Restoration' of 1868 (*see p. 121*). And even then it was supposed to remain co-equal with jumped up Edo, re-titled Tokyo – 'Eastern Capital'. For much of its history it was referred to simply as Miyako – Metropolis. Heian, like its predecessors, was modelled on the grid-plan Chinese capital Chang'an (now Sian/Xi'an), though it was not protected by walls but an encircling moat. Set on a broad plain, it was thought to be shielded from evil influences by low mountains to the east, west and north. Along with the idea of town-planning the Japanese had imported from China the practice of geomancy (*feng-shui*) which discriminated between auspicious and unlucky sitings for buildings. Rivers flowing down from these heights assured its water supply and ultimately linked it with the sea. The original structure plan envisaged a rectangle 4.5 km. from east to west and 5.2 km. north to south. It would be bisected by a grand north-south avenue, Suzaku Oji, 85 metres across, flanked by major temples at the southern end and culminating in a great palace enclosure at the northern end. Two markets, each occupying an entire city block, would be disposed symmetrically to the east and west. Each of the 1,200 city blocks (*bo*) was divided into 16 sub-units (*cho*) each of 1,450 square metres. As the site sloped gently away from the hills it was possible for each tree-lined street to have a stream of running water ducted alongside it. Apart from the two temples at the city's southern entrance other religious establishments were to be kept at a prudent distance, beyond the city's formal limits and in the foothills of the surrounding mountains. By the ninth century Kyoto had a population of about 100,000, of whom

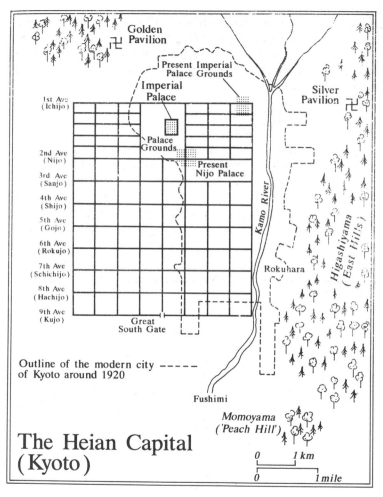

Golden
Pavilion

Present Imperial
Palace Grounds

Imperial
Palace

1st Ave
(Ichijo)

Present
Imperial
Palace

Silver
Pavilion

Palace
Grounds

Present
Nijo Palace

2nd Ave
(Nijo)

3rd Ave
(Sanjo)

4th Ave
(Shijo)

5th Ave
(Gojo)

6th Ave
(Rokujo)

7th Ave
(Schichijo)

8th Ave
(Hachijo)

9th Ave
(Kujo)

Kamo River

Higashiyama
(East Hills)

Rokuhara

Great
South Gate

Outline of the modern city
of Kyoto around 1920

Fushimi

Momoyama
('Peach Hill')

The Heian Capital (Kyoto)

0   1 km

0   1 mile

some 10,000 were aristocrats or officials. The rest provided the goods and services they required, establishing the city's character to the present day as a centre of learning , fashionable living and fine crafts. Even before the building of the capital the site was occupied by immigrant Korean silk-weavers.

DECLINE AND DISASTER

By the tenth century street crime, pillage and brawling by warrior-monks were already giving the lie to the city's self-congratulatory name. Fire, accidental or deliberate, remained a perennial curse. After a third major conflagration destroyed the Great Audience Hall of the palace in 1156 it was not rebuilt. The Onin War (1467–77, *see pp. 66*) virtually razed the entire city and little of its architecture now predates the seventeenth century, though much has been reconstructed to replicate previous structures as precisely as possible. The present Imperial Palace complex (located north-east of the original palace compound) was erected in 1855–6 after the destruction by fire of its 1790 incarnation.

The Fujiwara

For centuries the government of Japan was dominated by a single family whose leaders were emperors in all but name. Their power rested neither on military skill nor administrative competence but on their mastery of intrigue – in Sansom's words 'the game of skill with living pieces'. The very name that they themselves bore, Fujiwara, refers to the Wisteria Garden in which the founder of their greatness, Kamatari, hatched the conspiracy which, in 645, had destroyed the dominance of the Soga family at court and opened the way for the Taika Reforms (*see p. 20*). Kamatari's son further strengthened his family's position by marrying his daughter to the emperor, a practice henceforth assiduously continued by the Fujiwara whenever possible.

True Fujiwara dominance can be dated from 858 when Yoshifusa had his nine-year-old grandson enthroned as emperor, with himself as regent, the first commoner to hold this position. Over the next two centuries eight adult emperors were persuaded to take early retirement in favour of children, leaving the real power in Fujiwara hands.

Yoshifusa's nephew, Mototsune invented the new position of *kampaku* (chancellor) to become the sole link between the emperor and his bureaucracy. Mototsune's son, Tokihira, outmanoeuvred Emperor Uda's attempts to undermine the Fujiwara stranglehold and skilfully managed to frame and banish his chief rival, the brilliant scholar-poet Sugawara Michizane (845–903). (The Kitano Tenmangu shrine at Kyoto is said to have been built to appease the spirit of the wronged Michizane who became revered as a patron of learning. Generations of students in Japan have visited his shrine as part of their preparation for examinations.)

'CLOISTERED GOVERNMENT'

Fujiwara power reached its peak under the cultured Michinaga (966–1028) who obliged four separate emperors to marry his daughters; two emperors were his nephews and three his grandsons. Sei Shonagon (*see p. 45*) referred frequently to the splendour of his palace, which was the effective seat of government; and some scholars hold that Genji himself (*see p. 48*) is, in large part, modelled on him.

At the banquet to celebrate the marriage of his third daughter to his grandson, Emperor Go-Ichijo, Michinaga improvised a poem which likened his power to the perfection of a full moon. It was an ill-judged gesture of complacency as warrior families in the provinces had already begun to challenge the central government, refusing to pay taxes or acknowledge the authority of provincial governors. For a while the situation was stabilised by paying the Minamoto and Taira clans to bring troublemakers into line. This reliance on force revealed that the rot had begun to set in at the periphery. At the centre the Fujiwara hold on the imperial line was weakened by the failure of their women to produce male heirs who could be made emperors, and by the ingenuity of the Emperor Go-Sanjo (1034–73) in devising a system of 'cloister government' which turned the Fujiwara's trick of manipulating minors back against them. This procedure entrusted the performance of public ceremonial duties to minors who actually occupied the throne while real power was exercised from the seclusion of a monastery to which its previous, adult occupant had, in theory, 'retired'.

It was, however, more than a century before the collapse of Fujiwara power was complete and members of the clan continued to hold prominent positions at court and to excel as poets and painters. Fujiwara Takanobu established a new style of realistic portraiture. (Ironically the most famous of his surviving works is a likeness of Minamoto Yoritomo, founder of the dynasty which finally buried Fujiwara power for ever, *see p. 50*. It can be seen at the Jingo-ji in Kyoto.) Takanobu's son, Nobuzane, was the leading painter of thirteenth-century Japan and his half-brother, Fujiwara Teika (1162–1241, also known as Sadaie) was the country's greatest literary critic of premodern times. Teika, court poet and son of a court poet, was inspired by his father Shunzei's dictum of 'old diction, new treatment' and showed in his own huge output of 4,600 poems how classical language could be used to startling effect. He also had the unique distinction of being the first person to work on two imperially-sponsored anthologies of poetry. His personal collection *Single Poems by 100 Poets* is still treasured as an anthology and is used as the basis of the card-game traditionally played as part of Japanese New Year celebrations. Prince Konoe Fumimaro, Japan's prime minister 1937–9 and 1940–1, was a lineal descendant of the Fujiwara.

Tendai

In 804 the monk Saicho (767–822) journeyed to Mount Tiantai (in Japanese, Tendai – 'Heavenly Terrace') in China . There he was taught that the Lotus Sutra summarised all the Buddha's teachings and contained everything needed for salvation:
- all feeling beings are innately enlightened and share the Buddha nature and can achieve salvation
- the Buddhas and Bodhisattvas are constantly at work to assist progress to salvation
- philosophy and meditation are like two wings of a bird, both necessary.

Saicho described the intrinsic human potential for enlightenment as being like a lotus emerging from muddy water – 'The lotus flower implies its own emergence from the water, otherwise its blossom cannot open. . . . The deeper the water the taller the stalk will grow; its potential is limitless.' Tendai practice required strict monastic discipline, prayer, meditation, study of sacred texts and mastery of esoteric rituals. Nevertheless Tendai's promise of salvation for all stood in marked contrast to the austere teachings of existing Nara monasteries which reserved the path to nirvana for monks alone.

Saicho established Enryakuji monastery on Mount Hiei to the north-east of Kyoto. Proclaiming Buddhism to be the best protection for the state and capable of producing 'Treasures of the Nation' who would provide it with enlightened leadership, he was able to draw on the patronage of the court until Enryakuji became the greatest monastic centre in Japan, enrolling even younger sons of the imperial family as monks. Recruits followed a rigorous twelve-year training programme before being sent out as teachers and officials. Saicho also drew on the teachings of his great contemporary, Shingon, to permeate his doctrine with esoteric elements which would enrich its ritual and aesthetic aspects and thus its appeal to aristocratic patrons. He likewise incorporated local Shinto traditions to overcome lingering hostility to 'alien' teachings. Saicho's importance lies in vigorously combating the limitations of existing Buddhist teaching and adapting the faith to give it a national character; but Sansom loftily qualifies his achievement as that of 'an ardent rather than a profound spirit, whose energies were given scope by lucky circumstance'. Under Saicho's successors the esoteric element was further strengthened and Enryakuji continued to expand until by the twelfth century it had become immensely wealthy, with 3,000 buildings at its headquarters, vast land-holdings and a private army of warrior-monks whose turbulence helped to subvert the very court which had fostered its initial growth. Enryakuji's 'alumni' were to include such major Buddhist figures as Honen, Shinran and Nichiren, all of whom developed new sects which eventually undermined its dominance.

Shingon

The Shingon ('True Word') sect of Buddhism has some 12,000,000 followers and 12,000 temples, divided among forty-seven sub-sects.

Portrait of Kukai from the Toji temple in Kyoto

Shingon's founder, Kukai (774–835), is usually known in Japan as Kobo Daishi (Great Teacher Kobo).

Like Saicho the young monk Kukai accompanied the official mission to China in 804 in the hope of finding an approach to Buddhism more in tune with Japan's needs than the austere dogmas then taught in Nara. An excellent poet, superb calligrapher and fluent speaker of Chinese, Kukai lodged in Chang'an, where the famous master Huiguo greeted him like a lost son and made him his most favoured disciple. Kukai was immediately inducted into the mysteries of esoteric Buddhism:

> The abbot informed me that the esoteric scriptures are so difficult to understand that their meaning cannot be conveyed except through art. For this reason he ordered the court artist Li Chen and about a dozen other painters to make ten scrolls of the Womb and Diamond Mandalas and assembled more than twenty scribes to make copies of the Diamond and

other esoteric scriptures. He also ordered the bronze-smith to cast fifteen ritual implements. . . .

Shingon teachings may be crudely summarised thus:
- at the heart of all things is the transcendent Buddha, Vairocana (in Japanese, Dainichi Nyorai), who is shown at the centre of the Womb and Diamond Mandalas which Shingon art uses to represent the cosmos. (The Diamond symbolises hardness and therefore eternal truth, the Womb life, growth and change.)
- every reality is but an emanation from Dainichi and all other Buddhas and Bodhisattvas are but a manifestation of him (and thus, by extension, Shinto deities can likewise be embraced within this all-encompassing framework. Kukai rendered Dainichi's name with the same Chinese characters as 'great sun', enabling the Japanese to identify him with the supreme Shinto deity, Amaterasu, the sun goddess).
- to grasp the immanence of Dainichi in all things is to grasp the possibility of achieving Buddhahood in one's own body (i.e. without passing through countless reincarnations).

To assist the believer in achieving the realisation of Dainichi's immanence Shingon prescribes three ritual practices, representing the embodiment respectively of his thoughts, words and actions:
- meditation on the two mandalas which illustrate Dainichi's transformation into other forms of being
- repetition of secret 'true words' (*shingon*) which contained the essence of the sutras, the original texts of Buddha's teachings
- use of ritual hand gestures (*mudras*) to accompany incantations.

Shingon devotees were initiated and instructed through complex and colourful ceremonies which appealed strongly to the aesthetic tastes of the Japanese court. By 810 Kukai was able to introduce Shingon at Kyoto's greatest centre for monastic ordinations, Todaiji. In 816 he founded a monastery, Kongobuji, on wild Mount Koya, near modern Osaka. He interpreted its central plateau and eight peaks as symbols of the eight-petalled lotus shape of a mandala. In 823 his patron Emperor Saga granted him the Toji monastery in Kyoto, giving him a secure base in the capital as well. He received permission to train fifty monks here and the pledge that it would remain exclusively Shingon. By enduring austerities and mastering secret teachings Shingon priests (*yamabushi*) gained great prestige in the eyes of common folk and were credited with the power to work magic.

A LEGENDARY FIGURE

According to tradition Kukai eventually passed into deepest meditation, destined to awake at the advent of Maitreya, the Buddha of the Future. There are many legends of apparitions of Kukai performing acts of mercy or retribution. One tells how, in the guise of a beggar-priest, he asked for water in a drought-stricken village. After the peasants had readily shared what they had with him he struck the ground and created a bubbling spring. But on another occasion a villager laden with sweet potatoes refused him one and he turned them all to stones. He is also credited by tradition with such achievements as the introduction of tea to Japan and the invention of the *hiragana* syllabary, together with '*Iro Ha*', the poem which came to be thought of as 'the Japanese alphabet'. Its forty-seven syllables not only use all the sounds of the language except the final 'n' consonant but elegantly express the Buddhist preoccupation with the transience of existence:

> The colours bloom, disperse and fall.
> In this our world, who can endure?
> Today cross the distant peaks which are life's illusions,
> And dream no more misleading dreams nor give way to stupor.

His fame as a calligrapher endures in the idiom '*Kobo mo fude no ayamari*' (Kobo wrote clumsy characters) which expresses astonishment at a totally unexpected failure.

Kukai was evidently blessed with an extraordinary combination of charisma, creativity and tact. Even the fiery Saicho humbled himself to learn from him and be 'baptised' by him, although when one of his own disciples deserted him for Shingon it opened a breach which never healed.

Most of the eighty-eight temples which make up the famous pilgrimage route on Shikoku belong to the Shingon tradition and are believed to mark places visited by Kobo Daishi during his wandering period between leaving Nara in disenchantment and going to China. The seventy-fifth temple, Zentsuji, is held to mark his birthplace. Shingon temples are often guarded by terrifying sculptures of Myo-o, attendants of Dainichi, surrounded by hellish flames; their functions are, however, benevolent, to destroy passion and ignorance and to frighten away evil spirits. The most important, fierce Fudo, is a major figure in Japanese folklore.

Pure Land

The 'Pure Land' tradition of Buddhism was established in Japan by Honen (1133–1212), a Tendai-trained monk disillusioned with the élitism of Enryakuji. It focuses on worship of Amida (Sanskrit Amithaba – Infinite Light), the Buddha who presides over the Western Paradise, the Pure Land (in Japanese, Jodo). Followers of this tradition place their hopes of salvation on a vow made by Amida, promising that all who invoked his name with faith and sincerity would, after death, be reborn in the Western Paradise, a land free from pain and want, until they were ready for final enlightenment and nirvana. Statues of Amida are usually attended by those of Kannon, the goddess of mercy.

The Amida cult was known in Japan even before Tendai and Shingon but was for centuries confined to initiates. It was spread to laymen by the monks Kuya (903–72), Genshin (942–1017) and Ryonin (1072–1132) who preached the value of the chant '*Namu Amida Butsu*' (referred to in abbreviated form as the *nembutsu*) – 'I take refuge in Amida Buddha'. The great Michinaga (*see p. 36*) is said to have died chanting the *nembutsu* in Hojoji temple which he built in a typically lavish attempt to represent the Pure Land in earthly form.

Genshin's popular book *Essentials of Salvation* stressed that anyone could achieve paradise through total reliance on Amida's compassion and without the complex rituals or demanding meditation required by other sects. The monk Ippen (1239–89) popularised a *nembutsu* dance which is still performed at the summer festival of O-Bon when ancestral spirits are welcomed back to their graves.

Honen's achievement was, despite persecution and exile at the hands of Tendai, to establish Amida Buddhism as a mass-movement. The

Buddhist doctrine of '*mappo*' (The End of the Law) taught that an age of chaos would arise in which salvation through one's own virtue and efforts would be impossible. The turmoils attending the rise of samurai rule in the twelfth century seemed like just such an era and undoubtedly hastened the spread of the Amida cult among the disoriented poor. In their distress, a Western Paradise free from horror and hunger seemed quite desirable enough, never mind the ultimate Buddhist goal of non-existence. Honen's disciple Shinran (1173–1263) taught that it was necessary to say the *nembutsu* only once with absolute conviction to be saved, on the grounds that if salvation was due to Amida's compassion rather than one's own efforts once was entirely sufficient. Repetition was, however, commended as an expression of gratitude.

Shinran was an unashamed populist who justified his use of Japanese rather than Chinese script as follows:

> Country folk do not understand characters and are very slow. Therefore, in order to get them to understand I have written the same thing over and over again. Educated people will think it odd and deride me. But their abuse is irrelevant because my sole purpose in writing is to make my meaning clear to stupid people.

Shinran also proclaimed the Pure Land to be a state of grace which could be experienced in this life. (He was the first major Buddhist leader to renounce celibacy and had six children!) Shinran's followers established the most dominant group in the Amida tradition, the True Pure Land Sect (Jodo Shinsu) with headquarters in Honganji, Temple of the Original Vow, (Osaka) where Shinran's ashes lie. The most famous centre of the Amida cult is, however, the Byodo-in. Shinsu worship focuses on Amida to the exclusion of other deities and has abandoned monasticism, unlike other sects. It now claims some 13,000,000 followers.

THE PHOENIX HALL

The finest surviving example of Heian period architecture is to be seen on an island in a lotus pond at Uji, a few miles outside Kyoto. The Byodo-in, originally built as a retreat palace for Michinaga, was con-

An Amida Buddha made in 1053

verted to a Buddhist temple by his son Yorimichi in 1053. Its core, the 48-metre Hoo-do (Phoenix Hall), is said to take its name from the shape of its ground-plan, which resembles a bird. The main hall, which extends over the lake, is its body and tail, and the side-galleries its wings; until a fire in 1235 they projected much further forward . On the roof are two gilt-bronze phoenixes which symbolise rebirth in the Pure Land paradise of Amida, the western Buddha. Inside is a gilt wooden statue of Amida by the sculptor Jocho. In its combination of sweeping elegance and restrained splendour this building is felt to be a perfect representation of the spirit of its age.

The Byodo-in was the scene of the death of Minamoto no Yor-imasa, an early casualty of the Heike wars (*see p. 50*). Having chanted the *nembutsu* ten times he then composed a last verse:

> Like a fossil tree
> Which has never borne a flower
> Sad had been my life
> Sadder still to end my life
> Leaving no fruit. . . .

Having spoken these lines, he thrust the point of his sword into his belly, bowed his face to the ground as the blade pierced him through, and died.

'The Pillow Book'

Sei Shonagon was born around 965, the daughter of a scholar-poet and court official . From her mid-twenties until her mid-thirties she served as lady-in-waiting to the Empress Sadako. 'Shonagon' means 'Minor Counsellor', 'Sei' refers to the Kiyowara clan with which she was connected. Little more is certain about her. Murasaki Shikibu, who moved in the same court circles, referred to her scathingly as being gifted but arrogant and emotionally immature and predicted a well-merited downfall. Whether Sei Shonagon met such a fate is unknown; but her personality emerges vividly from her book which, in Sansom's neat phrase, 'gives a full picture of life at court and only the faintest hint of life outside'. When she did emerge from the confines of the palace complex her distaste for ordinary folk was clearly virulent and unconcealed: 'They looked like so many worms as they crowded together in their revolting clothes, coming so close that they almost touched me.' Perceptive but prejudiced, sophisticated but sentimental, she was warm to her intimates but callous towards inferiors, whether they were priests ('no more important than a block of wood') or dutiful, stay-at-home wives ('provincials'). Irritable and intemperate, fastidious and promiscuous, a show-off and a meddler, she had a ready wit and a retentive memory. She knew some of the easier Chinese classics but her mind was basically unburdened by abstruse learning and her prose was consequently uncluttered by obscure words and allusions. Japanese read her book for its style, not its structure, for it parallels the love life of its author – elegant but haphazard.

The title of *The Pillow Book* makes it sound like a sort of coy sex manual. Sei Shonagon was anything but coy about eroticism but would doubtless have found anything so explicit as a manual irredeemably gross. A pillow-book was in fact a sort of jotter, stored in the wooden neck-rest used by court ladies so that they could sleep, rather uncomfortably, with their hair hoisted clear of the floor. What in the West might be called a 'day book' served in Heian Japan as a 'night book' in which, on solitary evenings, one might record random anecdotes, snatches of poetry and acid observations on places and people.

Many passages in *The Pillow Book* expand discursively on some boldly opinionated initial assertion – 'Oxen should have very small foreheads', 'A preacher ought to be good-looking', 'The way in which carpenters eat is very bizarre'. Others are entirely devoted to the writer's evaluation of various types of tree, insect, illness, cloud, festival and wind instrument or else record in minute detail the most trivial incidents involving the emperor or empress. But the most remarkable feature of the entire composition is its 164 lists of objects, people or occasions which Sei Shonagon classifies as 'embarrassing', 'presumptuous', 'shameful', 'enviable' or 'awkward'. A single list may embrace a kaleidoscope of wildly diverse elements. 'Depressing Things' include a cold, empty brazier, a poor scholar with a string of female children, and a letter from the provinces without a gift. (An unaccompanied letter from the capital would at least have had the consolation of significant gossip.) 'Hateful Things' include a drowsy exorcist, a snoring lover, a hair on one's ink-stick and a pack of dogs barking in chorus. 'Squalid Things' range from the back of a piece of embroidery to the inside of a cat's ear, and 'Inappropriate Things' include moonlight on the snow-covered house of a common person. Some lists are placed in oppositional sequence – 'Things that give a clean feeling' (light on pouring water) and 'Things that give an unclean feeling' (snotty-nosed children), 'Things that lose by being painted' (beautiful characters in stories) and 'Things that gain by being painted' (mountain paths and villages). The very titles of the lists reveal the quite particular preoccupations of their compiler – 'Things that make one's heart beat faster', 'Outstandingly magnificent things', 'Things that arouse a fond memory of the past', 'People who look pleased with themselves', 'Things that give a pathetic impression' and, perhaps most revealing of all, 'Times when one should be on one's guard'.

Ivan Morris's Penguin edition of Sei Shonagon translates 185 selected passages, beginning 'In spring it is the dawn' and ending 'It is getting so dark'. They vary in length from a few lines to a dozen pages, making it the perfect bedside book – which is how it began. Sincerity was not one of the author's virtues so it is difficult to swallow the plaintive note on which she closes – 'Whatever people may think of my book, I still regret that it ever came to light.'

The great Orientalist Arthur Waley regarded Sei Shonagon's miscellany as 'the most important document of the period we possess'. There may have been dozens of other books like hers but hers is the only one to have survived. It is the earliest example of a genre known as *zuihitsu* – literally 'running brush', i.e. random notes – which has occupied an important place in Japanese literature ever since. *The Pillow Book* portrays a courtly society whose inhabitants, unmindful of past and future alike, lived in a present both eternal and evanescent, dreading the explicit, obsessed with complexities of precedent and the aesthetic niceties of such obscure pastimes as incense-blending and the spontaneous composition of thirty-one-syllable poems. 'Never,' Waley concludes in near-disbelief, 'among people of exquisite cultivation and lively intelligence, have purely intellectual pursuits played so small a part.' Capable of 'far surpassing the silliness of our own Middle Ages' they esteemed calligraphy above all other accomplishments, ranking it almost a virtue rather than a talent, valuing perfection of penmanship as much as fineness of face or figure. But, if they took life lightly, they also lived it delicately. They may often have been empty-headed but they were seldom heavy-handed.

The Tale of Genji

The Tale of Genji (*Genji Monogatari*) has been hailed as nothing less than the world's first real novel and the greatest fictional work of the

Japanese classical period. Even the urbane Sansom describes it as 'a remarkable romance which it is difficult to describe without superlatives...'. Given the limited opportunities for study and travel open to women it is all the more surprising that it was composed by one, albeit a courtier of high rank and a lover of Fujiwara no Michinaga. Denied access to mastery of Chinese characters, she was obliged to write it in phonetic script. Murasaki Shikibu began her work around AD 1000, just as Sei Shonagon was completing hers. Unlike *The Pillow Book* Murasaki's fifty-four-chapter Tale does have, if not a plot, at least a fairly focused theme, the life and loves of cultured, complex, sensitive Genji, 'the Shining Prince'. Genji, the emperor's favourite son but barred from succession, seeks, through exile and successive affairs, an embodiment of the mother who died when he was an infant. His first affair, with a wife of his father, the emperor, is clouded by its illicit nature. In Murasaki (Purple) he finds his greatest love – but she dies. Genji eventually returns to court and glories in royal favour but, after he marries, one of his wives produces a son, Kaoru, by another man. Genji eventually enters the priesthood. After his death the story, which covers a span of three-quarters of a century, follows, in darkened mood, the less successful amours of his supposed son. The strength of the book lies not in action but atmosphere; the author's great skill lies in her ability to convey with delicate precision the psychological states of its hundreds of different characters and the ever-changing beauties of the natural world. It is suffused throughout with '*mono no aware*', a sense of gentle sadness at the passing nature of all things and an acute sensitivity to the tragic implications of even a single gesture.

Genji enjoyed immediate popularity at the Heian court. Its reputation rapidly spread to the provinces where the female author of the *Sarashina Diary* (English translation *As I Crossed a Bridge of Dreams*) records her longing to go to the capital so that she could read the entire work. By the twelfth century *Genji* was being depicted in exquisitely decorative scroll paintings which can now be seen in the Tokugawa art museum in Nagoya and the Goto art museum in Tokyo. It has been the subject of commentary and analysis ever since. Adaptations of *Genji* have appeared as *Noh* and *kabuki* plays, novels, films, TV shows and even in cartoon form. Every Japanese student will at least have read selected passages from it, probably in modern Japanese, as the original text requires a detailed commentary for it to be comprehensible. The full version runs to a thousand pages and over a million words but its episodic nature encourages a leisurely reading. There are two major English translations, a free and lyrical version by Waley (1935–60) and a more precise and literal one by Seidensticker (1976).

The Rise of the Samurai

The rarefied atmosphere of the Heian court was better suited to breeding men for dilettantism than danger, and the Chinese-style claim to imperial supremacy over the whole land came to look increasingly threadbare within little more than a century of its proclamation. The system of conscripting peasants for military service was abolished as early as 792 and the last attempt at an official redistribution of land took place in 844. Few who professed their loyalty to the emperor proved capable of reconciling the advancement of their interests at court with the protection of his interests in the provinces. Provincial administration fell into the hands of 'deputies' who had bought their offices from courtiers, appointees who then resisted reassignment and made their office hereditary, and maverick scions of great courtly houses who had decided to go their own way. As central authority disintegrated these self-made men raised private armies to enforce tax-collection, uphold public order and extend the northern frontier against the aboriginals, adding conquered lands to their own estates.

Sometimes these private armies were turned against each other. When grouped in warrior leagues they could prove formidable as the Taira (also known as Heike) and Minamoto (also Genji) were ultimately to prove. As early as 935, Taira no Masakado, who claimed direct descent from Emperor Kammu, conquered most of the eight Kanto provinces and proclaimed himself emperor. At the same time Fujiwara no Sumitomo, sent to suppress piracy in the Inland Sea, likewise turned on the government. Only by using the armies of the Minamoto as their 'claws and teeth' could the Fujiwara crush the rebels and reassert control. The theory and reality of political power became more and more divorced. The Fujiwara could be circumvented by 'cloistered emperors', who posed as monks, while the 'real' emperors posed as emperors, whose regents posed as effective controllers of the bureaucracy. But the Fujiwara could not be ousted – and what did it matter anyway? Decrees might pour forth but the only people in a position to implement them were busy frustrating them in their own interests. By the time it lurched towards final collapse the Heian machinery of government had become so complicated that it could only survive so long as it was not expected to work. In the provinces local 'big men' began to realise that the only effective government was self-government.

THE HEIKE WARS

From the twelfth century the 'cloistered emperors' began to call upon the Taira in their efforts to outmanoeuvre the Fujiwara and their Minamoto strike-force. In 1156 a wrangle over the succession broke out between a cloistered emperor and a reigning emperor. The Fujiwara were split and Kiyomori (1118–81), astute head of the Taira, saw his chance to eliminate his rivals, killing off most of the Minamoto and making himself and his clan supreme at court. What had begun as courtly in-fighting ended as a decisive showdown between the real powers in the land. Incredibly, courtiers were caught in the cross-fire and fifty were executed in the early stages of the conflict, the first time in 350 years that capital punishment had been applied to 'cloud-dwellers'. A revolution was in the offing. The Taira awarded themselves court ranks and provincial estates, married into the imperial line, snubbed the existing establishment at will and generally behaved like insufferable upstarts. Meanwhile the Minamoto regrouped around their young leader, Yoritomo (1147–99). In 1180, when the Taira put a Taira-born infant, Antoku, on the throne, Yoritomo went onto the offensive, although the actual campaigning was led by his cousin Yoshinaka (1154–84) and his half-brother Yoshitsune (1159–89). In 1181 Kiyomori died of a fever so hot that his enemies said it came from hell as retribution. His death was a fatal blow to his prideful clan. Yoshinaka drove the Taira from the capital but then, suspected of potential treachery, was defeated by an army led by Yoshitsune. Yoshitsune in turn defeated the Taira at Yashima on Shikoku and finally brought them to destruction in 1185 in the sea-fight at Dan-noura, in the straits of Shimonoseki, between Kyushu and Honshu. The seven-year-old Emperor Antoku was drowned and the Taira leaders were either killed in combat, committed suicide or hunted down and put to the sword.

A TRAGIC HERO

The gallant and handsome Yoshitsune was subsequently driven to death by a jealous Yoritomo, anxious to secure his personal grip on power. Yoshitsune became for many Japanese the archetypal tragic hero and, with his loyal retainer, the warrior-monk Benkei, has been the subject of many stories and plays. (One legend holds that he fled to China and had a second career as Genghis Khan.) The Gikei-do shrine in Iwate prefecture is said to mark the site of his suicide.

The Heike (also Gempe) wars have proved a rich source for Japan's tradition of chivalric story-telling. The meteoric rise and catastrophic fall of the Taira is dramatically chronicled in the *Heike Monogatari* (*Tale of the Heike*) which constantly reiterates the illusory nature of power, '... the proud ones are but for a moment, like the dreams of an evening in spring. In the end even the mightiest are swept aside, as dust before a storm.'

Having established a seat of government at the strongly defensible coastal city of Kamakura, Yoritomo was awarded the title of *sei i tai shogun* (great barbarian-subduing generalissimo) in 1192, thus inaugurating seven centuries of military dictatorship. Yoritomo had neither the bravura of Kiyomori nor the reckless charm of Yoshitsune. He was cold, cautious and calculating – again and again it was to prove a winning formula in Japanese history.

CHAPTER FOUR

Shoguns and Samurai,
1185–1543

The Kamakura shoguns developed a peculiarly Japanese form of feudalism in which the administrative institutions of their '*bakufu*' ('tent government') paralleled or superseded those of the imperial court. Their reimposition of order favoured economic expansion. This was accompanied by the monetisation of the economy, at first largely through the importation of Chinese copper cash; a single mission in 1453 is recorded as having brought back some 50,000,000 copper coins. Regular markets, merchant guilds, wholesalers and money-lenders emerged to handle a growing volume of commerce.

The shift of the effective seat of government eastwards helped spread Heian sophistication to the provinces. Sculpture in particular flourished. The development of distinctively Japanese forms of Buddhism such as Nichiren and Zen represented a counter-current of national self-assertion against the established predominance of Chinese cultural norms. A sense of national identity, and indeed destiny, was further sharpened and refined by the effort required to defeat repeated Mongol attempts at invasion. Undermined by the strains of its defence efforts and brought down by imperial conspiracy, the Kamakura shogunate (1185–1333) was to be succeeded by that of the Ashikaga (1338–1573), centred (after 1378) on the Muromachi district of Kyoto. Their much weaker rule saw the country plagued by civil war, piracy and peasant rebellion and helpless to resist the (fortunately peaceful) intrusion of westerners. Loyalty was still praised but treachery more widely practised. Many laws were issued but little justice done. Ancient families were extinguished and 'sudden lords' exalted. Eager to advertise their new eminence they often proved lavish patrons of the artist and the

An elegant Jizo figure *ca* 1200–50 from the Todaiji temple, Nara

craftsman. Materially acquisitive, morally conservative and culturally adaptive, it was, as Sansom puts it with characteristic neatness, 'an age of ferment, but not of decay'.

A certain parallel can be drawn between the state of late medieval Japan and that of Renaissance Italy in the same period, as savage warfare and senseless destruction went hand in hand with the creation of significant new cultural forms – in Japan the splendour of the *Noh* drama and the gentle arts of flower-arranging, tea-ceremony and garden-design. Another parallel was the increasing standard of personal comfort expected by the better-off. In Italy this meant such niceties as forks and handkerchiefs, in Japan *tatami* (straw-matting) floor-coverings, soya sauce, tea-drinking and hot baths.

Government

The personal ascendancy of the Minamoto was short-lived. Yoritomo was succeeded by his sons, Yoriie and then Sanetomo, but real power passed to his widow and her father. They dominated a council of regency which set about entrenching the power of their family, the Hojo (ironically of Taira descent). With the assassination of poetry-loving Sanetomo in 1219 the Minamoto line ended. In 1221 the 'cloistered emperor' Go-Toba, supported by landholders from western Japan, attempted a coup against the eastern-based Hojo but his forces were easily crushed. He and his son were exiled, their leading followers executed and some 3,000 estates confiscated from the losers. These were used to strengthen the network of patronage on which the Kamakura *bakufu* depended. The post of *shogun* was henceforward formally filled by members of the imperial or Fujiwara families but government was actually directed by Hojo with the title of regent (*shikken*). The complexities of the governmental structure became ever more convoluted until, as Cortazzi explains in some wonderment: 'At times ... there was an Emperor and one or more ex-Emperors ... an imperial regent, a "dictator" (*kanpaku*), a titular shogun and a titular regent to the shogun (*shikken*), with the real power being exercised by a retired *shikken*.' Amazingly, for a time at least, it worked. The masking of effective authority by shadow office-holders has continued in Japan ever since and is not uncommon in big business to this day. Another distinctively Japanese tendency – a marked preference for collective decision-making by consensus – can also be traced back to the standard operating procedure of the Kamakura regime's three major offices of state – the *samurai-dokoro* (responsible for disciplining the 2,000 Minamoto vassals), the *mandokoro* (general administration) and the *monchujo* (court of arbitration).

More significant than the management of bureaucratic intricacies at the centre was the regime's achievement in establishing greater control over the provinces. Warrior vassals were appointed as constables (*shugo*) to take control of military recruitment and the suppression of disorder. Stewards (*jito*) were given charge of the lands directly under the control of the *bakufu* itself and bidden to collect taxes, expand cultivation, build roads and bridges and operate post stations. These appointees were bound to the ruling house by ties of personal loyalty as well as the profits of their office. The constables and stewards supplemented rather than supplanted imperial office-holders such as provincial governors but over time significantly upstaged them. The result of these innovations was, therefore, anything but a clear and comprehensive system of administration. Competing jurisdictions and personal rivalries created a semi-permanent situation of meddle and muddle, made worse by natural disasters which seem to have been more than usually frequent in the thirteenth century. On the other hand the *bakufu* did make earnest attempts to render justice as impartially as possible, issuing a systematised statement of feudal custom in 1232 as the Joei Code.

KAMIKAZE

Having seized most of China and Korea, the Mongol leader Kublai Khan determined to be suzerain of Japan as well. A first attempt at conquest was made in 1274 and a bridgehead established near Hakata in northern Kyushu. The Japanese were saved, not by their own ferocious efforts, but by a storm which wrecked the invasion fleet. In 1281 an expedition five times larger, consisting of two fleets, totalling 4,400 ships and 140,000 soldiers, tried again. Once again a bridgehead was established at Hakata. Once again fierce Japanese resistance prevented a break-out. Once again a storm annihilated the invaders. The Japanese hailed these typhoons as *kamikaze* (divine winds) and took their intervention as proof of heavenly protection over 'the Land of the Gods'. Nevertheless the regime felt it essential to continue to keep up its defence efforts. This involved the construction of such immense coastal fortifications and the mobilisation of so many labourers that agricultural output was severely crippled as a result. The drain on the nation's resources was offset neither by new lands nor by booty to compensate those who defended the country with their swords or, in the case of the Buddhist monasteries, with their prayers. The resulting discontent undoubtedly weakened Hojo authority as their regime slid towards bankruptcy.

Kamakura

Coastal Kamakura was chosen as the *bakufu*'s seat of government chiefly for strategic reasons. Its seven approach roads all went through steep mountain passes which could easily be defended. At the core of the city stood the Tsurugaoka shrine to the Minamoto's tutelary house deity – Hachiman, the God of War.

Although Kamakura expanded to a population of some 50,000 it never looked to rival Kyoto as a centre of urban sophistication. Indeed, Lady Nijo, the ex-mistress of a retired emperor, wrote witheringly of it as a place where local warlords visiting the shrine failed to wear the correct white pilgrim garb and turned up 'in everyday dress of various colours'. And as for the prospect of the city itself – 'Houses hugged the mountain slopes in terraced rows, huddled together like things stuffed into a pouch. I found this an altogether unattractive sight.' Kyoto courtiers may have become politically vestigial and economically marginal but Lady Nijo's disdain implies that their snobbish self-confidence was unimpaired.

Knights and Samurai

Samurai have been compared to the knights of medieval Europe. Some superficial similarities are obvious. Both were expected to display skill in arms, courage in battle and loyalty to their lord who, in turn, was expected to show generosity in rewarding his followers with booty and hospitality. Both knights and samurai were expected to prize personal honour, scorn hardship, cultivate self-control and despise wealth, but the cult of chivalry towards women and the religious zeal of the Crusaders would both have been quite alien to the Japanese warrior. Samurai women were expected to be every bit as tough and dutiful as their men and even to fight in case of necessity, wielding the fearsome, long-handled *naginata* (halberd). And, whereas knights often battled to extend the bounds of Christendom or wipe out heretics, Japanese warfare was invariably innocent of ideology. The religious beliefs of a samurai were largely a matter of individual conscience and consolation; they were expected to buttress, rather than conflict with, his primary obligations of service and honour.

Equally striking was the difference in knightly and samurai attitudes to the lord-vassal relationship. In Europe there was a contractual element which became increasingly explicit, whereas in Japan the duty of the follower was absolute and unconditional. Another major difference affected rights of inheritance. In medieval Europe the eldest son normally inherited his father's title and undivided estate as a matter of course, but in Japan a father retained the right to choose his successor and, if he thought his eldest offspring incapable, to disinherit him in favour of another son, a son-in-law or even a nephew. Naturally such decisions were not always accepted with equanimity. They were further complicated by the fact that a 'son' was sometimes older than the 'father' adopting him. Although both knights and samurai were expected to show benevolence towards the oppressed, knights were encouraged by the Church to spare the defeated whereas samurai were expected to seek death before dishonour. Those who did surrender could only expect torture and then slaughter at the hands of the victor. Many took their own lives on the battlefield rather than accept such a fate. By the twelfth century this practice had already become institutionalised as a ritual act of disembowelment, correctly termed *seppuku* but vulgarly known as *harakiri* (belly-slitting). Such suicide would, of course, be strictly forbidden to a western knight by the Christian church. To the samurai, however, it came to epitomise disdain for death and thus his very manhood.

Nichiren

The tendency of Buddhism to develop distinctively Japanese forms was strengthened in this period by the emergence of a new populist sect, named after its founder, Nichiren, and the spread of a strikingly different form of commitment, Zen, especially among the warrior class. Both represented a desire for a more direct and satisfying form of spiritual experience and thus a reaction against reliance on esoteric scriptures or complex rituals. But the former relied completely on the compassion of the Buddha for salvation, the latter entirely on the effort of the individual.

Whereas the promoters of Amidism (*see p. 42*) such as Honen, Shinran and Ippen, resembled revivalists in their approach, Nichiren Shonin (1222–82) was more like an Old Testament prophet or a

Savonarola. So sure in his beliefs as to reject all compromise, he campaigned to make his doctrines the official religion of the state and would have had non-believers killed as heretics. He dismissed the conventional *nembutsu* as a 'damnable practice' and excoriated Kobo Daishi (*see p. 39*) as 'the greatest liar in Japan'. Instead he substituted the chanting of the formula '*Namu myoho renge kyo*' – 'Praise to the Wonderful Law of the Lotus Sutra' – and made that text the core of his teachings. Twice exiled for his extremism, Nichiren modestly identified the Bodhisattva of Superb Action with himself and gained great prestige by prophesying the Mongol invasions. It is entirely appropriate that his name can be read in two ways, one meaning 'Sun Lotus', the other 'Japanese Buddhism'. By 1469 half of Kyoto practised Nichiren Buddhism but later persecutions persuaded the movement to redirect its focus from zealotry to education. One of Nichiren Buddhism's important modern descendants is Soka Gakkai, the 'Value Creating Society', founded in 1930. In the post-war period, it has sponsored its own political party, the Komeito (Clean Government Party), as well as its own university, publishing house and symphony orchestra.

Just as some scholars have drawn parallels between European and Japanese feudalism, so others have seen striking similarities between Christianity and the evolution of Buddhism in Japan with its growing emphasis on salvation through faith and an afterlife in paradise. Pushing the comparison even further they have also seen parallels with the Reformation in such developments as the organisation of religious observance around congregations rather than monasteries, the marriage of the clergy, vernacular translation of the scriptures and the merging of religious and national identities.

Zen

The term Zen (in Chinese *Ch'an*) comes ultimately from the Sanskrit *dhyana* (meditation). Zen arose in China in the sixth century and developed strongly in Japan from the twelfth century onwards. Zen aims to transmit the essence of enlightenment (*satori*) but not by such conventional methods as studying scriptures, performing rituals or doing good deeds.

The techniques employed by devotees of Zen range from deep meditation (*zazen*) as practised by Dogen (1200–53), founder of the Soto sect, to puzzling out riddles (*koan*) as recommended by Eisai (1141–1215), founder of the Rinzai sect, to physical 'shock treatment' involving loud screams or sudden blows with a hand or even a heavy stick. But all schools stress the value of a close personal link between pupil and master. Zen's contempt for nit-picking logic, its effort to reconcile self-control with spontaneity and even its off-beat sense of humour ('imagine the sound of one hand clapping', 'what was your original face before you were born?') all appealed profoundly to the warrior class.

TWO MASTERS

Zen ideals of gracefulness and understatement later came to exert an enduring influence in fields as diverse as calligraphy and archery, ink-painting and the design of ceramics, tea-ceremony and landscape-gardening. One of the most admired of all garden designers was the Zen adept Muso Soseki (1275–1351). As a wandering monk he incorporated natural scenery into the gardens he established around small mountain temples. Such fusion of the 'natural' and 'artificial' represents a typically Zen denial of the reality or meaning of categorical distinctions, so too does the artful selection and placing of rocks to imply that they too, being products of nature, also live and even 'grow'. In later life, as abbot of the Kyoto monasteries of Tenryuji and Rin-senji, Muso designed more elaborate landscapes. His final retreat at Saihoji is celebrated for a garden consisting principally of moss.

Zen's emphasis on salvation by self-help could promote the sort of eccentric individualism exemplified in the career of the 'mad monk' Ikkyu Sojun (1394–1481). He outraged the conventional by fre-quenting brothels, hob-nobbing with worldly merchant princes and collecting around himself a band of bohemian acolytes, including the artist Bokusai (d.1496) who both painted his portrait and wrote his biography. Another of Ikkyu's disciples was the priest Juko (Murata Shuko, 1422–1502) who served Yoshimasa as a consultant on Chinese art and pioneered the ritualised serving of tea in precious bowls in the calm surroundings of a small, plain straw-matted chamber. A refined calligrapher and accomplished poet in both Japanese and Chinese, Ikkyu was also a fiery preacher. Despite his unpredictability he was appointed abbot of Daitokuji temple in Kyoto where he used his wealthy contacts to finance extensive reconstruction work. In old age he continued to scandalise by conducting a very public affair with a blind woman entertainer.

Swordsmiths, Sculptors and Scholars

'The sword is the soul of the samurai' declares the Japanese proverb. The samurai's two swords were his badge of rank and the tools of his trade. During the Kamakura period the art of sword-making reached an unprecedented excellence. Given the new dominance of the military classes this is, perhaps, unsurprising. The high seriousness of the craft was signified by the fact that smithies were treated with the reverence normally reserved for shrines and the smiths themselves worked in a state of ritual purity guaranteed by Shinto rites. Individual blades were often given names and passed from father to son as family treasures. Straight-bladed iron swords had been imported from China and Korea as early as the third century AD. The deeply curved blade peculiar to Japan appeared by the tenth century and thereafter distinctive schools of sword-making began to develop. Swordsmiths learned to combine hard and soft steels to make a composite weapon which, in the words of one expert, combined the attributes of a hammer and a razor, being sharp enough to strike armour without shattering and weighty enough to slice through a man from shoulder to navel at a single blow. (Hip to hip was reckoned to be the hardest stroke to bring off.) Along the hardened edge of each blade is a crystalline pattern (*hamon*) produced by the process of tempering. Some patterns were likened to frost on the grass, others to stars in the sky. Swordsmiths perfected their own distinctive patterns to serve as marks of authentication and individual signatures. More prosaically blades were also marked on the *tang* (the end that fits into the handle) with characters identifying their provenance. Sub-division of the craft was eventually to produce specialist makers of scabbards and fittings such as guards and handles which could be changed to suit different occasions. Swords became a major export item to China, the embassy of 1483 alone taking some 37,000 of them.

A DYNASTY OF SCULPTORS

The other art which achieved new heights was sculpture, much of it made to replace images destroyed during the wars which brought the Minamoto to power. Japanese artists typically worked in wood or bronze rather than stone. The sculptures they produced were invariably painted and often decorated with eyes of crystal and jewelled crowns or metal swords. Most represented figures in the pantheon of Buddhist deities or saints but a significant innovation of the period was the realistic representation of individuals, such as great priest-teachers or statesmen, through portrait statues. The demonic guardian figures found at Buddhist temples, by contrast, are characterised by boldly

The Great Buddha at Kamakura

exaggerated facial features, postures and gestures intended to strike terror into the onlooker. Dramatic iconography emphasising the serenity and compassion of the Buddha or the horrors of hell was felt to be essential to convey the basic tenets of a subtle faith to the illiterate peasant masses.

The greatest sculptors of the age were Kokei, his son Unkei (d. 1223) and his son Tankei. All of Unkei's six sons became sculptors and their descendants continued to work in Kamakura as sculptors until the nineteenth century. The greatest sculpture of the age – in the most literal sense – was the 52-foot-high bronze Buddha cast in 1252 which remains one of Kamakura's most famous sights.

Other significant artistic developments of the era include the painting of fine picture-scrolls (*emakimono*) and the establishment by the potter Toshiro of a kiln at Seto for making Japan's first glazed wares. Toshiro (an abbreviation for Kato Shirozaemon Kagemasa) is said to have studied in China and is regarded as the father of fine ceramics in Japan, though he remains, historically speaking, a shadowy figure.

CHARTERS, SAGAS AND ESSAYS

Literature lagged behind the visual arts, for the military class was less learned in its accomplishments than it was cultured in its aspirations. Literacy was harnessed primarily to the purposes of the state to produce a proliferation of charters, registers and court reports which testify to the efforts of the shogunal regime to impose some sort of administrative order on the chaos of feudal realities. Composed in a peculiar mixture of colloquial Japanese and formal Chinese, these documents, blending native and foreign elements, albeit awkwardly, represent the emergence of Japanese in its national, written form.

Chanted tales of war satisfied the samurai appetite for literary diversion. Sansom dismisses the massive output of courtly poetry in this period as tired and pedantic, though he concludes generously that 'versifying at its worst is an amiable weakness and perhaps it helped to keep the spirit of poetry alive'. The most enduring works have proved to be occasional pieces and poems produced by the more reflective members of the religious orders. The best-known of these is *Hojoki* (*The Ten Foot Square Hut*) by Kamo no Chomei (d. 1216), a casualty of disaster and disorder, who reconciled himself to the loss of career and fortune and retired to mountain solitude. Successively a victim of fire, famine and earthquake, he found his consolation in the beauties of the seasons and his 'greatest joy in a quiet nap'.

The Ashikaga Shogunate

Exhausted by the effort to fend off the Mongols, incapable of rewarding supporters and impaired by a succession of sub-standard leaders, the Hojo lurched from one expedient to another in their efforts to restore the national finances, ordering debt-cancellations and the reversal of sales of over-mortgaged lands, and then cancelling the cancellations and reversing the reversals.

Scenting the decay of a dynasty, the Emperor Go-Daigo (1288–1339) repeatedly intrigued against the Hojo. In 1333 he managed to

A vivid painting of Ashikaga Takauji taken from a silk scroll, *ca* 1360s

escape from off-shore exile and, supported by Kyoto courtiers eager to regain their former eminence and western feudal magnates motivated by greed and envy of the easterners, rose once again. The Kamakura regime sent troops to crush the rising, among them an army led by Ashikaga Takauji (1305–58) – ironically a descendant of a branch of the Minamoto – who defected to the emperor's cause. When another general also turned his coat and marched into their very headquarters, the Hojo vacated the stage by committing suicide *en masse*.

COUP AND COUNTER-COUP

Go-Daigo's period of personal rule, known as the 'Kemmu Restoration', was short-lived. By showing exclusive favour to the charmed circle of court nobles he not only outraged his former warrior allies but revealed himself to be totally out of touch with the realities of political power. Unchastened by experience he compounded his folly by trying to levy a new national tax to pay for the building of an immense new royal residence. A counter-coup led by Ashikaga Takauji led to a see-saw war which, despite the heroic self-sacrifice of the emperor's most loyal champion, Kusunoki Masashige (d. 1336), forced him to flee to Yoshino in the mountainous area south of Nara. One significant by-product of this abortive attempt to turn back the political clock was the manifesto written by Kitabatake Chikafusa (1293–1354) – 'Record of the Legitimate Succession of the Divine Emperors' – which attempted to validate Go-Daigo's cause by an appeal to his genealogy. Its opening words – 'Great Japan is the land of the gods' – constitute an early assertion of the nationalistic doctrine that the nation's unique superiority derives from its unbroken line of emperors. Ironically this claim was being articulated at the very time when two branches of the imperial line were locked in a deadly struggle to decide which of them actually did represent an uninterrupted continuity with the mythic past.

TWO COURTS

At Yoshino a 'southern court' continued to exist for more than half a century while the throne of a 'northern court' at Kyoto was occupied by a succession of Ashikaga-sponsored puppets. The two imperial lines were reunited in 1392 by the third Ashikaga shogun, Yoshimitsu

(1358–1408), who also settled the seat of government in the Muromachi district of Kyoto. The era of the Ashikaga shogunate (1338–
1573) is therefore also known as the Muromachi period. In 1395
Yoshimitsu retired in favour of his young son, Yoshimochi (1386–
1428), to assure the succession but he continued to be the real head of
government and did not hesitate to treat the emperor and his circle
with insulting familiarity. A generous and discerning patron of the arts,
he dwelt in splendour in the famed Golden Pavilion (*Kinkakuji, see
p. 263*) which is now held to be one of Japan's greatest treasures. He
also made an immense personal fortune by reopening official trade with
China, all but suspended since the Mongol invasions. The Chinese
accepted trading relations only under the guise of payments of tribute
and in any case chiefly valued commerce with Japan not for itself but as
a way of pressuring the Japanese into controlling their pirate-infested
waters. Yoshimitsu's willingness to accept the Ming emperor's recognition of him as a subject 'King of Japan' has earned him the unanimous
derision of Japanese historians.

THE FALL OF THE DYNASTY

Ashikaga authority reached its peak under the calculating Yoshimitsu,
the drunkard Yoshimochi and his younger brother, the puritanical
Yoshinori (1394–1441), but it was never as complete as that attained by
the Kamakura *bakufu*. All three were ruthless and cruel but in an age
distinguished by the prevalence of such qualities they were not sufficient in themselves to guarantee hegemony. *Shugo* effectively ceased to
be removable appointees as they made their office hereditary. The great
feudal houses – Hosokawa, Hatakeyama and Shiba – entrenched
themselves in the central bureaucracy. Major regions, like Kyushu,
were virtually autonomous. Peasants, victimised by natural disasters,
inflation and extortion, or inspired by Buddhist visions of a just and
painless paradise, rose in revolt periodically. But it was succession disputes among the military classes which led to the most constant warfare
and ultimately sealed the fate of the *bakufu* itself.

The eighth shogun, Yoshimasa (1436–90), preferring courtly amusements to the increasingly grim realities of an inheritance sliding into
anarchy, decided in 1464 to designate his brother, Yoshimi, as his

successor. The very next year, however, Yoshimasa's wife presented him with a son and the demand that it should be granted the succession. The resulting quarrel dragged in rival factions on both sides, eager to settle old scores. The outcome was the Onin War (1467–77) which incinerated Kyoto and reduced Ashikaga authority over the provinces to a mere pretence. The later Ashikaga shoguns were largely the puppets of the Hosokawa and Japanese historians have dubbed their century of misrule *Sengoku Jidai* – the Era of Warring States.

Art among the Ashes

Despite the disorder of the age, economic development continued, albeit unevenly. The ports of Hakata, Sakai (Osaka) and Hyogo (Kobe) grew significantly. The castles at Odawara and Kagoshima became the nuclei of flourishing towns. As the water-wheel came into common use irrigation techniques improved. Better swords meant better farm-tools. The cultivation of barley, the increasing use of fertiliser and the spread of double-cropping all helped to swell the harvest. Regional specialisation in the growing of tea, flax and hemp, the introduction of skilled crafts such as the manufacture of paper, silk and cotton cloth, and the emergence of free-wheeling merchants who sought to buck an increasingly restrictive guild system, all imply the emergence of more market-oriented modes of production rather than a general practice of subsisting for survival.

Kurosawa's film *Seven Samurai* (*see p. 190*), set in this period, depicts a peasantry exposed to the most brutal bandit exploitation – but even he concludes that it is the peasants rather than the bandits that win through in the end. Perhaps, like the contemporaneous Wars of the Roses in England, the feudal scuffles of this era brought more in retribution upon their participants than they wrought in destruction upon innocent bystanders. The ability of communities to recover rapidly from arson and pillage and the increased popularity of large-scale and long-distance pilgrimage both imply economic as well as social resilience and the existence of a substantial surplus for 'investment' in purposes that were, in the narrow sense, 'non-productive' – i.e. cultural.

ZEN ASCENDANCY

The Ashikaga looked with special regard on the Rinzai sect of Zen Buddhism and recruited from a specially favoured group, the 'Five Monasteries' (*Gozan*), a succession of monks who served them as counsellors, curators, diplomats and tutors. If Zen was not actually the religion of the state it was certainly the philosophy of its usurpers for, if they seldom grasped its subtleties themselves, they often bowed to the advice of those who did.

Zen monasteries built in this period often embodied an austere Chinese style which itself echoed Indian influences. Chinese *objets d'art* and impressionistic ink-paintings of landscapes and other natural subjects were highly prized and inspired Japanese imitation. The monk Sesshu (1420–1506), who actually studied in China, became the acknowledged supreme master of the exacting art known as *suiboku-ga* (water and black ink paintings). The economy of line and suggestion of mass and depth which he achieved in a few bold brush-strokes are also embodied in the Zen-inspired 'dry landscape' (*kare-sansui* – dry mountain water) gardens, like those at Ryoan-ji and Daitoku-ji in Kyoto, where rocks and white sand replicate the impression of flowing water.

NOH

In the field of performing arts the most significant achievement was the elaboration of the *Noh* drama from naïve song, dance and mime routines to accompany religious or village festivals to the level of *yugen* – sublime beauty. This was chiefly the work of the actor Kan'ami (1333–84) and his producer son Zeami (1363–1443), whose good looks attracted the homosexual attentions and generous patronage of shogun Yoshimitsu. Zeami, a theatrical genius, not only wrote some ninety plays but also set out his dramaturgical theories in twenty-one treatises. The Zen principle of 'non-action' provided him with a rationale for acting which was self-consciously non-realistic and symbolic. The highly stylised performances of *Noh* often deal with the supernatural or with madness and thus feature angels, ghosts and demons, but their essence lies far more in style than in substance. Plot development is much less important than the relentless intensification of a single emotion to a point of concentration and climax. *Noh* still enjoys a devoted following among cognoscenti although, of the 2,000 plays known to have been written, texts survive for only 800 and of these less than a third are still in the active repertoire. Much study is required by the uninitiated to appreciate a *Noh* performance as more than a gorgeously-costumed mystery, but this is less true of the *kyogen* ('mad words') interludes used to punctuate the serious and sad set-pieces. *Kyogen* ranges from the satirical to the slapstick and often derides the pretensions of authority figures such as priests or village elders. Direct, simple and sometimes cruel, it represents the humour of the underdog.

The most noteworthy literary innovation of the Muromachi period was the fashion for *renga*, a linked-verse form which gave its exponents the chance to show off both deep learning and ready wit. Usually one person would offer the opening three lines of a stanza, which a second would complete with two more. These last two would then be taken up by a third person as the opening lines of a new verse and so on. A typical session of competitive versification would produce a hundred stanzas. Accomplished practitioners could manipulate their 'spontaneity' to link the separate verses around a developmental theme such as the passage of the seasons. The *renga* vogue spread from courtiers to monks, samurai and even merchants. The more colloquial forms became the forerunners of the humorous *senryu* of the Edo period (*see p. 105*).

Paradoxically this age of topsy-turvy catastrophe also witnessed the gradual formalisation of the elegant tea-ceremony and the founding of organised schools to perpetuate and refine the delicate arts of incense-burning and flower-arranging (*ikebana*).

CHAPTER FIVE

The Christian Century,
1543–1639

The general anarchy which grew out of the Onin War (1467–77) continued for over a century as feudal lords, freelance adventurers and even leagues of villages, banded together for mutual protection, struggled against each other for survival or local supremacy. The nature of warfare changed decisively with the introduction of firearms, the construction of massive castles and a shift from cavalry, fighting with sword and bow, to infantry, fighting with pike and gun. Japanese historians have dubbed the Darwinian process of mutual rivalry *gekokujo* – 'those beneath overthrow those above'. The ultimate demise of the Ashikaga shogunate illustrates the process clearly enough. For over half a century (1490–1568) the vestiges of shogunal authority were exercised by the Hosokawa family, until they were usurped by their retainers, the Miyoshi (1558–65), who were in turn displaced by their vassals, the Matsunaga (1565–8). The abandonment of Kyoto by the last Ashikaga in 1573 effectively marks the final end of the dynasty.

This minuet of treachery at the supposed heart of government was, however, largely irrelevant to the larger course of events. Japan's future destiny was being shaped by clashes between great provincial warlords and their determination to bring 'all the country under one sword'. Three men, very different in their personalities and backgrounds but alike in their guile and ruthlessness, accomplished the work of national reunification. One analogy holds that Oda Nobunaga (1534–82) hacked out the stones, Toyotomi Hideyoshi (1537–98) cut them to shape and Tokugawa Ieyasu (1543–1616) set them into place. The contrast in their characters is summed up in a story that they were once infuriated by a songbird which refused to sing. Oda threatened to kill it,

Toyotomi vowed to force it to sing – but Ieyasu knew that if he had the patience to wait long enough it would sing of its own accord.

The process of national reunification was complicated by Japan's first contacts with Europeans, contacts which resulted in an invasion which was less political and economic than cultural and technological. Its main carriers were merchants and missionaries and they brought with them such novelties as guns, spectacles, clocks, carpets, perspective oil-painting, tobacco, sweet potatoes, bread – and Christianity.

Oda Nobunaga

Oda Nobunaga began his career of conquest as a minor leader of a minor clan who held the castle of Nagoya. He took part in his first battle at the age of thirteen. A warrior by bent, he was quick to recognise the value of

Himeji Castle which was completed in 1617. Famous for its elegance, its appearance resembles many castles of the past, such as Nobunaga's Azuchi Castle

the gun and the first to grasp its battle-winning potential when used *en masse*. He was also the first to use iron-clad ships.

It was Nobunaga who was responsible for establishing the last Ashikaga, Yoshiaki, in power, and then deposing him when he tried to be more than a puppet. When the militant monks of Mt Hiei, whose great temple complex overshadowed Kyoto, attempted to stand against him he reduced it to ashes and massacred all its inhabitants. Between 1576 and 1579 he used an army of slave-labourers to build a magnificent castle at Azuchi, overlooking Biwa, Japan's largest lake. The foremost painter of the day, Kano Eitoku (1543–90) was employed to fill it with golden screens of unprecedented splendour. By 1582 a small town with a free market had grown up around the castle walls but in that same year Nobunaga fell victim to one of his own generals. Moving to join forces engaged in countering a threat in western Japan he paused to enjoy a tea-ceremony at the Honnoji temple in Kyoto. Here he was surrounded by units under the command of Akechi Mitsuhide. After a ferocious but futile resistance Nobunaga ended his bloody career with Wagnerian bravura, disembowelling himself while the ancient temple crashed around him in flames. By the time of his death more than half the provinces of Japan, including the central region around Kyoto, had been brought under his rule. By instituting new land surveys, abolishing tolls and beginning to disarm the peasantry he also laid the foundations on which his successors were to build a new Japan of order and prosperity.

'MONKEY'

Nobunaga was soon avenged by the ugly little man he had himself nicknamed 'Monkey'. Toyotomi Hideyoshi soon revealed himself as anything but small in his ambitions. A foot-soldier with a genius for siegecraft, he had risen swiftly in Nobunaga's service and felt fully competent to continue what his master had begun. In 1587 he celebrated the success of a huge punitive expedition into southern Kyushu by staging a lavish ten-day tea-ceremony at the Kitano shrine in Kyoto. From 1588 onwards he accelerated the process of disarming the peasantry by instituting an intensified 'sword hunt' (*katana gari*). By 1590 Hideyoshi's supremacy was recognised from one end of the country to the other. In the same year he ordered the taking of a census as the basis of a new system of land-holding and taxation. Henceforth payment of taxes would no longer be in cash but in rice. This made it possible to tie the extraction of surplus much more closely to the actual productive power of the land and to relate income directly to military potential by estimating how great an army could be provisioned from the yield of a specific estate. Farmers' rights to cultivate the land were guaranteed but the price for security was the loss of freedom. They were forbidden to neglect any of their land or leave it. To confirm the separation of social classes a decree of 1591 obliged craftsmen and merchants to live in towns and forbade them residence in villages. Henceforth each man, at least in theory, was bound from birth to follow the occupation of his father. The petrification of the social order had begun.

Hideyoshi's administrative reforms were accompanied by the slighting of many castles, the issue of new coinage, a take-over of all gold and silver mines and foreign trade and the establishment of a uniform system of weights and measures.

INVASION OF KOREA

In 1592 Hideyoshi resigned the regency in favour of his nephew and began to build himself an extravagant residence at Fushimi, near Kyoto. Its elaborate Chinese-style gate survives at Nijo castle in Kyoto. In the same year Hideyoshi also set himself to conquer the rest of the world – i.e. China. The first step was the invasion of Korea.

The Japanese invaders swept aside feeble resistance until the Korean king appealed for Chinese assistance and the Korean navy rallied under the redoubtable Admiral Yi. Although they beat off the first Chinese counter-attack, the Japanese were soon weakened by Korean guerilla resistance and their lack of naval forces. They were relentlessly forced back from the borders of Manchuria, abandoning first Pyongyang and then Seoul. Attempts to broker a negotiated settlement foundered and in 1597 Hideyoshi despatched another invasion force of 100,000. Again the pattern of initial success and subsequent retreat was repeated. Hideyoshi's sudden death in September 1598 led to the immediate abandonment of this hugely destructive and ultimately abortive enterprise.

Historians have long debated whether the Korean expeditions were ultimate proof of Hideyoshi's megalomania or a shrewd attempt to divert turbulent military energies from disturbing the peace he had so painfully achieved in Japan itself. Whatever their motivation they had two certain outcomes: an enduring legacy of enmity between the two countries and, paradoxically, an enrichment of Japanese culture through the immigration of Korean master-craftsmen, especially potters and printers.

A Shogun at last

Having nominated his nephew Hidetsugu as successor, the childless Hideyoshi had suddenly found himself a father in 1593. In 1595 Hidetsugu was banished and ordered to commit suicide while his family and most trusted retainers were massacred to root out any possibility of further challenge to the newly-designated successor, the infant Hideyori. In the summer of 1598 doting, dying Hideyoshi established a five-strong council of regency to ensure the succession of his son. Guardianship of Hideyori was entrusted to Tokugawa Ieyasu, who had, through all the twists and turmoils of the previous half-century of bloodshed, managed to come out on the right side of both Nobunaga and Hideyoshi.

Ieyasu had spent much of his childhood as a hostage. Calculation came as second nature to him. The many sayings attributed to him reveal the temper of his heart – 'Turn your attention to distasteful duties', 'Consider anger as an enemy', 'Regard discomfort as normal and you will not be troubled by want'. To demonstrate his loyalty to Nobunaga, Ieyasu had arranged the deaths of his first wife and eldest son when they were suspected of plotting against his overlord. To bind himself to Hideyoshi he had given him a son to adopt and married his middle-aged sister. By the time Hideyoshi died Ieyasu was the largest single landholder in the country, with twice as much as the next nearest to him. Reneging on his pledge to protect Hideyori's succession, Ieyasu prepared to seize supreme power for himself. He secured the backing of four other feudal chieftains and crushed his opponents in one of the most decisive encounters in Japanese history – the battle of Sekigahara, fought on 21 October 1600.

SETTLING THE DYNASTY

Ieyasu's victory enabled him to confiscate eighty-seven estates from the defeated and distribute them amongst his own followers. He also took control of Kyoto and with it the person of the emperor. In 1603 he had himself proclaimed shogun. Hideyoshi's peasant origins had disqualified him from appointment to such high honour but Ieyasu claimed descent from the Minamoto, founders of the Kamakura shogunate. Nijo castle was completed in the nominal capital as a palatial residence from which the shogun's deputy could keep a watchful eye on the emperor and court. Meanwhile Edo in eastern Japan was rapidly built up as the stronghold of Tokugawa power (*see p. 84*).

In 1605, to ensure the continuance of the new dynasty, Ieyasu resigned as shogun in favour of his third son, Hidetada. In typical Japanese fashion the old tyrant remained the real ruler of the country, albeit living for the most part in discreet seclusion. Ieyasu knew that the security of his regime could not be guaranteed while Hideyori and his disgruntled supporters remained alive. The final confrontation between the two sides involved a lengthy siege (1614–15) which culminated in the sacking of the immense Osaka Castle and the suicide of Hideyori amid the carnage. (A large part of the artistic output of Kano Eitoku was an incidental casualty of the inferno.) The present Osaka Castle is a replica. Ieyasu's last political accomplishment was to issue regulations to guide the governance of feudal domains and the imperial court. After his death he was enshrined in a mausoleum so gorgeous that it has given rise to a proverb, 'Never use the word "magnificent" until you have seen Nikko!' (*see p. 267*). Elevated to the status of a Shinto *kami* he was also hailed as 'Tosho Daigongen', a manifestation of the Buddha in the incarnation of Healer.

Newcomers

Europeans first came to Japan by accident when a Chinese junk, with Portuguese passengers, was driven ashore on the island of Tanegashima.

While the crew repaired the ship the Portuguese strolled along the shore shooting at duck. The Japanese had never seen a gun before; within six months they had learned how to manufacture them. Technology transfer dates back to the very beginning of the relationship between Japan and 'the West'.

The initial impressions that Japan and its people made on Europeans are of considerable interest in the light of the subsequent relationships between the two cultures. One of the earliest (*ca* 1565) accounts in English combines condemnation and respect in a curious mixture:

> The extreme part of the knowen world unto us is the noble Iland Giapan.... This country is hillie and pestered with snow, wherefore it is neither so warm as Portugal, nor so wealthy ... wanting oyle, butter, cheese, milk, eggs, sugar, honey, vinegar.... Nevertheless in the Iland sundry fruites doe growe, not much unlike the fruites of Spaine: and great store of silver mines are to be seen therein. The people are tractable, civill, wittie, courteous, without deceit, in vertue and honest conversation exceeding all other nations lately discovered, but so much standing upon their reputation, that their chief Idole may be thought honour. The contempt thereof causeth among them much discord and debate, manslaughter and murther.... They live chiefly by fish, hearbes and fruites, so healthfully that they die very old.... No man is ashamed there of his poverty ... so much do they make more account of gentry than of wealth. The greatest delight they have is in armour.... They feed moderately but they drink largely.

The first Englishman to know the Japanese at first-hand summarised their character more concisely: 'The people of this Iland of Iapon are good of nature, curteous above measure and valiant in warre....'

'SOUTHERN BARBARIANS'

Traders, bringing guns, were quickly followed by priests, bringing the gospel. Japanese came to call these newcomers *namban* – 'southern barbarians' – because they usually arrived from the south, making their first landfall in Kyushu. Vivid painted screens, depicting the aliens wearing bizarre, baggy pants and sporting protuberant noses, are representative of what has become known as *namban* art.

For half a century the Jesuits had a virtual monopoly on the missionary enterprise. Their leader, St Francis Xavier, pronounced the

St Francis Xavier painted by a Japanese artist after a Western original

Japanese to be 'the best people yet discovered' and proclaimed them to be 'the delight of my heart'. The missionaries set about their task with industriousness and discretion. Acutely aware of the cultural gulf between the traditions of Christendom and those of Japan, they analysed their situation with meticulous thoroughness. The Italian Vicar General, Alessandro Valignano, declared that 'Japan is a world the reverse of Europe'. His colleague, the Spaniard Luis Frois, author of the first *History of Japan* to be written by a Westerner, carefully listed the topsy-turvy customs that confronted them:

> With us it is not very common that women can write; the noble ladies of Japan consider it a humiliation not to be literate.
> In Europe the men are tailors, and in Japan the women.
> We believe in future glory or punishment and in the immortality of the soul; the Zen bonzes (monks) deny all that and avow that there is nothing more than birth and death.
> We bury our dead; the Japanese cremate most of theirs.

People in Europe love baked and boiled fish; the Japanese much prefer it raw.

We mount a horse with the left foot first; the Japanese with the right.

Our paper is only of four or five types; the Japanese have more than fifty varieties.

We consider precious stones and decorations of gold and silver as being valuable; the Japanese prize old kettles, ancient and cracked porcelain. . . .

Despite their bewilderment the Jesuits persevered, producing a Portuguese-Japanese dictionary and dressing in saffron robes like Buddhist priests. Father João Rodrigues' *Arte da Lingua de Iapan*, a treatise of 480 pages, represents the first systematic attempt to analyse the complexities of Japanese grammar-which was alleged by some of his brethren to be an invention of the devil, invented of a purpose to hinder the propagation of the gospel. The Jesuits also operated a printing-press. Most of its titles were religious textbooks; but one combined simplified versions of *Aesop's Fables* and the *Heike Monogatari*. (Coincidentally printing with moveable type was introduced from Korea, where it had also been pioneered, in the very same decade.)

PROFIT AND PERSECUTION

In the absence of any strong central government the Jesuits were relatively free to spread their doctrines and gained much encouragement from those Japanese nobles who saw conversion to Christianity as a painless pathway to profitable commerce with the Portuguese trading-base at Macao, on the southern coast of China. They also valued trade with westerners as a source of guns, armour and cannon.

From 1570 onwards Nagasaki, on the western coast of Kyushu, developed as a Jesuit-dominated port. Nobunaga welcomed the Christians as a counterweight to the influence of the militant Buddhist sects and by the year of his death there are reckoned to have been some 150,000 Japanese converts to the faith. This represented an astonishing success considering that there were at that time perhaps not more than twenty European fathers, assisted by thirty local aides. Two years later the first Japanese envoys to Europe arrived in Lisbon – four Christian boys aged thirteen and fourteen, despatched by three Christian lords of Kyushu. In Madrid they were received with honour by Philip II and in

Rome by Pope Gregory XIII himself. Throughout their odyssey they behaved with conspicuous decorum. Their momentous journey ended with their safe return eight years after their departure.

The prospects for the new faith began to darken as Hideyoshi became concerned about its concentrated influence in newly-subjugated Kyushu. Offers made by a visiting Jesuit official to support the warlord in his career of conquest alarmed him as he realised that the missionaries might have temporal power as well as spiritual objectives. It was all too easy to conjure up a nightmare scenario in which Christianised warlords called in the aid of foreigners to contest his supremacy. In 1587 Hideyoshi suddenly required all his vassals to seek his permission before giving their allegiance to the alien religion. He also decreed that all missionaries should henceforth leave Japan. This order was not rigorously enforced. Indeed, the number of proselytisers actually increased with the arrival of Franciscans, taking advantage of a Vatican decision to breach the Jesuit monopoly. Fired with zeal and impetuousness, the Franciscans, mostly Spanish, soon fell out with the tactful Jesuits, who were mostly Portuguese. The friction between them deepened the odium in which they were held by the increasingly erratic Hideyoshi. In 1597 he abruptly ordered the crucifixion (upside down, like common criminals) of twenty-six Christians. They met their fate with fortitude. The crackdown was a portent of what was to come. But it was not heeded.

SERVANT OF THE SHOGUN

In 1600 yet another kind of newcomer arrived in Japan: Protestants. The Dutch ship *Liefde*, piloted by an Englishman, William Adams (1564–1620), washed up on the shores of Kyushu, her skeleton crew reduced to skeletal condition. A month later Adams was interviewed, via a Jesuit interpreter, by Ieyasu himself:

> The king [i.e. Ieyasu] demanded of me, of what land I was, and what moved us to come to his land, being far off. I showed unto him the name of our country, and that our land had long sought out the East Indies, and desired friendship with all kings and potentates in way of merchandise, having in our land divers commodities which these lands had not. Then he asked whether our country had wars? I answered him yea, with the Spaniards and

Portugals. He asked me in what did I believe? I said, in God, that made heaven and earth. He asked me divers other questions of things of my religion, and . . . what way we came to the country. Having a chart of the whole world I showed him, through the Strait of Magellan. At which he wondered and thought me to lie. . . . And having asked me what merchandise we had in our ship I showed him all. In the end, he being ready to depart, I desired that we might have trade of merchandise, as the Portugals and Spaniards had. To which he made me an answer, but what it was, I did not understand. So he commanded me to be carried to prison. . . .

Adams' confinement had a happy issue. Ignoring with contempt Jesuit demands that the castaway be crucified as a heretic, Ieyasu saw in him a valuable source of political information and technical expertise. Adams soon became the shogun's tutor in mathematics, gunnery and cartography and was raised to samurai status with the rank of *hatamoto* which conferred right of personal access and audience with the country's supreme ruler. No other foreigner has been so honoured before or since. Adams acquired a sizeable estate, married a Japanese wife and had the singular satisfaction of displacing the Jesuit Rodrigues as the shogun's official interpreter. In 1611 he negotiated the inauguration of commercial relations between Japan and the Netherlands and in 1613 did the same for Britain. Later he led a commercial embassy to the Philippines on Ieyasu's behalf. He also built the first western-style ships in Japan and has therefore been subsequently honoured as the founder of the Japanese navy. A ceremony commemorating this achievement is still performed annually at his grave on a hill overlooking the Yokosuka naval base. Adams' extraordinary career provided the inspiration and central character for screen-writer James Clavell's best-selling novel *Shogun*.

THE CLOSING OF JAPAN

William Adams' last years were clouded by the loss of his privileged position and a general decline in the status of Europeans. In his last years even the far-sighted Ieyasu became irritated by the foreigners, their squabbles and their intrigues. Christianity was once again proscribed. Seventy Jesuits sailed away, but almost forty went underground. With the support of a hundred Japanese assistants they committed themselves to sustaining the surviving faithful.

Ieyasu's death deprived Adams of a powerful protector. Hidetada had little use for Adams personally, was inclined to favour Japanese over foreign merchants and was rabidly hostile to Christianity. Whereas Ieyasu had seen advantage to be gained from playing on and profiting from the rivalries of Catholic against Protestant, Spaniard against Portuguese, English against Dutch, his successor drew little satisfaction from the game of divide and conquer. In the year of his father's death Hidetada confined foreign trade to the ports of Nagasaki and Hirado. Adams attempted in vain to re-establish the trading privileges of his countrymen. He did not succeed and died in 1620. The English East India Company, having lost its last major asset, faced up to its failure and wound up its Japanese operations three years later. The Spanish were expelled the following year for their continued support of missionary activity under the cover of trade.

The persecution of Christians became increasingly severe. The foreigners had won converts but they had also made enemies: their dismissal of Buddhism as idolatry had naturally antagonised its priesthood; their criticisms of divorce, concubinage and sodomy had outraged many samurai as insolent meddling. Their condemnation of usury had irritated the merchants, the more so as the entire missionary effort was financed by profits siphoned off from trade conducted in Spanish and Portuguese ships – trade which Japanese merchants wanted for themselves. The aliens were also tainted by the shortcomings of their secular countrymen. Did they not kill and eat useful animals, like horses and oxen? Did they not deal in slaves?

In 1622 fifty-one Christians were martyred at Nagasaki. In 1623 the new shogun, Iemitsu, had fifty more burned at the stake to mark his assumption of office. All Japanese were required to register at Buddhist temples as proof of loyalty. Torture to secure apostasy was systematised. Suspected Christians were required to trample on images of the Virgin and Christ (*fumie*). Professed Christians were immersed in boiling hot sulphur. (The Roman Catholic Church recognises 3,125 martyrdoms in Japan in the years 1597–1660.)

In 1635 Japanese ships were forbidden to sail abroad, children of mixed marriages were deported and an artificial island, Dejima, was built in Nagasaki harbour to house, or rather impound, the last tolerated foreign merchants. Japanese living abroad were forbidden to return home and the construction of ocean-going ships was banned. The final act of this tragedy was played out in 1637–8 when the peasants of Kyushu's Shimabara peninsula rose in revolt against the oppression of their local lord and 37,000 of them took refuge in an abandoned castle. Many, though not all, were Christians. In defiance they sang hymns and flew banners marked with the cross. The Dutch, eager to prove that their interests were commercial rather than spiritual, loaned a ship to the Tokugawa shogunate to bombard the rebels into submission. The castle fell. The defenders, regardless of sex and age, were massacred. The Dutch were confirmed in the favour of the authorities.

When the Portuguese fleet arrived as usual in 1639 its ships were forbidden to unload. In 1640 a mission of seventy-four arrived to plead for the resumption of the trade; sixty-one were executed and the rest spared only to tell the tale. The Dutch, immured on Deshima, remained. Apart from them, Christians were not tolerated in Japan. Nevertheless *onando-buppo* ('backroom Buddhism') survived and in the very different world of 1865 some 20,000 'hidden Christians' were to be uncovered.

Splendour versus Serenity?

'Sudden riches breedeth insolence' observed Francis Bacon (1561–1626), English statesman, judge and philosopher. Apart from being an almost exact contemporary of William Adams his involvement with Japan was minimal – but his maxim hits the mark exactly as far as Japanese warlords are concerned. Arrivistes seem compelled to affirm their arrival. Nobunaga's Azuchi castle has given its name to an era; 'over the top' will suffice as a rough translation. Hideyoshi performed the tea-ceremony with utensils made of gold and had a tea-room whose walls and ceiling were lined with gold-leaf. Somehow, one has the feeling, he didn't quite get the point. His tea-master, the Sakai merchant Sen-no-Rikyu (1522–91), a proponent of the natural and simple, is generally acknowledged as the aesthetic arbiter of the age. Hideyoshi ordered him to commit suicide, allegedly because he would not give up his daughter to the tyrant's harem. To be fair to Hideyoshi he did recognise the talent of master-potter Chojiro who used clay dug near the warlord's residence to make rough-and-ready-looking tea-bowls authenticated with the character *raku* – enjoyment.

CROSSES AND COOKERY

Even an autocrat like Hideyoshi was relatively powerless to command the whims of fashion. Many Japanese flaunted Portuguese garments or dangled rosaries as eye-catching accessories. The Japanese word for a button (another western novelty) is *botan*, taken straight from the Portuguese. Craftsmen incorporated crosses and other Christian motifs into the decorative designs on tea-bowls, lacquer boxes and sword-fittings. Even the kitchen was invaded by the craze for foreign fads. *Kasutera* sponge-cake, a local Nagasaki speciality, is thought to derive its name from Castile and the Japanese for bread – *pan* – is clearly from the Portuguese. Nowadays most Western visitors to Japan delight in a visit to a restaurant specialising in *tempura* dishes – delicate portions of fish and vegetables deep-fried in a light egg-flour batter. The word may come simply from the Portuguese for cooking, *tempero*, or alternatively from the word temple, with the implication that it was invented by Christian missionaries who were either concocting something tasty for Fridays and other fast days or just pining for some fried dish to punctuate the monotony of a fat-free Japanese cuisine based on boiling and grilling.

CHAPTER SIX

The Closed Country,
1639–1853

The long *Pax Tokugawa* brought a stability which enabled the country to make good the ravages of civil strife. Prosperity fostered spectacular urban growth and a brilliant new popular culture which reached its apogee in the period known as Genroku (1688–1704). It saw the birth of the *haiku*, the *kabuki* drama, the plebeian novel and the wood-block print as well as the founding of the Ura Senke school of tea-ceremony, which is today Japan's largest. The enjoyment of elegance among the leisured classes popularised the art of growing miniature trees (*bonsai*) and landscape gardening. Architectural critic Kawazoe Noboru claims Edo as the world's first 'garden city', supporting a substantial industry of full-time horticultural suppliers.

Japan's seclusion was not total. There was a Chinese merchant colony in every port and the Dutch brought not only imports but also news of the outside world. These foreigners were, however, only tolerated because they limited themselves strictly to commerce and that commerce was itself limited to petty luxuries which could be dispensed with if necessary. The country's entire foreign trade was managed through the thirty Chinese vessels which were allowed to call annually and just two Dutch ones.

The Tokugawa regime attempted to freeze society for its own good. By placing severe limitations on foreign influences it fostered a process of cultural involution which made Japan more intensely Japanese at the very time when more outward-looking countries, like Britain, were becoming more cosmopolitan. To Engelbert Kaempfer, the German physician who served with the Dutch East India Company in the 1690s, Tokugawa policy seemed like the fulfilment of a natural destiny:

... it seems nature purposely designed these islands to be a sort of a little world, separate and independent of the rest, by making them of so difficult an access, and by endowing them plentifully, with whatever is requisite to make the lives of their inhabitants both delightful and pleasant, and to enable them to subsist without a commerce with foreign nations.

Making a Metropolis

THE POWER BASE

In 1590 Edo was an obscure fishing-village with a broken-down castle. A century-and-a-half later it was the biggest city in the world. This phenomenal urban explosion was the direct outcome of a sequence of deliberate political decisions which began when Hideyoshi assigned Ieyasu the governorship of the eight provinces of the Kanto plain. Ieyasu could have chosen to headquarter himself either in the castle-town of Odawara, which was nearly as wealthy as Kyoto itself, or in the old shogunal capital of Kamakura. Instead he decided to base himself at Edo, a neglected nowhere at the farther edge of what was still regarded as a semi-civilised region. Why?

Edo did have some clear advantages. It stood at the crossing-point of a number of major highways and at the innermost point of a large, calm bay where port facilities could be built. And the very fact that Edo was so undeveloped meant that the site afforded room for massive expansion. Its chief defect was the paradox of an inadequate water supply combined with severe waterlogging. To make it habitable for any substantial number of inhabitants would require large-scale civil engineering projects to build bridges, dig canals and alter the course of existing rivers. These were among Ieyasu's earliest priorities. His other main concern was to refortify the castle, established back in 1457, but now so sadly decayed that it sported the absurdity of a thatched roof. Sixteen temples were summarily cleared out of its precinct to enlarge the fortified area, which was henceforth to be encircled with a double moat.

THE CAPITAL

Once Ieyasu had become shogun in 1603 Edo was upgraded from a regional power base to the effective seat of national government, although Kyoto remained in theory the official capital. The city designers now laid out an extensive system of moats, spiralling out from the castle, which lay like a spider at the heart of its web. These waterways eased the transport of bulk goods, acted as firebreaks and defensive barriers and helped to tackle the problem of flood-control. The earth from the canals was used to stabilise marshy areas. At the hub of the road system a new bridge, Nihonbashi (Japan Bridge) was built in. (It remains the zero point from which all distances are measured.) For its defences the new city relied, not on walls, but on a system of defence in depth depending on winding roads, staggered crossings, gated precincts, guard stations (*tsujiban*) and blind alleys to delay and confuse any intrusive force.

In 1617 an officially-regulated red-light area (*Yoshiwara*) was established near Nihonbashi; it was later relocated near Asakusa where some 3,000 licensed ladies of pleasure were divided between about 200 establishments. There was only one gate – to prevent the girls leaving and to frustrate customers attempting to abscond without payment. In 1619 bells to ring out the hours were set up. In 1624 a theatre district was laid out.

Social space and physical space were closely correlated. The *daimyo* built their mansions with spacious gardens on the hills of the Yamanote area. The New Otani hotel, the Akasaka Prince Hotel and the University of Tokyo all now occupy the sites of former *daimyo* mansions. The merchants, craftsmen and labourers who served the samurai crowded together in low-lying, waterside Shitamachi, modern Tokyo's downtown and home of the 'Edokko' – its own kind of Cockney, chirpy, street-wise and a born survivor of the urban jungle.

In 1657 a huge fire gutted much of the city. In rebuilding it the planners gave a new priority to disaster prevention, creating earthen wall barriers and open spaces to act as firebreaks and tightening building regulations to require tiled rather than thatched roofs. An accurate new survey of the metropolis was also prepared as a basic aid for future urban planning. Further major fires occurred in 1772 and 1806.

THE WORLD'S BIGGEST VILLAGE

By 1725 Edo had a population of about 1,300,000, half of whom were samurai, occupying two-thirds of the city's 70 square kilometres. fifty thousand monks, priests and temple servants occupied a generous sixth of the total. As another 5 per cent was open space this meant that 600,000 commoners were crammed into just an eighth of the total area. In the temple districts the population density was 5,000 per square kilometre, among the samurai 14,000, among the commoners an incredible 70,000 – over three times the level of modern Tokyo's highest density of settlement, Toshima Ward.

Edo by now far outstripped any other city. Kyoto with a population of 400,000 covered only 21 square kilometres. It owed its continued importance not so much to the presence of an impoverished court as to its educational and religious establishments and significance as a centre of luxury manufacture. Osaka with a population of 300,000 spread over 14 square kilometres ranked third, deriving its prosperity from control of the national commerce in rice and associated products such as sake and soy sauce. Other towns with a population over 50,000 included Nagoya, Kanazawa, Sendai and Kagoshima.

The Social Order

CONFUCIAN PRINCIPLES

The social order was, at least in theory, just that – orderly. Japan had endured over a century of chaos and Tokugawa rule was intended above all to establish and maintain peace and stability. It was based quite consciously on Confucian principles and in particular on the interpretation of them by Chu Hsi (1130–1200), a Chinese philosopher of the Sung dynasty.

Society was held to consist of four main social categories, ranked in order of precedence and usefulness – warriors, farmers, craftsmen and merchants. Some occupations – such as doctors and priests – did not really fit neatly into this system. Others were in a sense outside it. Actors, *geisha* ('accomplished person') and prostitutes were in a little make-believe world of their own, superficially glamorous but often cruel.

OUTCASTS

Beggars, bandits and other riff-raff had put themselves outside the security that went with conforming to law and convention. And there were substantial outcast groups such as the *eta*, who were regarded as ritually unclean, and *hinin* ('non-humans'), people deprived of normal social status as a punishment for some totally abhorrent act such as patricide and put to forced labour or degrading tasks such as handling dead bodies or diseased persons.

Eta were condemned to work as tanners and butchers, occupations classified as polluting by Shinto and impious by Buddhism. Their origin is obscure; possibly they were descended from prisoners of war spared from slaughter after defeat. Popular prejudice attributed them with various physical deformities such as having six toes. It is quite possible that the disabled and disfigured were forced into their ranks by social rejection. *Eta* lived in separate ghettoes and were subject to curfews and various avoidance rituals to keep them apart from ordinary people; their outcast status was formally abolished in 1871 when they were reclassified as *shin heimin* (new common people). In practice they became known as *burakumin* ('people of special hamlets') and have continued to be subject to social, though no longer legal, discrimination in matters of education, housing, employment and marriage. Their modern descendants number some three millions, clustered together in some 6,000 segregated communities and mostly engaged in leather working (shoes, drums and baseball gloves) and construction.

In theory each person was born and died within the status-group of their parents. In practice things were not quite so tidy. Samurai could lose caste, particularly if their lord were disgraced. Some were driven by impoverishment to renounce their status. Merchants could be awarded the right to bear arms, the mark of a warrior. *Hinin* could be readmitted to society in return for some particularly meritorious act, such as saving the life of a magistrate.

Emperor and Shogun

At the pinnacle of society was the emperor himself, so far above mundane matters that he seemed scarcely of this world at all. The Tokugawa shoguns treated emperors with outward respect, filled up their days with ceremonial duties and gentlemanly pastimes and kept them under close and constant surveillance. Their movements were restricted and their contacts controlled. Their society was limited to the 140 courtly families who inhabited the imperial precinct and they were allowed a moderate, but not over-generous, income. In effect they were prisoners in their own palace. So secluded were their lives that foreign visitors to Japan at both the beginning and end of the Edo period either regarded the emperor as some sort of pope or, in many cases, remained quite unaware of his existence.

In practice, therefore, it was the shogun in Edo who was top dog. This designation is not entirely inappropriate as the fifth shogun, Tsunayoshi (1646–1709), held canines in such esteem that he required his subjects to address them as 'Mr Dog' and banned the formerly common amusement of using them for archery practice. Born in the year of the dog, he was told by a priest that his childlessness was probably a punishment for having killed one in a previous existence, hence his compensatory programme of shelters and free meals for stray mutts. The historian and magistrate Mitsukuni (1628–1700), whose name became a byword for justice, is said to have sent the hides of twenty dogs to the shogun as a protest against this whimsy.

DAIMYO

Immediately answerable to the shogun were the *daimyo* ('great name') who ruled the 250 *han* (clan domains) into which the country was divided. They fell into two broad groups, *fudai* and *tozama*, inner and outer, depending essentially on whether they had proclaimed their allegiance to the Tokugawa before or after the battle of Sekigahara (*see p. 74*). *Tozama* lords were excluded from serving in the shogunal government. The physical pattern of land-holding was arranged to reflect the underlying realities of the political order. The estates of many 'outer' lords were literally on the fringe of the national territory in the far north and west. All the land within a day's march of Edo was held either by the Tokugawa directly, or by their branch houses or by their most trusted vassals. The shogun was not only the largest single landowner, holding more than a quarter of all cultivated land as his personal estate; he also controlled the major communication routes, port facilities and precious metal supplies.

To qualify for *daimyo* status a feudal lord had to have land sufficient to produce an annual yield of 10,000 *koku* of rice, one *koku* being the amount needed to feed an adult male for a year. The holdings of the greatest *daimyo* ran to over a million and about fifty had estates yielding 100,000 or more. Holdings below 10,000 conferred the rank of *hatamoto*, with the privilege of personal access to the presence of the shogun. In the mid-seventeenth century there were some 5,000 of them. A revenue of 260 *koku* or less defined a samurai as *gokenin*, fitted to serve as a minor bureaucrat; in 1800 their numbers were estimated at 20,000. Control of *daimyo* was exercised through a system of spies and hostages. Marriages and the building of bridges and fortifications were subject to strict shogunal supervision; that apart, *daimyo* were left pretty much to run their domains as they wished. Only if their rule proved so incompetent or oppressive as to threaten national security would direct intervention ensue. Disputed successions were, in practice, the most frequent cause of shogunal involvement in *han* politics. In the first forty years of the seventeenth century seventy *daimyo* were removed from power or demoted and over a third of the cultivable land reassigned.

A key feature of the control system developed by the Tokugawa was the requirement of 'alternate attendance' (*sankin kotai*). For part of their time *daimyo* were allowed to reside on their own estates but periodically they were required to come to Edo to attend upon the shogun in person. This obligation necessitated both the expense of maintaining a suitably prestigious residence in the capital and much time and trouble in organising the impressive retinue required to escort the attendant lord on his journeys to and fro. These journeys had to be taken according to a specified route and timetable and subject to periodic inspections to ensure that no attempts were made to smuggle guns into the capital or hostages out of it.

SAMURAI

Warriors were afforded first place in the social order because they defended it from attack and enforced its sanctions. They were expected to possess the virtues of courage and loyalty, obedience and frugality. Until the practice was officially forbidden in 1663, many senior retainers demonstrated their devotion to their liege lord by committing suicide when he died. General Nogi did this on the death of Emperor Meiji as recently as 1912.

In the *Buke-sho-hatto* (Laws for Military Houses) issued by Ieyasu shortly before his death he urged samurai to cultivate their skills with 'both the sword and the brush'. Unlike Europe's military aristocracy they were supposed to be literate as well as proficient in arms; this was not a mere matter of good form but a professional skill. Most samurai spent much of their time on administration, which necessarily involved record-keeping and correspondence – though some die-hards regarded facility with numbers, the merchant's expertise, with deep suspicion. Military skills were honed by formal instruction, practice and hunting. Occasionally they were required in earnest. The *Pax Tokugawa* was punctuated by some 2,000 peasant rebellions which were usually provoked by over-taxation in a hard year. (A saying of the times likened peasants to oil-seeds – the more you squeeze the more you get.) The standard procedure was to execute the ringleaders and then remit the extortion until the village economy had recovered sufficiently for it to be reimposed.

Frugality appears to have been a requirement honoured by samurai as much in the breach as the observance. Exposure to the pleasure quarters and commerce of great cities opened the way to temptation. Many samurai raised cash by mortgaging their future rice-allowances and fell deeply into debt, placing themselves at the mercy of the merchants they despised.

Acutely aware of their superior status, samurai had the right to protect themselves by summary execution (*kirisute-gomen*) of any social inferior who insulted them. This was not an error which could easily be committed by accident; samurai were quite clearly distinguished, not only by their assertive manner, but also by the two swords they carried and their distinctive hair-style. The long sword (*katana*) was used for fencing, the short one (*wakizashi*) for taking heads or committing suicide. Hair was worn tied back in a top-knot, the brow and dome of the head being shaved bare.

Hagakure (Hidden among Leaves), a confidential summary of the warrior code compiled around 1700, adjures the samurai to cultivate self-control and dignity at all times. Every day should be lived as though it might be the last, for a true warrior should be ever prepared to sacrifice his life at an instant. Cherry blossom symbolised the ideal attitude for it falls in full bloom rather than withering on the branch. Samurai accounted for over 5 per cent of the total population, a much higher proportion than the nobility and gentry in Europe. Although they were a caste apart and concentrated mainly in castle-towns their very numbers helped to diffuse a familiarity with military values throughout society.

FARMERS

In theory peasants, who accounted for over 80 per cent of the population, ranked second only to warriors. Confucianism was based on a sound appreciation of the desirability of a full rice-bowl. In practice the peasants seldom ate the rice they grew and were often obliged to fill themselves with barley or millet and usually forbidden the pleasures of sake, tobacco and even tea. (Ironically the poor man's substitute, *mugicha* – barley tea, is nowadays taken chilled as a summer drink by all classes.) The virtues expected of peasants were obedience and diligence. Common sense and duty alike called upon them to waste nothing, fallen leaves should be gathered for compost and human excrement should be recycled onto the vegetable patch.

Every head of household had to belong to a group of five (*goningumi*) whose members were mutually responsible for each other's actions. If any one failed to pay his taxes or committed a crime the rest were obliged to make him pay up or own up and face the consequences. If they failed to do so the punishment fell on them. Associations like these were revived and used to mobilise the population as recently as the Second World War.

MISERY AND OPPORTUNITY

For most peasants life was very hard – if the harvest failed they starved. Ecologically speaking Edo Japan was virtually a closed system. Although surplus rice might be traded from one end of the country to the other (e.g. Niigata to Osaka) by coastal shipping, there was no possibility of importing food on a large scale in a bad year. Female infanticide was sometimes a cruel necessity, euphemistically referred to

A scene of farming and silk production

as *mabiki* – weeding out the rice seedlings. There were large-scale famines as a result of repeated harvest failures in 1732–3, 1783–7 and 1833–6. All were accompanied by riots and risings. But these were explosions of wretchedness not abortive attempts at revolution.

The economic expansion of the Edo period did, however, offer opportunities for the enterprising. Villages near big cities could prosper by supplying the food and raw materials they needed, such as cotton and silk, and some peasant households undoubtedly became quite well off. The possibilities for social advancement are well illustrated by the career of Ninomiya Sontoku (1787–1856). Orphaned as a child and dispossessed of the family farm by disastrous floods, he succeeded through sheer hard work in restoring his household to solvency by the time he was twenty-four. His energy and initiative brought him to the notice of the Odawara clan who set him to reinvigorate agriculture throughout their domains by organising engineering projects and bringing new land into cultivation. This he did, visiting some 600 villages and constantly preaching the gospel of diligence and frugality. He also required his masters to content themselves with fixed incomes and reinvest surpluses in projects that would benefit the cultivators. Eventually he was taken up by the Tokugawa themselves and after his death his philosophy was spread by the Hotokusha, a society he established for that purpose. During the militarist period of the 1930s his example and doctrines were lauded as still worthy of emulation. Even though this unsought for association may have tainted his memory for the post-war generation, Japanese of all persuasions still greatly admire the man who persists against the odds and selflessly puts the common interest before his own.

In one respect, at least, peasants were better off than their betters. Samurai marriages were invariably arranged. Peasants, subject to parental approval, could marry whom they chose. That said, marriage in any social class was looked upon more as a union of families than of individuals. A girl who failed to produce children might be discarded. In some areas marriages were not formally registered until the fourth month of a pregnancy. And a new wife who failed to defer to her mother-in-law was quite likely to be sent back home, whatever her husband's views on the matter.

CRAFTSMEN

Townspeople did not produce their own food, which made them less worthy than the peasantry. They did, however, produce useful things. Status was related to product, with swordsmiths at the top and makers of fine ceramics pretty near it. What they did required great technical skill and their customers were among the highest in the land, while makers of everyday goods for everyday people ranked correspondingly lower.

MERCHANTS

Merchants came at the bottom of the heap because Confucian economic theory held them to be essentially parasitic. They produced nothing. Paradoxically many became extremely wealthy and in Osaka developed their own bravura life-style. (The local greeting there is still 'Are you making money?') The complex currency system which employed gold, silver and copper coins, enabled them to manipulate exchange rates to advantage. Lending money to samurai or managing *han* finances could also prove profitable, though not likely to enhance a reputation. Conventional opinion held commerce to be essentially corrupting. Samurai wisdom regarded trade as the only kind of contest in which victory was dishonourable. Merchants were likened to a folding screen, neither being able to stand up unless they were crooked. Given such antagonistic social attitudes the expansion and sophistication of the economy in the Edo period seems all the more remarkable. Regional specialisation in the production of highly specific types of pottery and textiles would, of course, have been impossible without the services of the men who managed their distribution and marketing.

Captain Vasilii Galownin, a Russian sailor who had the misfortune to be held captive in Japan for two years around 1811, observed shrewdly that:

> The class of merchants . . . is very extensive and rich . . . though their profession is not respected, their wealth is. . . . The commercial spirit of the Japanese is visible in all the towns and villages. In almost every house there is a shop. . . . In their regard to order, the Japanese very much resemble the English; they love cleanliness and the greatest accuracy. All goods have in Japan, as in England, little printed bills on which are noted the price, the use, and the name of the article, the name of the maker . . . and often something in their praise. Even tobacco . . . tooth powder and other trifles are wrapped up in papers . . . .

MERCHANT PRINCES

The larger-than-life extravagance of the great merchant princes was such that characters like Kinokuniya Bunzaemon (1669–1734) became almost legendary figures. His most famous business coup came about when a spell of stormy weather cut Edo off from the orange-growing districts of the warm south just before New Year's day. Mandarins were held to be indispensable for the ritual celebrations which traditionally accompanied the inauguration of a new year. The wily entrepreneur saw the chance to make a killing, chartered a ship and tantalised its crew with the promise of such a bonus that they risked their lives to make the delivery, thus bringing him huge profits. A more reliable source of income came from the fires that so regularly ravaged the city that they were known as *Edo bana* (flowers of Edo). Kinokuniya Bunzaemon did very nicely as a timber trader, supplying the lumber constantly needed for rebuilding. He is said to have been so rich that at the festival which required householders to scatter roasted soybeans to drive demons from their homes he would use gold coins; and whereas most families changed their *tatami* (straw floor-mats) every several years he had his changed right through the house every day.

By the eighteenth century there were some 200 merchant houses valued at over 200,000 gold *ryo*. Taking one *ryo* to be roughly equivalent to one *koku* this meant that there were perhaps ten times as many merchant princes as *daimyo* of comparable wealth. But the shogunal government never really cracked the problem of how to use their expertise to promote economic expansion which could be taxed and directed to the broader public benefit. Attempts to co-opt merchants into official policy-making usually proved to be a short route to increased corruption.

One living legacy of Edo enterprise is the mighty house of Mitsui, a world-wide business empire which began as a draper's shop in seventeenth-century Edo. Low margins, high volumes and strict insistence on cash not credit laid the foundations of greatness. The shop itself is the lineal ancestor of swanky Mitsukoshi, 'the Harrods of Japan'. The Sumitomo Corporation can likewise trace its ancestry to a Kyoto dealer in iron goods and drugs.

Picture the Past

HANGA AND UKIYO-E

The coloured woodblock print is both one of the most characteristic products of the Edo period, and thanks to its brilliance and detail, a beguiling and informative source of information about it. Print artists came to specialise in depicting 'The Floating World' (*ukiyo*) – the pleasure quarters and the courtesans and actors who worked there. Their characteristic products are therefore often referred to as *ukiyo-e* (floating world pictures) although the general word for prints is *hanga*. Among the pleasures illustrated in *ukiyo-e* are watching a parade of gorgeously-dressed geisha, shooting darts from a blow-pipe for prizes from a stall, eating and drinking on a river-boat on a summer evening, watching *kabuki* or *sumo* and viewing cherry blossom.

Printing from woodblocks dates back to 764 when Empress Koken ordered the mass-production of Buddhist sutras so that they could be distributed to temples throughout the country. Woodblocks were later used for printing pictures of Buddhist deities to be used as objects of veneration or souvenirs of pilgrimage. The first complete book printed by this method dates from 1346.

The printing of pictures of secular subjects by means of woodblocks dates from the seventeenth century. At first they were of one colour only, usually red or black. Although they seem rather crude compared to the masterpieces of the late Edo period their age and rarity now make them valued collector's items. Indeed, all genuine Edo-period prints are now highly esteemed, which is ironic considering that Japanese connoisseurs once held them in contempt and would scarcely have classified them as 'art' at all. Woodblock prints were produced to illustrate storybooks and calendars, as promotional material for theatres, brothels and restaurants, as greeting cards, and as cheap gifts and souvenirs.

MASTERS OF THEIR CRAFT

The first great master of the medium was Moronobu (1618–94), who trained originally as a textile designer and produced some two dozen sets of *shunga* ('spring pictures') to illustrate books of erotica. (A government ban on such publications in 1722 naturally increased the demand for them.) Torii Kiyonobu, the son of a *kabuki* actor, pioneered theatrical subjects and founded a dynasty of printmakers, of whom Torii Kiyonaga (1752–1815) was to pioneer the depiction of landscape in print form. The first truly multi-coloured print (*nishiki-e* – brocade picture) was produced by Harunobu (1724–70) in 1765, some seventy years before multi-colour printing by chromolithography first appeared in Britain. Early colour prints had as few as three blocks – one to establish the compositional outlines in black and two more to fill in areas of colour. As the technical competence and ambition of artists and engravers increased the number of blocks used could be as many as fifteen, all of which had to be keyed in to one another with absolute precision. The standard size for prints was 38 x 25 cm.

Harunobu specialised in small portraits (28 x 20 cm.) of slim young ladies, though he also produced sets of prints of poets, festivals and flowers. His storming success inspired a host of imitators, though he struggled manfully to maintain his supremacy, turning out almost a thousand such pictures in the last six years of his life. Another specialist in depicting female subjects was Utamaro (1754–1806), although his early works were of animals, birds, insects and plants. He invented the 'head and shoulders' portrait. Both men were also prolific producers of *shunga*. Sharaku (*fl*. 1794–5), Shunsho (1726–92) and Toyokuni (1769–1825), by contrast, were best known for portraits of actors. Sharaku produced 145 ultra-dramatic actor portraits in a great outburst of creativity from May 1794 to February 1795; but virtually nothing more is known about him. Shunsho became an accomplished painter late in his career. Toyokuni trained two of the most popular artists of the late Edo period, Kunisada (1786–1864) and Kuniyoshi (1797–1861). Kuniyoshi's output includes some wonderfully weird portraits of legendary warriors and highly idiosyncratic landscapes influenced by Western painting styles. Kuniyoshi's fascination with military themes is said to reflect Tokugawa efforts to revive traditional martial virtues in the face of a growing awareness that western countries might attempt to breach Japan's traditional policy of isolation.

HOKUSAI AND HIROSHIGE

The woodblock artists whose works are best known in the west are Hokusai (1760–1849) and Hiroshige (1797–1858), both of whom came to concentrate on landscape subjects, a field which developed rapidly after Dutch merchants made Prussian blue pigment available in Japan, greatly extending the range of blues and greens an artist could use. Hokusai studied under Shunsho but eventually broke away from theatrical subjects such as 'Chushingura' (*see p. 107*) to create a set of prints illustrating the nation's most awesome natural feature: 'Thirty-six Views of Mount Fuji'. The picture of 'The Great Wave at Kanagawa' which forms part of the latter cycle is one of the few Japanese works of art to have acquired the status of a visual cliché in the West. A brilliant cartoonist with a great gift for humorous observation Hokusai came to sign himself as 'the old man mad about painting'. His restless curiosity

Mannen Bridge at Fukagawa from the 'Thirty-six Views of Mt Fuji' by Hokusai

led him to move house no less than ninety-eight times in the course of a
long and prolific life. Hiroshige, like Hokusai, was born in Edo, of
which he produced more than a thousand views. His best-known
work, however, is the print series 'Fifty-three Stations of the Tokaido'
which illustrates wayfaring life on the Great Eastern Route between
Edo and Kyoto and includes a number of stunning snow scenes. In all
he was to produce twenty sets of views of the Tokaido as well as series
depicting Kyoto and Osaka. His total output is estimated at over 10,000
print designs as well as paintings and book illustrations.

The arrival of Westerners after 1853 prompted the development of a
print school at Yokohama, chronicling the extraordinary appearance
and doings of the newcomers and then of the changes wrought by
Japanese attempts to imitate them. The foremost practitioners in this
genre proved to be Yoshitora (*fl. ca* 1850–80) and Sadahide (1807–73).
Their successors experimented eagerly with the bright new pigments
originating in the industrial chemistry of the West. Some connoisseurs
have viewed the results as the sad degeneration of a fine tradition.

'JAPONISME'

Woodblock prints first became widely known in the West in the mid-nineteenth century when they were used as wrapping-paper for export porcelain from Japan. In 1862 Sir Rutherford Alcock, Britain's first ambassador in Japan, exhibited his personal collection of prints in London. The 1867 Paris Exposition Universelle included over 100 such prints and in 1890 the École des Beaux Arts organised an exhibition which included no less than eighty-nine prints by Utamaro alone.

The woodblock print had an immediate and lasting impact in Impressionist circles in France, where in 1872 the critic Burty dubbed the craze '*Japonisme*'. Monet is known to have owned a copy of Hiroshige's 'Wisteria Blooms over water at Kameido' and his celebrated picture of the bridge and lily-pond of his garden at Giverny is so closely based on it that it could be seen as a 'homage' to the Japanese master. Degas, Pissarro and Van Gogh were also keen collectors. In the angularity of his perspective and eye-catching foregrounds Toulouse-Lautrec perhaps came closest to capturing the style and spirit of *ukiyo-e* and his familiarity with the world of cabarets and the *demi-monde* gave him an entirely appropriate subject-matter for his posters.

The London-based American painter, James Whistler, was including Japanese prints as props in his portraits as early as 1864; he also based pictures on them. The 'Nocturne in Blue and Gold: Old Battersea Bridge' bears more than a passing resemblance to an Edo bridge depicted by Hokusai. The enthusiasm of artists was matched by that of collectors, the French novelist Zola being one of the keenest. One ironic outcome of this is that some of the greatest collections of prints are not in Japan but in London, Paris and Vienna.

In Japan itself the tradition of woodblock printing was reaffirmed by the establishment in 1931 of the Nippon Hanga Kyokai. The foremost modern exponent of the art was Munakata Shiko (1909–75) (*see p. 151*).

Painting

In their enthusiasm for the coloured woodblock print Westerners have perhaps been liable to neglect the achievements of the painters of the Edo era. 'Serious' art focused on landscape and aspects of natural history, such as birds and flowers. The human figure was used only to tell a story or indicate a scale or a mood, rather than as a subject in its own right. Invariably such figures were simplified, conventionalised, even stereotyped. As Oliver Impey, the art historian, has observed:

> In *Ukiyo-e* figures achieve a new prominence, but even here the interest is on the scene and on the depicted person's reaction to the scene, not upon the figure. The great portraits of statuesque *oiran* (courtesans) ... are really fashion plates as much as portraits, and much of the genre painting of the Edo period is more about what people wear than what they are.

The vertical hanging-scroll (*kakemono*) and horizontal hand-scroll (*makimono*) continued to be the typical formats for small-scale subjects, sliding doors (*fusuma*) and folding screens (*byobu*) for larger ones. In that sense painters were, in effect, also illustrators and interior designers. An additional, peculiarly Japanese, format was the folding fan of paper or silk, which offered the artist the challenge of unusual perspectives. Perspective as such continued to be understood in the Chinese rather than the Western sense – vertical and variable rather than geometric and fixed. The higher up a picture an object is shown, the further away it is supposed to be, and it is not assumed that the viewer is static, looking into a single vanishing-point; rather he looks down at the lower portions of the picture and up at the rest. Shadows therefore tend to be conspicuous by their absence in Japanese painting. Towards the end of the Edo period a small group of artists, known as Rangakusha, and led by mathematician Shiba Kokan (1747–1818), experimented with Western conventions, but their wholesale acceptance had to wait until the late nineteenth century when Japanese artists rushed to 'catch up' with the West in this as in so many other respects.

KANO, TOSA AND RIMPA

The two most important schools of painting were the Kano, who worked under the patronage of the shogun and *daimyo*, and the Tosa, who worked for the imperial court but also accepted commissions from wealthy commoners. Associated with Tosa was the Rimpa school which specialised in stunning decorative effects. Concentrated in the village of Takagamine, it was much patronised by the discerning Kyoto aristocracy. Its founding-father was Koetsu (1558–1637), an astonishingly versatile talent who earned his living as a professional appraiser of swords and excelled as a calligrapher and amateur designer of lacquerware and ceramics. The gorgeous screen paintings of 'Irises' (Nezu Art Museum, Tokyo) and 'Red and White plum blossom' (MOA Museum, Atami) by his successor Korin (1658–1716) are among the best-known works of art in Japan today. A few outstanding talents, such as 'the two-handed swordsman' Musashi (1584–1645), the Buddhist layman Jakuchu (1716–1800) and eccentric Rosetsu (1754–99), belonged to no school but their own.

Kano Tan'yu (1602–74), who started painting at the age of four, was regarded as the supreme exponent of classical academic technique, while his contemporary, Tosa Mitsuoki (1617–91), concentrated the aesthetic wisdom of the age in a single sentence – 'The essential point of painting can be summed up in one word: lightness.' Understatement and restraint, even in the use of vivid colour, were to be the watchwords of the truly accomplished artist. Artistic training consisted of copying the works of acknowledged masters for ten or twenty years. Originality of treatment and subject-matter were frowned on. Inevitably it proved a formula for formalism and ultimate decline.

Artisans as Artists

Engelbert Kaempfer, bearing in mind, no doubt, that European readers of his impressions of Japan would assume their own culture to be superior in matters of technology and manufacture, went out of his way to inform that they were wrong:

> As to all sorts of handicrafts, either curious or useful, they are wanting neither proper materials, nor industry and application, and so far is it, that they should have any occasion to send for masters from abroad, that they rather exceed all other nations in ingenuity and neatness of workmanship.

The peace and prosperity brought by Tokugawa rule created a class of *nouveaux-riches* (*nariagari-mono*) who constituted a buoyant market for finely-crafted goods such as ceramics, lacquerware and fine textiles. Even personal accessories such as carved clothes toggles (*netsuke*) and the boxes which served as pockets in kimono (*inro* – 'seal basket') became ingeniously-wrought minor works of art.

POTTERY

The popularity of the tea-ceremony stimulated the demand for fine ceramics, and the Korean potters who came to Japan as a by-product of Hideyoshi's abortive attempt to conquer their country brought with them exciting new techniques and styles which stimulated imitation and rivalry. The cult of calculated rusticity meant that there was as keen an appreciation of rough, unglazed earthenwares as of delicate porcelain. Great artists co-operated eagerly in the production of ceramics. Korin did underglaze paintings for his brother Kenzan (1663–1743), and the talented calligrapher Koetsu also produced particularly fine tea-bowls. Pottery also became a significant export to Europe during this period. The main centre for porcelain production was Arita in Kyushu. The wares produced there became known as Imari, from the name of the port through which they were shipped. The collapse of the Ming dynasty in China in 1644 disrupted the regular source of blue and white ware used by Dutch merchants and Imari output filled the gap. In Europe it was soon being imitated at Delft, just as the brightly over-glazed white porcelains known as *kakiemon* were subsequently imitated at Meissen, Chelsea and Bow.

LACQUER AND WEAPONRY

Banquet and boudoir alike created a demand for lacquer-wares, durable, heat-resistant and suitable for many kinds of decorative treatment. Tables, trays and bowls for serving food, boxes and chests to hold make-up, medicines or writing-materials could all be delicately incised or lavishly treated with gold or mica fragments to produce the effect known as *maki-e* ('sprinkled picture'). Chests of drawers and writing-cabinets in the European style were also made for export.

Paradoxically the *Pax Tokugawa* led to no diminution in the demand for arms and armour though the emphasis in their production shifted markedly from practical use to luxurious decoration as they were needed, not for battle, but for parade and the hunt. *Daimyo* and their retainers delighted to dazzle the lowly with the splendour of their accoutrements, from helmet to stirrups. Many armours were even created in deliberately anachronistic styles, harking back to the 'great days' of feudal anarchy. Even merchants, technically forbidden to bear more than small personal side-arms, were enthusiastic as connoisseurs and collectors, though they tended to be more interested in intricate scabbards and sword-furniture than in the actual quality of the blades themselves.

TEXTILES

Textile production in the Edo period embraced an immense range of materials from inexpensive stencilled or resist-dyed cottons to hand-painted or gold-embroidered silks for court wear. The flat surface of the kimono ('the thing worn') suits it admirably for imaginative decoration and the elaborate social distinctions of the age created a need for many kinds of specialised garments indicative of status or occupation, though differences in the dress of men and women were singularly blurred for a society which placed such emphasis on strictly demarcated gender roles. Indeed, *kabuki* actors (always male) specialising in female roles were often among the leading trendsetters of their day. The broad waist-sash (*obi*) became an item of particular elaboration.

Designers eagerly absorbed motifs taken from China, Europe and even, via the Portuguese, Indian chintzes. Sumptuary laws issued in 1682 and reissued in 1683 signally failed to curb extravagance in dress. Merchants fearful of reproof simply indulged themselves with garments outwardly dull but lined with expensive fabrics exquisitely worked. The brilliance of the costumes used in *Noh* drama and the bravura fashions of the pleasure-quarters were doubtless further constant provocations to self-indulgence.

Literacy and Literature

The Japanese took over from China the Confucian respect for those who had managed to master the complexities of the written language. A fine calligraphic hand has always remained one of the most admired of all accomplishments. Edo period exponents include the Emperor Go-Yozei (1571–1617), the Zen priest Hakuin (1675–1768) and the noted painter-poet Buson (1716–83). They were widely imitated. Edo alone is said to have had over 800 teachers of calligraphy.

What distinguished the era, however, was the great increase in the number of ordinary townspeople (*chonin*) who attained a basic grasp of reading and writing. Some estimates place the figure as high as 40 per cent. Collectively they constituted a new level of readership which demanded entertainment which was direct, realistic, even earthy. Japanese term the fiction written for them *gesaku* ('stories written for amusement'). One of the first to cater for this demand was the novelist Saikaku (1642–93) who dashed off stories which are saucy but shallow. He was evidently gifted with an extraordinary facility with words. On one occasion he entered a poetry marathon and composed non-stop for twenty-four hours. His *Life of an Amorous Man* is a fifty-four-chapter account of an erotic odyssey from the age of seven to sixty which ends with the bi-sexual hero sailing into the sunset with a boat-load of aphrodisiacs bound for an island populated only by women. *Five Women Who Loved Love* is rich in savage irony – one heroine who starts a fire to create a diversion so that she can be with her lover ends up herself being burned alive for arson. *The Japanese Family Storehouse or The Millionaire's Gospel Modernized* and *This Scheming World* are full of cynical advice to businessmen on how to turn every opportunity to advantage. (Japanese salarymen still read success manuals avidly.)

Other Edo period popular classics include the ghost stories (*Tales of Moonlight and Rain*) of Akinari (1734–1809) and *Shanks's Mare* by Ikku (1765–1831) which recounts the comic misadventures of two middle-aged likely lads who take leave of their wives for a walking tour along the Tokaido. Another literary landmark, outstanding not least for its length, is the 106-volume novel written by Bakin (1767–1848), containing 300 characters and written over a period of twenty-eight years.

HAIKU

The most important literary innovation of the Edo period was the *haiku*, a seventeen (i.e. 5-7-5)-syllable poem perfected by Basho (1644-94). *Haiku* are poetic snapshots, rich in puns and inner echoes and invariably containing, by reference to some suitable plant or creature, an allusion to the season of the year. As Cortazzi neatly puts it, 'It is not so much what they say as what they suggest which matters.' Some of

Basho's finest *haiku* are to be found in his travel journal *The Narrow Road to the Deep North*. When he came to the place where Yoshitsune died (*see p. 51*) he encapsulated his sadness thus:

> Summer grass
> All that remains
> Of warriors' dreams.

Issa (1763–1827) pioneered the inclusion of slang in his *haiku*. His tragic life is mirrored in the sympathy for small creatures and the poor evident in many of his 20,000 verses.

Senryu is a variant form of *haiku*, also having seventeen syllables, but omitting the seasonal allusion in favour of wry comments on the human predicament. The greatest *senryu* of the period were collected in an anthology running to twenty-four volumes.

THE TALE OF THE FORTY-SEVEN RONIN

This is the best-known saga of samurai days and has inspired at least a hundred and fifty modern novels and films as well as countless television versions, some of which elaborate it into an epic lasting dozens of episodes. The outline of the story is as follows: In 1701 Asano Naganori, lord of the Ako domain in the then Harima province (now part of Hyogo prefecture) was ordered to serve as one of the shogun's representatives to meet envoys bringing New Year greetings from the emperor in Kyoto. To prepare himself appropriately he was obliged to receive instruction in the correct etiquette from the shogun's *chef de protocol*, the greedy and conceited Kira Yoshinaka. Unfortunately Asano (or in some versions his steward) omitted to demonstrate his gratitude in advance by offering Kira a substantial fee/gift/bribe. Kira then behaved so arrogantly towards Asano that the latter, outraged, drew his sword and slashed at his tormentor. The swift intervention of another courtier deflected the blow and Kira escaped with a slight wound. But Asano had already signed his own death-warrant by daring to draw a weapon within the precincts of the shogun's residence. Asano was condemned to commit *seppuku*, his estate was confiscated and his entourage of samurai dismissed and cast adrift as *ronin* (literally 'wave men', i.e. having no direction, masterless). Kira went unpunished.

Asano's chief retainer, Oishi Yoshio, dutifully supervised the hand-over of the estate, hoping that the house might be re-established under Asano's younger brother. When it became clear that this was not going to happen he plotted vengeance and united forty-six other loyal samurai in a secret blood-oath to pursue the vendetta. Realising that Kira would take extraordinary precautions against a possible revenge attack the conspirators lay low and waited to throw off suspicion. Oishi himself set an extreme example by giving himself over to drunkenness and debauchery, enduring the insults of other samurai for his apparent gutlessness.

After two years the *ronin* judged that Kira believed himself to be safe from retribution and decided to strike. Disguised as a detachment of firemen (so that they could carry ladders without arousing suspicion) the conspirators passed through deserted, snowy streets on the night of 14/15 December 1702 and stormed Kira's mansion. Dragging him from his hiding-place they beheaded him, took the head to the grave of their master at Sengakuji temple and calmly awaited their fate.

The authorities were faced with a dilemma. The conspirators had showed to the highest degree qualities most admirable in a warrior – loyalty, daring and, not least, dogged determination. Many admired them, from the common people to the shogun himself, and the head of the Hosokawa clan, into whose custody they were placed, treated them as honoured guests and offered to take them on as his own vassals. On the other hand their action was a clear defiance of the judgment passed upon their lord and, in the view of the shogun's senior counsellors, must be punished.

It was more than a month before a decision was reached. The shogun even took the unusual step of appealing to the abbot of Ueno for his advice but he came down on the side of the death sentence on the grounds that the *ronin* had achieved a peak of spotless honour and, should they live on, some at least would be bound to tarnish their glory by a lapse of one sort or another. In the end there was a sort of compromise: rather than being executed as common criminals the offenders would be permitted to die like heroes by their own hand. They did so on 4 February 1703. (Only Chikara, Oishi's son and the youngest of the conspirators, was spared.) They now lie beside their master at Senkaguji in Tokyo's Minato district. For long a place of pilgrimage in their memory, it is now a major tourist site.

INTO LEGEND

The first dramatisation of this story appeared within twelve days of its occurrence. In 1706 Chikamatsu Monzaemon wrote a puppet drama about the incident and in 1748 it was presented in a fifteen-hour *kabuki* version as *Kanadehon Chushingura* – 'The Treasury of Loyal Retainers'. Prudence decreed that, to avoid the displeasure of the censor, the details of when the incident occurred and to whom should be falsified; but everyone knew just who was actually being referred to.

To most Japanese the story can be taken at face-value as a demonstration of supreme self-sacrifice. But another interpretation criticises the *ronin* as lacking true 'sincerity' and having altogether a too calculating view of their obligations. A true samurai, they insist, should have hurled himself into an act of revenge, no matter how hopeless, as soon as he had heard of the humiliation of his lord. A man of honour 'must not live under the same sky as one who has injured his lord or his father'. Whether or not the act 'succeeded', on this view, matters far less than that it was made with complete commitment, regardless of consequences. This is the true samurai spirit. The enduring significance of the knowingly futile gesture is discussed and illustrated at length in Ivan Morris's fascinating book *The Nobility of Failure: Tragic Heroes in the History of Japan*.

The Stage

Noh plays continued to be the preserve of the aristocracy but had already begun to stagnate into traditionalism. Prosperous city-folk wanted something much racier. They got it in two new theatrical forms – *kabuki* and *bunraku*.

Bunraku is a puppet drama in which puppets about two-thirds life-size are each manipulated by three masked operators. It grew out of an older tradition of *joruri*, chanted storytelling to musical accompaniment. *Bunraku* plays sometimes had comic scenes but tended to be tragic or heroic. *Bunraku* was particularly strong in Osaka where Chikamatsu

Monzaemon (1653–1724), known as 'the Shakespeare of Japan', was responsible for providing it with a classic repertoire of almost a hundred plays. Typically they are concerned with the conflict between passion (*ninjo*) and duty (*giri*). In twenty of his plays the dilemma is resolved by double suicide; the most famous of these, *The Love Suicides at Sonezaki* (1703), is based on a real incident, was written in three weeks and has been frequently adapted for both stage and screen. It inspired such an outburst of similar tragedies that the authorities felt bound to clamp down by decreeing that any surviving partner would be judged a murderer and the corpses of such persons exposed like common criminals for samurai to test their swords on. Writers were forbidden to use the words 'love suicide' as a title.

Chikamatsu's *Battles of Coxinga* includes in its account of the famous pirate's adventures a duel with a tiger, extensive eye-gouging and the agony of a female character who undergoes a brutal 'Caesarian' in full view of the audience. Chikamatsu also wrote some thirty *kabuki* plays but preferred writing for puppets on the grounds that they stuck more closely to his texts than actors usually did.

KABUKI

Kabuki is said to have begun with the seductive entertainments of a Kyoto shrine-servant, O-Kuni. Her success inspired imitators to form female troupes whose performances were often no more than an advertisement for more intimate forms of diversion. In 1629 the government banned such goings-on only to find it rapidly replaced by an all-male version which promoted the desirability of pretty youths instead of pretty girls. The government banned that in 1652. Mature *kabuki* remained all-male but came to depend on the thespian prowess of its actors rather than on their physical charms. Ichikawa Danjuro (1660–1704) founded an outstanding dynasty of star performers; his lineal descendant today is the twelfth of that name. He pioneered what became the characteristic style of acting through exaggerated postures and gestures (*aragato* – 'rough stuff'); ironically he died in truly melo-dramatic circumstances, stabbed in his dressing-room by a rival actor jealous of his talent.

Developed *kabuki* made extensive use of wildly extravagant cos-

A *Kabuki* actor in the part of a samurai

tumes and boldly stylised, mask-like make-up (*kumadori*). It achieved a
hectic pace of action by means of colourful scenery, revolving stages,
hidden trapdoors and other stunning stage-effects. Drums, flutes and
clappers were often used to heighten the tension. A runway (*hanamachi*)
which passed right through the audience to join the action at stage right

was much used to effect dramatic entrances and exits or to enable two different scenes to take place simultaneously. Many *kabuki* plays were taken over from *bunraku*. The trials of the tragic Yoshitsune (*see p. 51*) provided a favourite subject. Another was the career of the just official Ooka Tadasuke (1677–1751) who was famed for tempering the savagery of the criminal law and once made an exactly parallel judgment to that of Solomon when two women quarrelled over the custody of a child. With scant regard for propriety *kabuki* also made a hero out of Nezumi Kozo (executed 1832), a cat-burglar, nicknamed 'Mouse Boy' for his ability to deceive and escape pursuers. Because his victims were usually rich merchants he was attributed with the democratic generosity of a Robin Hood; in fact his thefts subsidised a bottomless appetite for drink and gambling.

Both *bunraku* and *kabuki* can still be seen today, the latter being much the more popular.

Scholarship and Science

As Confucianism was the official ideology of the regime, its professional experts enjoyed both power and prestige – though the Sage's inconvenient passion for meritocracy was ignored in the interests of heredity and hierarchy. There were other intellectual currents, however, which were to nurture the seeds of challenge to the prevailing orthodoxy. The *kokugaku* ('national learning') movement began as a scholarly attempt to re-evaluate ancient Japanese poetry. Under Hirata Atsutane (1776–1843) the unique mythology of Shinto was commandeered to 'prove' the inherent superiority of Japan and its people. From this poisonous principle much misery would one day flow.

A quite contrary movement was represented by scholars of *rangaku* ('Dutch learning', i.e. Western culture) which was stimulated by the partial lifting of the ban on the importation of dangerous books in 1722. Works of a political or religious nature remained forbidden but practical treatises, especially on technological subjects such as agriculture, navigation, surveying or gunnery, were allowed. The first scientific account of human anatomy to be produced in Japan was a medical atlas, already more than a century old when it was translated from the Dutch by Sugita Gempaku (1733–1817) despite the handicap of having no dictionary. In 1811 the shogunate established a special translation institute. Although there was considerable interest in applied sciences, such as medicine, ballistics or cartography, the appetite for pure science was limited.

Many scholarly triumphs were the product of purely individual effort, rather than institutional patronage. The first accurately surveyed map of all Japan took Ino Tadataka (1745–1818) seventeen years of solo slog after he retired from a lifetime of service to a failing sake business. The ingenious Hiraga Gennai (1726–79) devised a hand-cranked electrical dynamo, a thermometer and a process for making asbestos cloth but was treated as an eccentric and embittered by the indifference shown towards his inventions.

The absence of a true 'scientific spirit' may indeed have been one of the intellectual shortcomings of the era; but the equal absence of religious fanaticism in some sense compensated for this. When Japanese did encounter Western science and technology with full force their response to it was unhindered by obscurantist attachment to old dogmas.

New Light on a Dark Age?

History is the propaganda of the victors. New regimes rarely resist the temptation to rubbish the immediate past, justifying their own assumed authority by contrasting their shining ideals with the incompetence and corruption of their ousted predecessors. The modernisers of the Meiji period (1868–1912), hustling Japan towards 'civilisation and enlightenment' on Western lines, denigrated the Edo period as stagnant and benighted. As recently as 1950 the philosopher Watsuji Tetsuro published an analysis of its legacy entitled *National Seclusion: Japan's Tragedy*.

The emergence since then of 'development theory' has led to a reconsideration of such negative views. Conceding the rapidity with which technical progress and institutional change were achieved after 1868 the revisionists argue that, far from retarding economic expansion, the achievements of the Edo period were just what made Meiji Japan's uniquely successful leap forward possible. They catalogue an

intriguing list of factors favourable to further change. Under Tokugawa
rule the cultivated area was more than doubled. Cotton, silk, tea,
indigo, sweet potatoes and tobacco were developed as major crops,
substituting for previous imports and, in the case of silk, providing a
future export vital to earn the foreign exchange needed to pay for
imported technologies. Aided by voluminous encyclopaedias of agricultural wisdom the Japanese peasant was almost certainly the most
advanced farmer in Asia. Techniques of manufacture in ceramics, paper
and textiles improved so much that they constituted what has happily
been dubbed 'an industrious revolution'. Improvements in mining
turned Japan from a net importer of specie metals to a significant
exporter. An extensive network of roads and coastal shipping routes
was established. Most townspeople attained at least a modest level of
literacy. The *rangaku* scholars constituted a small but strategic intellectual resource from which a technocratic élite could be developed.

On the other hand the Tokugawa regime was undoubtedly afflicted
by severe structural problems with which it grappled in a confused way.
The population increased to the point at which a marginal failure of
food-supply could cause huge price rises and condemn the weakest to
famine. Persistent tinkering with the tax system and the coinage and the
issuing of a stream of sumptuary laws proved useless to remedy the
situation. Yoshimune solemnly decreed that no one should have more
than ten palanquins at a wedding reception. His successors repeatedly
tried to turf go-getting peasants out of the towns and back to their
villages and suppress inflation by passing laws against it. None of this
could help an economic system which had more or less reached the
limits of its potential and was burdened with an immense and largely
unproductive miltary class whose privileged position was apparently
immovably entrenched. As Beasley has emphasised, 'Even at the end of
the period samurai values still had a central role, if only as objects of
satire or debate.'

A series of disastrous harvests in the 1830s led to a large-scale popular
uprising in Osaka in 1837. Ominously it was led by a former official of
the shogunal government. The Opium War of 1839–42 witnessed the
humiliation of proud China by a British expeditionary force. In Japan a
Confucian scholar noted presciently, 'How can we know whether the

mist gathering over China will not come down as frost on Japan?' In 1852 the *Edinburgh Review* confidently declared that 'the compulsory seclusion of the Japanese is a wrong not only to themselves but to the civilised world'. In 1853 that policy was finally challenged in a decisive confrontation. The government of the shogun might have wished to uphold the traditional policy of isolation but it would soon become clear that it no longer had the strength to do so.

Chinese gateway, Nijo Castle, Kyoto

CHAPTER SEVEN

Revolution and Modernisation,
1853–1912

Japan's long isolation was forcibly ended by outside intervention in 1853. After a decade and a half of political confusion a brief but bloody civil war destroyed the shogunate and installed a new regime. This 'Meiji Restoration' was a revolution in everything but name. The new government of Japan undertook a programme of rapid modernisation to equip the nation with the armed forces and economic strength to resist the imperialist ambitions of Western powers. So successful was this programme that Japan itself, far from becoming their victim, joined their ranks.

Japan's headlong transformation from 'backward feudal isolation' to 'Great Power' status in half a century is conventionally depicted as a triumph of national unity and will. There was also a darker side: resistance to change was swept aside or crushed by force. Harsh labour exploitation and pollution of the environment were unhappy by-products of Japan's first 'economic miracle'. Westerners were ambivalent in their response to these changes. Most took for granted the virtues and superiority of their own culture and regarded its adoption by Japan as both desirable and inevitable. Some were prescient enough to fear its consequences. Others regretted the destruction of a 'Lotus Land'. Rudyard Kipling's brief stay made him such a warm Japanophile that he facetiously suggested that the whole country should be put under a glass case as too pretty to be part of the real world. Basil Hall Chamberlain, who became the first Professor of Japanese at Tokyo University, summed up this attitude with poignant pungency: 'Old Japan was like an oyster; to open it was to kill it.'

The Coming of the Barbarians

Throughout the centuries of isolation foreign ships had periodically visited Japanese shores unbidden, either seeking shelter and provision, or in the attempt to establish more lasting relationships. All had been fended off, sometimes by gifts, sometimes by gunfire. The determination of the United States to send an expeditionary force which would not be fended off rested on its recent conquest of California. As a Pacific power the US henceforth looked forward to the profitable expansion of its whaling industry and of its trade with China. Both of these involved the passage of American ships through Japanese waters. Americans thought it entirely reasonable that such ships should be provided by the Japanese with fresh water, provisions and repair facilities. They believed, moreover, that by 'opening' Japan they would be conferring upon it two undeniable benefits: American merchants would blaze a trail for American missionaries, bringing the gospel of

A caricature of Commodore Perry of the 'North American Republican State' from an 1854 woodblock print

Jesus Christ as well as the gospel of Free Trade. American aggression was thus bolstered by both practical and moral justifications.

On 8 July 1853 an American squadron of four ships under the command of Commodore Matthew Calbraith Perry anchored in Tokyo Bay. The shogunate, forewarned by the Dutch, knew that they were coming. But no one had told the local fisherfolk, who fled for the shore 'like wild birds at a sudden intruder'. That night a flaming comet passed through the sky. Perry righteously construed this as an omen 'that our present attempt to bring a singular and isolated people into the family of civilised nations may succeed without resort to bloodshed'. Implicit in this piety was the clear intention to shed blood if necessary; but first the commodore would try swagger. When he finally deigned to go ashore to meet the shogun's representatives Perry was escorted by two huge black sailors ('the best-looking fellows of their colour that the squadron could furnish') plus an escort of marines and a very noisy band. As the official chronicle confessed, '. . . all this parade was but for effect.' Having presented their demands, the Americans sailed away, pledging to return the following year for an answer.

The Americans returned, as promised, bearing gifts – and with twice as many ships. The gifts for the shogun, clearly intended to impress, included an entire miniature railway, complete with 350 feet of 18-inch track, a telegraph with three miles of wire, two boats, an iron stove, a telescope, numerous weighty tomes of history, law, Congressional debates etc., a virtual cellarful of drink and a small armoury of weapons. Every Japanese official was presented with what were evidently regarded as the most representative products of a higher civilisation: a clock, a sword, a rifle, a revolver and five gallons of whisky. The Japanese reciprocated with a selection of bronzes, lacquer, ceramics and textiles which the Americans thought 'a poor display, not worth over a thousand dollars'. To underline their superiority the Americans then put on displays of close-order drill and fire-fighting, staged a mock attack on a ship and fired off a broadside of their heaviest guns. These proceedings were followed by a lavish disbursement of naval hospitality ('. . . when clean work had been made of champagne, Madeira, cherry cordial, punch and whisky I resorted to . . . a mixture of catsup and vinegar which they seemed to relish with equal gusto') – and rounded off with a 'nigger-minstrel' entertainment.

What the Japanese made of this final proof of the advanced state of American culture is not recorded, but Perry got a treaty and within a few years so had the rest of the Western powers. The initial treaties of friendship, in effect promising hospitality to travellers, were soon enlarged, under Western pressure, into trade agreements granting far greater rights.

In the course of this diplomacy the shogunate revealed its fundamental feebleness, first by its unprecedented decision to consult both the *daimyo* and the emperor before acceding to the treaties, and secondly by the implicit admission that it could not hope to combat the superior military technology represented by Perry's 'Black Ships'. The basis of Tokugawa authority, the right to rule in the name of the emperor as 'great barbarian-subduing generalissimo', had been exposed as a sham.

First Impressions

Britain's first permanent diplomatic representative in Japan was Sir Rutherford Alcock; his account of his tour of duty, *The Capital of the Tycoon,* was long held in great esteem by his countrymen, though it provoked his (far abler) colleague A.B. Mitford to observe sourly of his boss that he would 'have been a greater man if he had never written a book about a country which he did not understand, or a grammar of a language which he could neither read nor write'. Be that as it may, Alcock's characterisation of Japan as 'topsy-turvy' land was to remain an enduring image in the minds of Western readers:

> Japan is essentially a country of paradoxes and anomalies, where all – even familiar things – put on new faces, and are curiously reversed. Except that they do not walk on their heads instead of their feet, there are few things in which they do not seem, by some occult law, to have been impelled in a perfectly opposite direction, and a reversed order. They write from top to bottom, from right to left, in perpendicular instead of horizontal lines; and their books begin where ours end, thus furnishing examples of the curious perfection this rule of contraries has attained. Their locks, though imitated

from Europe, are all made to lock by turning the key from left to right. The course of all sublunary things appears reversed.... I leave to philosophers the explanation – I only speak to facts. There old men fly kites while the children look on; the carpenter uses his plane by drawing it to him, and their tailors stitch from them; they mount their horses from the off-side – the horses stand in the stables with their heads where we place their tails, and the bells to their harness are always on the hind quarters instead of the front ... and finally, the utter confusion of sexes in the public bath-houses, making that correct, which we in the West deem so shocking and improper, I leave as I find it – a problem to solve.

The Japanese were no less eager to read about the West than Westerners were to learn about Japan. A description of London in a *Compendium of Famous Places in Barbarian Countries* (1862) eschews Alcockian drollery in favour of upbeat enthusiasm and a character-istically Japanese appetite for facts and figures:

There are a great many buildings and the whole population is prosperous. The river is spanned by a large bridge 1800 feet long and 40 feet wide.... The bank of the river is dominated by an imposing fortress.... The mouth of the river is so choked with ships that one would believe one was on dry land. The population is large and the number of students normally at university is never less than several tens of thousands. The women are extremely lustful and the men are both shrewd and cunning. To fulfil their ambitions they build large ships with which to sail the oceans of the world. They trade in all manner of goods and make enormous profits for them-selves. They have 28,000 merchantmen with 185,000 officers on board. The monarch's ship has 40 cannons and there are eight hundred or more ships with 120 cannons each....

Such naive impressions have their British counterpart in the *Sketches of Japanese Manners and Customs* published by Lt J. M. W. Silver on his return from serving with a detachment of marines guarding the British legation. His book carries no pretensions to scholarship and, indeed, follows no discernible logic at all, starting with 'Festivals and Holidays' and ending with 'Love of Flowers' and giving as much attention to 'Fires and Fire Brigades' as to 'The Court of the Mikado'. More shocked by mixed public bathing than by brutal public execu-tions, Silver commented with unaffected candour on whatever struck him as curious or surprising. As keen a sportsman as most healthy young men of his time, he found the national sport of Japan particularly odd:

> Their principal athletic amusement is wrestling … and pairs of brawny fellows are to be frequently met with of an evening in the outskirts of towns and villages, either crouched down in the preliminary attitude, which resembles that of angry fighting-cocks, or dragging one another to and fro like frogs struggling over a choice morsel. The game is necessarily a dragging and pulling one, its grand object being to force the opponent beyond a certain boundary. . . .
>
> The professional wrestlers are generally men of Herculean proportions. From constant practice they attain a muscular development that would eclipse that of our prize-ring champions; but their paunchy figures and sluggish movements render any further comparison impossible, as they neither practise nor appreciate what we call training. Size and weight are prized more than activity in the limited arena to which their performances are confined; so, instead of walking down superabundant flesh, they endeavour to increase it . . . .

And, if the sumo wrestlers were for Silver a paradox, the behaviour of their fans was little less than an outrage:

> Thundering plaudits greet the hero of the occasion, who presently strolls about among the assembled multitude, attended by his. . . servant who collects the offerings with which they liberally reward his exertions. When money fails, articles of clothing are frequently bestowed – and sometimes too freely, as it is by no means unusual for both sexes to half denude themselves at these exhibitions; and it is a favourite joke with the women to send their male friends to redeem the articles from the wrestler.

The Crisis of the Shogunate

The political events of the years between 1853 and 1868 proved to be complex, contradictory and confusing. Many samurai, and not least those whom the Tokugawa had excluded from power, took up the cry '*Sonno joi!*' ('Revere the Emperor! Drive out the barbarians!'). The 'unequal treaties' not only allowed foreigners rights of residence and property, they also bound Japan not to impose protective tariffs against foreign goods and to allow foreigners to be tried for criminal offences in their own consular courts. These curtailments of Japan's sovereignty in its own land were deeply humiliating. Opposition to the shogunal policy of appeasement began to coalesce around the imperial court in Kyoto, which became a focal point of intrigue. The Tokugawa, internally divided as to the best course of action, fumbled between concession and repression in their attempts to retain control of the situation. In 1862 they relaxed the obligation for *daimyo* to make 'alternate attendance' (*see p. 89*) upon them; when they later tried to reimpose it their orders were ignored. The ineptitude of the shogun's government managed to irritate the foreign powers while alienating its own allies and failing to silence its critics. The *tozama* houses of Satsuma and Choshu, who had long been excluded from government under the Tokugawa, began to emerge as leaders of the internal opposition, despite their long-standing rivalry with each other. Both had their estates in south-western Japan, far from the traditional centres of political life, both were subject to punitive bombardment by the Western powers after attacking their subjects or shipping. Both were convinced by this bloody experience of the necessity to modernise Japan's armed forces and industry along western lines. They began at once to modernise their own. In both fiefs radical young samurai were eager to speed up the pace of change and force the country's crisis to a resolution. Gradually their discontents began to crystallise into a coherent revolutionary programme: to overthrow the shogunate and replace it with a government, headed by the emperor, which would undertake a national reformation.

In 1866 the Tokugawa made a last attempt to assert their power by sending an army to subdue the combined forces of Choshu and Satsuma. It was beaten. In the same year shogun Iemochi died. His successor, Yoshinobu (1837–1913), decided not to risk another fight and accepted the suggestion of the lord of Tosa, that he should resign his office. Confident that his vast estates would ensure him inclusion in any new political set-up Yoshinobu was entirely wrong-footed by his opponents. In 1867 Mutsuhito (1852–1912), a youth of fifteen, succeeded to the throne, surrounded by courtiers who favoured the Satsuma–Choshu alliance. Yoshinobu, having given up his office, was

Emperor Meiji (1852–1912)

now faced with the prospect of losing his estates as well. His forces marched on Kyoto. The armies of Choshu, Satsuma and Tosa, now united under an imperial banner, defeated him and took Edo without a battle. In January 1868 the leading *daimyo* were summoned to Kyoto to be informed that direct rule by the emperor had been 'restored'. The 'reign name' for the new era (and posthumously the emperor) would be *Meiji* – 'Enlightened Rule'.

In April Edo was occupied by the emperor and renamed *Tokyo* ('Eastern Capital'). Sporadic fighting continued in northern Japan until the summer of 1869 but the rule of the Tokugawa, the longest shogunal dynasty in the history of Japan, was done for.

THE CHARTER OATH

In April 1868 a Charter Oath, carefully drafted by the leaders of the Restoration, was issued in the name of the new emperor. Its main aim was to win the allegiance of the political classes; the masses were curtly informed to obey the instructions on village noticeboards as per usual. The very brevity of the Oath conferred an aura of grandeur upon it while the vagueness of its phrasing left its propagators with plenty of room for manoeuvre:

1. Deliberative assemblies shall be widely established and all matters decided by public discussion.
2. All classes, high and low, shall unite in vigorously carrying out the administration of affairs of state.
3. The common people, no less than the civil and military officials, shall each be allowed to pursue his own calling so that there may be no discontent.
4. Evil customs of the past shall be broken off and everything based upon the just laws of nature.
5. Knowledge shall be sought throughout the world so as to strengthen the foundations of imperial rule.

As a manifesto this promised much but specified little.

The new regime moved cautiously at first and made much of its obedience to the emperor to secure the obedience of others. An embryo administration of ministries and departments was set up on Western lines. A mint was established to issue an imperial coinage. Commoners were ordered to adopt family names. The old feudal domains were abolished and replaced by prefectures (at first their borders were often the same and so were their governors).

'Enrich the Country, Strengthen the Military'

In 1871 a large and high-ranking delegation, led by a court noble, Iwakura Tomomi (1825–83), was despatched to the West to renegotiate the 'unequal treaties' signed by the shogunate. The ambassadors were brusquely informed that this was entirely out of the question but the outcome of the 'Iwakura Mission' was much more positive than negative.

Okubo Toshimichi of Satsuma saw the smoke-laden sky above London as 'a sufficient explanation of England's wealth and strength'. When he learned that 'this great growth of trade and industry in the cities has all happened in the last fifty years' and that only forty years previously railways, steamships and telegraphs were all unknown he became convinced that, through effort and education, Japan could in time 'catch up'. Overwhelmed by their first-hand experience of the West the Japanese emissaries returned with the resolve to push ahead with radical reforms faster than ever.

The overall slogan for the policy of modernisation was *Fukoku Kyohei* (Enrich the Country, Strengthen the Military). Its components ranged from adopting the solar calendar to building railways, from compulsory education to compulsory military service, from permitting marriage across class lines to abolishing the right to wear swords in public. Such revolutionary changes were bound to provoke resistance. Farmers resented being deprived of their sons' labour by the demands of the schoolteacher and the drillmaster. Samurai resented their loss of status under a regime which could find employment for only a minority of them as teachers, policemen, officials or officers in its new Western-style army. Raging inflation compounded popular discontent.

There were riots and more seriously there were rebellions. The last and most dangerous took place in 1877. With double irony it occurred in Satsuma and was led by a hero of the Restoration, Saigo Takamori (1827–77), who passionately believed that the wholesale adoption of Western ways was threatening the moral core of the nation's character. His 40,000 malcontents gave the government forces a hard fight of it but were eventually overcome by what were, in their eyes, peasants in outlandish uniforms. Saigo committed suicide after a last stand of heroic futility. In 1891 he was granted a posthumous pardon in recognition that his action had been motivated by outraged integrity, not personal ambition. 'The Great Saigo' remains a Japanese hero to this day.

THE EDUCATOR

Fukuzawa Yukichi (1835–1901) has been called the most influential private individual in Meiji Japan. Although often invited to enter government service, he refused, in the belief that one of the things his country needed most was an intelligentsia independent of official patronage. He made a huge contribution to creating such a class by founding Keio, one of Japan's most prestigious universities, and *Jiji Shimpo*, one of its most influential newspapers – and by writing over a hundred books. Fukuzawa aimed to achieve the transformation and strengthening of Japan by 'sweeping away blind attachment to past customs' in favour of a thoroughgoing adoption of Western civilisation and the scientific principles upon which he believed it to be based:

> Schools, industries, armies and navies are the mere external forms of civilisation. They are not difficult to produce. All that is needed is the money to pay for them. Yet there remains something immaterial, something that cannot be seen or heard, bought or sold, lent or borrowed. It pervades the whole nation and its influence is so strong that without it none of the schools or other external forms would be of the slightest use. This supremely important thing we must call the spirit of civilisation.

Born the younger son of a poor Kyushu samurai, Fukuzawa realised early that he would have to make his own way in the world. In 1854 he moved to Nagasaki to master Dutch, the established language of communication with the West. When he later discovered that English was the dominant European tongue he manfully set himself to master that as well. His open enthusiasm for alien culture exposed him not merely to ridicule but to personal danger from the xenophobes provoked by Perry's forceful opening of Japan. When he achieved fame in later life as an enthusiast for 'things Western' he was for years at a time unable to leave his house at night for fear of assassination.

Fukuzawa's avidity to learn and his skill in languages enabled him to accompany the earliest Japanese missions to the USA (1860) and Europe (1862). In his *Autobiography* he recorded his amazement at the extravagance and bizarre behaviour he witnessed:

> ... there seemed to be an enormous waste of iron everywhere. In piles of rubbish, along the seashore – everywhere – I found lying old oil tins, empty cans and broken tools. This was surprising, for in Yedo, after a fire, there would appear a swarm of people looking for nails in the ashes....

The affluence of a hotel lobby was another shock:

> ... we noticed ... the valuable carpets which in Japan only the more

wealthy could buy from importers' shops at so much a square inch to make purses and tobacco pouches with. Here the carpet was laid over an entire room – something quite astounding – and upon this costly fabric our hosts were walking in the shoes they wore in the street!

Fukuzawa was equally puzzled when no one could answer his enquiries about the descendants of George Washington, or seemed very bothered about the question:

... I knew that America was a republic ... but I could not help feeling that the family of Washington would be revered above all other families. My thinking was based on the reverence in Japan for the founders of the great lines of rulers.... So I remember the astonishment I felt at receiving such casual answers....

In Britain Fukuzawa was mystified by fox-hunting, ballroom-dancing and the concept of a 'Loyal Opposition'. It was always institutions that interested him most, although foreigners insisted on trying to impress him with demonstrations of their latest gadgets or most powerful engines. What Fukuzawa wanted to know was how a hospital, a bank or a post office worked. Upon his return he wrote *Conditions in the West* in three volumes (1866–70); its straightforward style helped it to become a best-seller and made him famous. 'Fukuzawa books' became a synonym for progressive learning. They also helped to popularise such alien concepts as 'rights' and 'liberty' for which Fukuzawa and fellow-enthusiasts for Western culture had to coin Japanese equivalents. The unfamiliar notion of (economic) competition, for example, was rendered by combining the Chinese characters for '(running) race' and 'fight'.

DEBATE AND DISILLUSION

Fukuzawa became a leading member of the Meirokusha (Sixth Year of Meiji Society) which promoted public understanding of Western culture and reform proposals through discussions and publications. He was therefore a pioneer of the unaccustomed art of public debate in Japan. In 1875 he published *An Outline of a Theory of Civilisation* which characterised Japan as 'semi-civilised', on a par with China and Turkey, and therefore inferior to the West ' in literature, the arts, commerce and industry, from the biggest things to the least'. He advocated the adoption of parliamentary government, mass-education, modernisation of the language and improvements in the status of women. But, although he was an ardent progressive, Fukuzawa remained a fervent patriot and saw no contradiction between nationalism and inter-nationalism:

> Japan and the Western countries lie between the same heaven and the same earth. They are warmed by the same sun and their peoples have the same human feelings.... Thus countries must teach and learn from each other, pray for each other's welfare and mix with each other.... We need not fear to oppose all the battleships of England and America for the sake of what is right.... A country should not fear to defend its freedom against inter-ference even though the whole world is hostile.

In his later years Fukuzawa became increasingly disenchanted with the aggressive imperialism of Western powers and dismissed their claim to be 'spreading civilisation' as a hypocritical screen for racism and exploitation. The outrageous behavior of Western residents in Japan's treaty ports provoked him to angry and contemptuous rebuke:

> They tell me that all foreigners believe in a future life but I should judge that only very few of those in our open ports will succeed in getting to heaven. They eat and drink and then leave without paying.... They accept payment in advance... and then fail to deliver.... They fire guns near people's houses, force their way through private by-ways, gallop about on their horses....

As for the self-styled 'Law of Nations', Fukuzawa saw clearly that it applied: 'only to those that happen to be Christian countries.... For whatever excesses Westerners may commit in Eastern countries, no one would dream of lifting a finger against them.'

In a series of pamphlets on *The Encouragement of Learning* Fukuzawa argued that 'when men are born they are by nature equal... The distinction between wise and stupid comes down to a matter of edu-cation'. At Keio Fukuzawa aimed to pioneer 'practical learning that is close to ordinary human needs'. Dismissing traditional scholars as useless 'rice-eating dictionaries' he developed an institution which was to produce generations of business leaders – though remarkably few bureaucrats. Summarising his career in his *Autobiography* Fukuzawa concluded modestly that 'my success was not due to my ability, but it was by reason of the time that I came to serve....'

'Civilisation and Enlightenment'

Official endorsement of the adoption of Western customs dates from about 1870. In 1871 the Tokyo municipal authorities banned public nakedness in deference to Western notions of modesty. The Imperial Court discarded its traditional silks in 1872 in favour of the serge and gold braid favoured by European monarchies. For centuries respectable married women in Japan had shaved off their eyebrows and blackened their teeth with a mixture of vinegar and iron filings; in 1873 the empress appeared in public sporting her own eyebrows and white teeth. The craze for *bummei kaika* (civilisation and enlightenment) reached its climax in the 1880s. The fashionable and ambitious glutted themselves on unfamiliar dairy products and beef, albeit the latter was coyly referred to as 'mountain whale'. In 1883 the government opened the *Rokumeikan* (Pavilion of the Deer's Cry), a building in the European style where officials and confidants of the Meiji regime could join with Western diplomats and visitors to enjoy such pastimes as ballroom dancing, music recitals, billiards and bazaars in aid of charitable causes. More seriously a Western-style criminal code, based on that of France, was adopted in 1883, a European-style peerage in 1884 and Cabinet government in 1885. More alarmingly an agitation for 'popular rights' began under the leadership of Itagaki Taisuke (1837–1919), founder of the rurally-based Liberal Party, and Okuma Shigenobu (1838–1922), creator of the business-based Progressives and founder of what later became Waseda University. (Both men were to survive assassination attempts and to serve together in Japan's first party-based government, Okuma being Prime Minister and Itagaki Minister for Home Affairs.)

REACTION

The need for a more considered approach to reform was voiced by a young intellectual, Kuga Katsunan, in the newspaper *Nihon* (Japan):

We recognise the excellence of Western civilisation ... and we respect
Western philosophy and morals... Above all, we esteem Western science,
economics and industry. These, however, ought not to be adopted simply
because they are Western; they ought to be adopted only if they can
contribute to Japan's welfare.

If for 'welfare' one reads 'strength' these sentiments become an echo of
government thinking. A reaction against frivolity and radicalism – real
or imagined – was soon enshrined in official policy. In 1887 a Peace
Preservation Law granted the police extensive powers of supervision
over political activity. Teachers and students, as well as civil servants,
were forbidden to attend political meetings. In 1889 a Western-style
Constitution was promulgated. Designed by Ito Hirobumi (1841–
1909), the emperor's most trusted adviser and a fervent admirer of
Bismarck, it was modelled on German lines, with a weak parliament, a
strong executive and special influence for the military. It was made
abundantly clear to the Japanese that this new political framework was a
gracious gift from his august majesty, not an expression of popular
sovereignty. About one in eighty Japanese men were qualified to vote.

The emperor himself took the keenest interest in the creation of the
Constitution, attending every single one of the drafting sessions in
person. He was equally closely concerned with the composition of an
Imperial Rescript on Education. Issued in 1890, it established the
fundamental principles of the Japanese school system until 1945. Its
exhortations combined a traditional Confucian regard for filial piety,
respect for parents, elders, teachers, policemen etc. and benevolence
towards neighbours, with a novel emphasis on civic obligations:
'...advance public good and promote common interests; always
respect the Constitution and observe the laws; should emergency arise,
offer yourselves courageously to the State.'

The samurai virtues of unswerving loyalty, unquestioning obedience
and unflinching bravery, once the special obligations of a privileged
caste, were henceforth to become the ideals of the entire nation.

Economic Development

The official exhortation to 'Enrich the country, Strengthen the Army' implied the closest possible relationship between the two strands of this policy of national self-strengthening. Japan needed to modernise its economy to make the nation powerful, not to make its people affluent. The Meiji regime gave early attention to establishing a framework for economic development, setting up a western-style postal system in 1871 and a national bank in 1872. Model factories were founded and later sold off to the private sector. Some, making glass, cement, matches and paper, were intended to further a policy of import-substitution. The silk-mill set up at Tomioka with French instructors in 1872 was to create an export industry to provide Japan with a crucial source of foreign exchange to pay for essential imports of foreign technology. The government attached such importance to this venture that its initial labour force consisted almost entirely of girls recruited from the samurai class. It never made a profit while in government hands but it did serve as a vital training centre for the industry which eventually accounted for a third of Japanese exports. By 1882 there were some 2,000 factories in operation, but mostly on a small scale, for they employed only 60,000 workers in total. The development of heavy industry had to wait upon the stimulus provided by the Sino-Japanese war of 1894–5 (*see p. 142*), which led to the birth of the giant government-sponsored Yawata steelworks and the production of Japan's first domestically-built railway locomotive.

Enthusiasm for industry did not imply neglect of agriculture, which remained by far the largest employer of labour and the supplier of food to a rapidly growing population and raw materials such as silk and cotton for export-led industries. Tea was also a valued crop and became the nation's second largest export item. The land tax continued to be the government's main source of revenue and was collected even more rigorously than it had been in feudal times. The new regime was strong in resisting the temptation to borrow money abroad and only two substantial loans were raised on the London market; one paid for the nation's first railway, which ran nineteen miles from Tokyo to Yokohama and was built by a twenty-nine-year-old Scot who worked himself into an early grave; the other loan stabilised the government's shaky finances at the time of the Satsuma rebellion (*see p. 123*). A national commitment to financial self-reliance meant that ultimately it was the peasants who paid for Japan's industrialisation, for taxation on industry itself was deliberately kept low to encourage initiative and experiment. Rural resistance to taxation, schooling or conscription was ruthlessly crushed. On the other hand assistance to peasant enterprise was offered through agricultural advice schemes and prizes for outstanding achievements, either in improving traditional techniques or in successfully introducing novel activities such as dairying.

ENTERPRISE AND PROTEST

The abolition of feudal restrictions on the sale of land, movement of people and choice of occupations released a surge of energy and ambition in all quarters. Samuel Smiles' *Self-Help*, translated as early as 1871, was the gospel for the age and none practised the new doctrine more fervently that Shibusawa Eiichi (1840–1931), a small-town boy who became president of the First National Bank and helped to found some 500 different companies and trade organisations. Self-consciously distancing himself from the despised image of the selfish and deceitful Edo-period merchant he trumpeted the patriotic value of his activities. Another self-made millionaire was ex-samurai Iwasaki Yataro (1835–85) whose shipping line, NYK, became the launch pad from which the Mitsubishi business empire diversified into shipbuilding, mining, warehousing, real estate and banking.

Established enterprises were not content to let newcomers make all the running. Mitsui managed to finance both sides during the struggle to overthrow the shogunate and later benefited substantially from the privatisation of government-funded model enterprises, acquiring a paper mill, textile factories, the company that installed Tokyo's first electric lights in 1883 and a machine works that is the ancestor of today's Toshiba electronics corporation. The specialised branch it set up in 1876 to handle foreign commerce acquired a stranglehold on Japan's coal business, supplied half the nation's machinery imports and developed its own shipping line. It is now Mitsui Bussan, one of the world's largest trading corporations. Recognition of the Mitsui group's efforts in supporting the war effort in 1894–5 (*see p. 142*) came with the elevation of its head to the rank of Baron Mitsui.

The reckless pursuit of economic growth went virtually unchecked by legislation to protect either workers or the environment. Fearless Tanaka Shozo (1841–1913), simultaneously a rebel and a traditionalist, was one of the few who railed against abuse and exploitation. The self-educated son of a peasant, he mounted a dogged campaign against the copper mine which polluted the food, water and land of his community. Proclaiming boldly that 'to kill the people is to kill the nation' he coined one of the modern world's first conservationist slogans in his declaration that 'the care of rivers is the Way of Heaven'.

Yatoi

The importation of Western culture and technology necessarily involved the importation of Western experts as instructors. They were addressed to their faces as 'honourable foreign expert' and referred to behind their backs as 'live machines'. Some of these *yatoi* (foreign employees) were already in Japan and were poached from their Western employers, some volunteered themselves, most were purposely recruited or even 'head-hunted'. In the earliest days the Japanese found themselves inundated with *ikasama* (honourable frauds) who, according to the biographer of the formidable British Minister Sir Harry Parkes (1828–85), 'belonged to the vast array of unclassified humanity that floats like waifs in every seaport. Coming directly from the bar-room, the brothel, the gambling saloon ... they brought the graces, the language and the manners of those places into the school room....'

In all some 4,000 *yatoi* were employed, of whom about half were British, the next largest contingents being French, American and German. More than half of the British were employed on public works projects and most of the rest by the navy and shipping departments. Whereas the British were mostly engineers and sailors, the French were bureaucrats and soldiers, the Germans doctors and policemen and the Americans teachers and agriculturalists. Most were young, able and enthusiastic, eager for responsibility and often entrusted with it. According to Georges Bousquet, the first lawyer to be hired by the Justice Ministry: 'Young students of fine arts build palaces, bank clerks handle large credits, army captains perform duties which would weigh heavily on the shoulders of a general....'

Japanese policy was to pay the *yatoi* well, work them hard and get rid of them as quickly as possible. (Only one was ever referred to in an official statement as 'indispensable', W. W. Cargill, the British director of government railways and telegraphs.) Just as Japan was anxious to avoid becoming dependent on foreign loans so it was also aware of the need to achieve self-sufficiency in technical and administrative skills. Many *yatoi*, thus discarded, found the rest of their professional lives an anti-climax. Henry Dyer returned to his native Scotland still young enough to take on dozens of worthwhile causes and projects but never found anything that stretched him as much as what he had done in Japan when he set up what became the Engineering School of Tokyo University.

At the height of the *yatoi* programme, their salaries absorbed no less than 10 per cent of the entire budget of the Ministry of Education. In 1874 there were about 500 of them. By 1879 the figure had been halved and by 1885 halved again. The investment certainly paid off. The last course to be taught in English at university level – the strategically vital discipline of naval architecture – closed in 1910. In less than half-a-century Japan had absorbed and indigenised virtually the entire technical heritage of the Western world up to graduate level.

MASTERS AND MENTORS

In Japan itself many of the Westerners who helped to lay the foundations of the modern nation are still remembered with awe and respect; in their native countries their names are often quite unknown. In Sapporo, where American William S.Clark, founder of the Agricultural School, stayed a mere nine months, his memory is honoured with a dashing equestrian statue, worthy of Custer, and inscribed with his parting advice – 'Boys, Be Ambitious!' A few examples must suffice to illustrate the extraordinary careers and influence of these pioneers.

Weighing in at seventeen stone, Ulsterman Dr William Willis, official physician to the British legation, must have inspired awe in many Japanese. During the civil wars which overthrew the shogunate he treated hundreds of casualties on both sides, instructing Japanese doctors in Western surgical techniques as he did so. (Most of the wounds, he noted, were caused by firearms, very few by sword-cuts.)

In the course of his professional duties he also dealt with cholera, malaria, rabies, smallpox and an outbreak of venereal disease which afflicted the British diplomatic mission and its garrison so severely that the Foreign Office asked him to prepare a special report on the problem and propose remedial steps for its solution. Willis later went on to found a medical school in Kagoshima after which he departed to pioneer Western medicine in Thailand.

W. E. GRIFFIS

Willis' sojourn in Japan lasted fifteen years. The American W.E. Griffis lasted only four before his contract as a teacher was abruptly terminated; but this skilful self-publicist remained the United States' leading 'Japanologist' for more than half a century. His initial motives for going to Japan were a mixture of curiosity and cupidity as he hoped to combine teaching with continuing to study for the ministry and accumulating material for a book and money for a nest-egg at the same time. Fukui, capital of Echizen, came as a salutary shock ('. . . the scales fell from my eyes. . . . I was amazed at the utter poverty of the people . . .'). Undaunted, he set himself high aims, from writing a chemistry textbook to eliminating the drinking of sake and 'the promiscuous bathing of the sexes'. The eagerness, idealism and diligence of his young samurai students humbled his initial vanity and led him to write to *Scientific American* in admonitory tone:

> The Japanese simply want helpers and advisers. They propose to keep the 'bossing', officering and all the power in their own hands. . . . Nearly every appointee comes here 'to revolutionise' his department, but the Japanese don't want that. They want the foreigners to get into the traces, and pull just so fast as, and no faster than, their mighty enterprises can bear . . . if a man means real hard work . . . and is willing to help without 'taking charge' of everything, let him try Japan. If he expects that the Japanese people wish to make him a Secretary of State . . . he had better stay at home. . . .

Within less than a year Griffis had wangled himself a job in Tokyo. He was staggered at what had taken place during his brief rural exile:

> Tokio is so modernised that I scarcely recognise it. No beggars, no guard-houses, no sentinels. . . . The age of pantaloon has come . . . carriages

numerous.... Soldiers all uniformed.... New bridges span the canals.
Police in uniform.... Gold and silver coin in circulation.... Old Yedo has
passed away for ever.

Having taught geography, physiology, literature and law, having
written textbooks and guide-books and preached at the Union Church
of Yokohama, Griffis returned home to write *The Mikado's Empire*. It
became the standard American work of reference on Japan and went
through a dozen editions. In his book Griffis lambasted the Western
powers for their arrogance and duplicity in dealing with Japan but his
love of the country did not blind him to the shortcomings of its people
– 'Love of truth for its own sake, chastity, temperance are not characteristic virtues.' In 1908 Griffis was awarded the Order of the Rising
Sun, Fourth Class.

BASIL HALL CHAMBERLAIN

England's equivalent of Griffis was perhaps Basil Hall Chamberlain,
whose much longer sojourn saw him rise from instructor in English at
the Navy school to Professor of Japanese at Tokyo University, where
he pioneered the study of early Japanese history, poetry and language.
Judged too delicate to complete a university course in England he had
arrived in Japan by chance in 1873 in the course of a round the world
voyage intended to restore his health. He stayed on until his retirement
in 1911. Chamberlain became greatly irritated by the publications of
globe-trotters who proclaimed themselves instant experts on Japan after
a six-weeks stay. He condensed his own encyclopaedic knowledge into
a delightful dictionary-style vade-mecum, *Things Japanese*. It first
appeared in 1890, eventually went through six editions and is still in
print, and still an absolute gem of deep learning and sardonic humour,
as the following brief quotations will testify:

> [sumo] wrestlers must be numbered among Japan's most characteristic
> sights, though they are neither small nor dainty, like the majority of things
> Japanese. They are ... mountains of fat and muscle, with low sensual faces
> and low sensual habits ... their feats of strength show plainly that the
> 'training' which consists in picking and choosing among one's victuals is a
> vain superstition.

The Japanese 'admire scenes, not scenery'; '... tea and ceremonies are perfectly harmless, which is more than can be affirmed of tea and tattle'; 'Cleanliness is one of the few original items of Japanese civilisation ... the nude is seen in Japan, but not looked at.'

Chamberlain also revised the *Handbook for Travellers to Japan*, published by John Murray and first drafted by the eminent diplomat, Sir Ernest Satow (1843–1929). Much of the advice remains eminently sensible – 'With regard to boots, it is advisable to wear such as can be pulled off and on easily ...'; '... officials must not be insulted by the offer of a tip'; 'The conditions of travel in this country do not lend themselves to intricate arrangements'; 'Take visiting cards with you. Japanese with whom you become acquainted will often desire to exchange cards'; 'Above all, be constantly polite and conciliatory in your demeanour'; 'Many travellers irritate the Japanese by talking and acting as if they thought Japan and her customs a sort of peep-show set up for foreigners to gape at....'

ERNEST FENELLOSA

What Chamberlain did for Japanese literature, the American Ernest Fenellosa (1853–1908) did for Japanese art. He was initially invited to Japan by Tokyo University zoologist Edward Morse (1838–1925) whose *Japanese Homes and their Surroundings* (1886) was to introduce Western readers to the unsuspected subtleties of Japanese domestic architecture. Initially a teacher of economics and philosophy Fenellosa subsequently devoted himself to reassessing the plight of the arts. When the mania for 'things Western' was at its height Fenellosa had the cultural detachment to use his position at the Education Ministry to re-establish courses in Japanese painting in the schools and to alert the government to safeguard against the wholesale exportation of *objets d'art* by foreign collectors, including many of the *yatoi* themselves. He also helped to found the school that became the Tokyo University of Fine Arts and Music (Geijutsu Daigaku). Fenellosa worked closely with Okakura Kakuzo (1862–1913), a pioneer of modern museum curatorship, who threw new light on Japanese aesthetics in *The Book of Tea* (1906). Fenellosa died abroad and was temporarily interred in London's Highgate cemetery where his headstone may still be seen. Devoted

Japanese students arranged for him to be reburied in Miidera, over-looking Lake Biwa.

JOHN MILNE

John Milne (1850–1913) came to Japan as a mining expert. The day he arrived in 1876 he experienced an earthquake. Despite the distractions of his teaching duties he perfected an accurate seismometer to monitor earth tremors, organised the world's first seismological congress and founded the Seismological Society of Japan. Decorated twice by the emperor and awarded the title of Professor Emeritus, 'Earthquake Johnny' sealed his commitment to Japan by marrying the daughter of a Buddhist priest.

Gaijin

The Japanese term for a foreigner is *gai-koku-jin* (literally 'outside-country-person); nowadays this is normally abbreviated to *gaijin*, a term originally carrying pejorative overtones but so widely accepted by *gaijin* themselves that it has come into general currency. The original *gaijin* community of the 1860s consisted of diplomats and 'commercials' but they were soon joined by idealists, opportunists and plain riff-raff. Like the *yatoi* a number of these newcomers were to make outstanding contributions to inter-cultural understanding.

James Curtis Hepburn (1815–1911) practised medicine in New York and preached the gospel in China before arriving in Japan to continue his evangelism. As the formal ban on Christianity was still in force when he landed he set himself to compiling a Japanese–English dictionary in the entirely correct belief that it, in due course, would prove an invaluable tool for the task of converting the Japanese. Hepburn found ready informants to hand among the pupils of the English language class taught by his wife. The result of his labours was published in Yokohama in 1876. He went on to make a Japanese translation of the Bible and to found a school which grew into the prestigious Meiji University. The Hepburn method of rendering Japanese in Roman characters remains widely used to this day.

Achievement on the missionary front, as such, was more limited.

The Japanese welcomed many aspects of Western culture eagerly but Christianity, despite the vigorous efforts of Catholic and Protestant alike, won few adherents. In 1907, after more than thirty years of evangelism, there were still only 140,000 Christians in Japan. Hepburn arrived in Japan with the education and self-confidence of a professional man. Fellow-missionary John Batchelor (1853–1944) was a Sussex lad with only elementary schooling yet this equipped him to become a world authority on the Ainu, among whom he lived for sixty years, compiling the first Ainu–English–Japanese dictionary. He lies buried in the Uckfield churchyard which he once tended as a gardener's boy. John Reddie Black (1816–80) came from his native Scotland via Australia to become editor of the infant *gaijin* community's English-language weekly *Japan Herald* in 1861. In 1872 he went on to found a Japanese-language newspaper with the reassuring title of *Nisshin Shinjishi (Reliable Daily News)*. Black's book, *Young Japan*, was one of the first accounts to be written by a journalist rather than a diplomat; initially published in Yokohama it later came out in London and New York as well.

INTERPRETER OF JAPAN – JAPANESE INTERPRETER

No *gaijin* went further than Lafcadio Hearn (1850–1904) in identifying with his adopted country. Half Irish-English, half Greek-Maltese and wholly rootless, Hearn drifted from Britain through the United States and on to the West Indies in search of an earthly paradise. As soon as he landed in Japan in 1890 he knew that he had found it. The tone of his essay 'My First Day in the Orient' is one of uncritical ecstasy

> ... everything Japanese is delicate, exquisite, admirable.... The bank bills, the commonest copper coins, are things of beauty. Even the piece of plaited coloured string used by the shopkeeper in tying up your last purchase is a pretty curiosity ... on either side, wherever you turn your eyes, are countless wonderful things as yet incomprehensible.

Within a few years he was bemoaning the relentless transformation of his new-found refuge: '... how utterly dead Old Japan is, and how ugly New Japan is becoming.' Where other Westerners saw drains and telegraph poles as encouraging evidence of the dawning of a better way of life Hearn was appalled at their impact on 'this detestable Tokyo . . . square miles of indescribable squalor. . . . To think of art or time or eternity in the dead waste and muddle of this mess is difficult.' Hearn stands out as one of the very few Westerners who not only did not praise Japan's modernisation but actually deplored it.

Eventually Hearn adopted a Japanese name, Koizumi Yakumo, and Japanese nationality and married a Japanese wife. He became fascinated by Japan's myths, legends and folklore and set himself to record and celebrate what he regarded as an endangered heritage. His books, with titles like *In Ghostly Japan, Glimpses of Unfamiliar Japan* and *Gleanings from Buddha Fields*, found an eager readership in the West and in the decade leading up to his death he was one of the most influential interpreters of Japan's culture to the outside world. His last work was modestly entitled *Japan: An Attempt at Interpretation*. Hearn's romanticism contrasts sharply with Chamberlain's gruff bark that 'when a man is forced to live in Lotus-land, it is Lotus-land no longer'. Chamberlain did, however, generously praise Hearn's swan-song as a labour not merely of love but also of learning, though Hearn never actually managed to decipher Japanese well enough even to cope with a newspaper, let alone classical texts. Had he been alive to read it he would therefore have been deeply moved by the homage of his Japanese biographer, who praised him as a *Japanese* writer through whom: '. . . the old romances which we had forgotten ages ago were brought again to quiver in the ear and the ancient beauty which we buried under the dust rose again with a strange yet new splendour.'

Even before Hearn's death Japan had begun to produce its own cultural interpreters, foremost among them Nitobe Inazo (1862–1933), whose *Bushido: The Soul of Japan* was written in English and published in 1899. Nitobe argued that the samurai ethic provided the moral basis of the Japanese social order. Of samurai stock himself, it was natural that he should take such a view. And he was writing at a time when, through the novel institutions of mass-education and conscription, ex-samurai teachers and army officers could be said to have been 'samuraising' peasant Japan with the honour code of their caste. Whatever the validity of Nitobe's argument it scored a singular success, passing, in six years, through ten editions in English, nine in Japanese, and being translated into languages as diverse as Czech, Norwegian and Marathi. Nitobe, a graduate of Sapporo Agricultural College, had studied in the United States and Germany and taken an American wife. His distinguished career later embraced service as an agronomist in Taiwan, professorships at the Imperial Universities of Kyoto and Tokyo and finally the post of assistant Director-General of the League of Nations.

Globe-Trotters

'It is strange to be in a clean land, and stranger to walk among dolls' houses. Japan is a soothing place for a small man.' Thus Rudyard Kipling writing in 1889, by which time Japan had become a well-established stop-over on the Victorian globe-trotter's circuit. Many contented themselves with curio-hunting in the treaty-ports of Kobe and Yokohama or made brief forays to 'do' the shrines of Kyoto or Nikko. Perhaps they were wise to limit their ambitions. As Victoria Manthorpe has noted:

> For most tourists the cherry blossoms, Mount Fuji, the temples, shrines, and the picturesqueness of the people were what they had come to see. After all, the food was difficult if not downright unpalatable. One needed an interpreter or a guide, or both. The winter and summer climates were extreme. Though there were European-style hotels in the big cities, if you ventured into backwaters you would find yourself staying in teahouses with paper walls, no heating, no furniture, and no privacy. If you went too far off the beaten track ... you were likely to find conditions very rough indeed....

ADVENTURER VERSUS AESTHETE

Bolder spirits scorned such problems as trifles, accepting Chamberlain's dictum that 'the real Japan' could only be found where the railways ended. This was certainly true of Isabella Bird (1831–1904). Yet another of those indestructible spirits bidden to take a world tour to repair an allegedly feeble constitution she had already climbed a volcano in Hawaii and ridden across the Rockies in winter before lighting on Japan, where she set off to explore the remote north – '... my route was altogether off the beaten track, and had never been traversed in its entirety by any European'. Miss Bird's record of her trail-blazing odyssey, *Unbeaten Tracks in Japan*, comes peppered with acerbic snap-judgments: 'The Japanese are the most irreligious people that I have ever seen – their pilgrimages are picnics, and their religious festivals fairs'; '. . . as may be expected, suicide is more common among women than men'; 'Yokohama does not improve on further acquaintance'; 'No view of Tokyo . . . is striking, indeed there is a monotony of meanness about it. . . . It is a city of "magnificent distances" without magnificence'; 'Yezo (Hokkaido) is to the main island of Japan what Tipperary is to an Englishman. . . . Nobody comes here without meeting with something queer and one or two tumbles.'

The art critic George Rittner's rather precious passion for 'Japo-naiserie', by contrast, was unchecked by any trace of Miss Bird's sturdy scepticism:

> No country in the world is probably so artistic as Japan. . . . Should a stream not harmonise with a mountain it will have its course altered; should an inartistic tree have the insolence to grow on a hillside covered with mauve and white azaleas it will be cut down. . . . Nothing may look out of place.

Kipling had had some harsh words to say about the impact of American missionaries who put up 'clapboard churches . . . for whose ugliness no creed could compensate'. Rittner hit out at their compatriots as tourists – ' The Americans, I believe, are chiefly responsible for the decline of Japanese art.'

If Rittner's effusive praise or prejudice often teetered over into sheer silliness he was by no means the worst offender in that respect. *Queer Things About Japan* by the experienced travel-writer Douglas Sladen was less awful than its title might imply (its success led inevitably to *More Queer Things About Japan*) but *Three Rolling Stones in Japan* achieved a truly remarkable level of sustained and offensive fatuous-ness:

> Even the beggars were jolly fellows and smiled at us with quite unprofes-sional cheerfulness. It is a curious sensation to be accosted by a hilarious hunchback who shows you his hunch as if it were the best joke in the world. . . . It is impossible to take anything seriously in Japan; everything seems made on purpose to be laughed at.

A JAPAN DIARY

It is ironic that while even trivial impressions of Japan could find a ready market among Western readers one of the most fascinating first-hand accounts should remain unpublished for sixty years after the death of its author, Richard Gordon Smith (1858–1918). Smith, a keen hunter, naturalist and collector, with a private income and a constitution as robust as his opinions, used foreign travel as an escape from a loveless marriage. His eight huge leather-bound diaries became jam-packed with hand-scrawled notes, hand-coloured sketches, photographs, post-cards and every kind of ephemera, from pressed flowers to tram-tickets. Perhaps surprisingly for a huntin'-shootin'-fishin' type he became a devoted student of Japanese mythology, faithfully recording folk-tales and commissioning local artists to illustrate them. These came to fill a further five volumes and formed the basis of his *Ancient Tales and Folklore of Japan*, published by A & C Black. Victoria Manthorpe has put together a handsomely-illustrated edition of his impressions and experiences as *The Japan Diaries of Richard Gordon Smith* (1986).

The Path to Empire

Japanese expansionism awakened only gradually. Until the Meiji Restoration the northern island of Hokkaido, which now accounts for over 20 per cent of the national territory, was not even formally part of the realm. Apart from a single clan domain it was left to the native Ainu – and was, theoretically at least, wide open to Russian occupation. The Meiji regime therefore hastily incorporated it into the state and set up a development agency to promote its settlement and exploitation, assisted by a team of *yatoi* consisting largely of Americans.

In 1874 an armed expedition was sent against Formosa (Taiwan) to punish the locals for the murder of fishermen from the Ryukyu Islands (Okinawa); by claiming the obligation to protect their inhabitants Japan was implicitly claiming sovereignty over the Ryukyus as well. They had been under loose Satsuma rule for centuries. In 1879 they were incorporated into Japan, despite protests from China.

The year 1874 saw the Meiji government's first major internal crisis over an issue of foreign policy. Alarmed by military analysts who argued that the Korean peninsula constituted 'a dagger pointed at the heart of Japan', a clique headed by Saigo Takamori (*see p. 123*) pressed for its pre-emptive annexation. Saigo even volunteered to lead an embassy there in the hope of provoking his own assassination to provide a *casus belli*. Those who advised against precipitate action were strengthened by the support of the recently-returned Iwakura mission (*see p. 122*), whose experiences had convinced them that Japan would have to undergo far-reaching military modernisation before being in a position to risk adventures overseas. The counsels of caution prevailed and Saigo retired to Satsuma in disgust to crusade for a revival of traditional martial valour.

THE SINO-JAPANESE WAR

Korea was not a colony of China but a tributary state which had for centuries acknowledged the cultural overlordship of the 'Celestial Empire'. Alerted by the scale of Japan's rearmament, China began to take an active interest in defending the integrity and independence of her client. Japan, still unwilling to risk outright war, compromised over incidents which might have led to conflict in 1882 and 1884. In 1885 both countries agreed that neither would send troops to Korea without informing the other. The element of mutuality in this agreement clearly implied that China had tacitly renounced any pretension that Japan was anything other than a fully independent state, to be dealt with on equal terms. In 1894 Korea requested Chinese assistance to suppress a rebellion. Japan quickly rushed in its own troops and declined to withdraw. Fighting ensued between Chinese and Japanese forces by land and sea but lasted less than a year. A treaty signed at Shimonoseki in April 1895 bound both countries to recognise Korean independence. China ceded to Japan Formosa (Taiwan), the Pescadores Islands and the Liaodong peninsula, agreed to pay a huge indemnity in gold to offset the expenses of the campaign and offered a range of economic concessions of benefit to Japanese commerce.

Japan, which had, in the aftermath of its own legal and constitutional reforms, just renegotiated the extra-territoriality clauses of the 'unequal treaties', thus signalled its emancipation by imposing even harsher humiliations on her formerly revered mentor. Unwilling to acknowledge Japan as a first-league player in the imperialist game of beggar-my-neighbour, Germany, France and Russia then combined to force Japan to return the Liaodong peninsula to China. Japan had no option but to yield before such a daunting alliance, though her compliance provoked large-scale and violent riots in Tokyo and an admonition from the emperor himself to 'bear the unbearable and suffer the unsufferable'. As if to rub salt in the wound, Russia in 1898 forced China to give it a lease on the peninsula and proceeded to build up Port Arthur as an ice-free naval base.

Despite these cruel disappointments the war boosted the international image of 'Jap the Giant Killer' and, in Taiwan, gave it a major asset to be developed as a market, an outlet for surplus population and, in the longer run, a source of rice and raw materials. Victory also had the effect of enhancing the prestige and power of the military in shaping national policy. Japanese military prowess was further displayed during the 1900 'Boxer Rising' in China, when Japanese troops played the leading part in the international force which rescued the foreign nationals besieged in Peking's diplomatic compound.

THE RUSSO-JAPANESE WAR

Japan's international position was greatly improved in 1902 by the signing of the Anglo-Japanese alliance. Both sides agreed to aid the other in the event of it being in conflict with two or more powers and to stay neutral in the event of it being at war with a single power. Britain, dismayed by its diplomatic isolation during the Boer War (1899–1902), henceforth felt able to redeploy some of its naval strength from the China coast to counter the growing German naval threat in European waters. Japan was assured that, in the event of a war with Russia, the threat of British intervention would prevent the French from coming to the aid of the Tsar.

Thus bolstered, the Japanese could now take a firmer line against the continuing build-up of the Russian presence in Korea and south Manchuria. Having made careful preparations they finally abandoned the lengthy and inconclusive negotiations they had entered on to find a mutually acceptable adjustment of interests. In February 1904 Japanese ships attacked and severely damaged squadrons of the Russian Pacific Fleet at anchor in Port Arthur. The London *Times*, overlooking the Japanese omission of a formal declaration of war, hailed the strike as 'an act of daring'. The British-trained Japanese fleet subsequently annihilated the Russian Baltic Fleet after it had sailed half-way round the world to come to battle. The Tyne-built ships of Admiral Togo (1848–1934), 'the Nelson of Japan', sent virtually every enemy vessel to the bottom of Tsushima Strait in less than an hour. The land-war was more of a slogging-match. The Russians, fighting at the end of a tenuous supply-line stretching through thousands of miles of wilderness, could scarcely bring their huge manpower advantage to bear effectively. The Japanese were so weakened by their efforts in the field that their officer corps was badly depleted and their domestic economy brought to the verge of collapse. Both sides were relieved to accept the mediation of the United States President Theodore Roosevelt and sign a treaty of peace at Portsmouth, New Hampshire in September 1905. Russia accepted Japanese primacy in Korea and turned over its economic interests in south Manchuria (including the prized Liaodong peninsula), as well as the southern half of the island of Sakhalin.

The absence of a war indemnity tarnished the agreement in the eyes of the Japanese public; but the victory of an Asian power over a European one heartened the leaders of movements for independence from colonial rule from one end of Asia to the other. Ironically Japan soon revealed its own attitudes to colonialism by reducing Korea to protectorate status and forcing the abdication of its king. The assassination of newly-appointed 'resident-general' Ito Hirobumi by a local patriot in 1909 showed that the Koreans were unwilling to accept the radiant benevolence of Japanese rule with humble gratitude. Japan responded by annexing Korea outright in 1910, thus inaugurating half a lifetime of antagonism between the two nations. No western power protested. In 1911 Japan at last resumed the right to impose its own tariffs unhindered by the 'unequal treaties'. Japanese could scarcely be blamed for drawing the conclusion that to be accepted as a fully 'civilised' nation, on a par with the western powers, it was essential to behave as aggressively as they had.

CHAPTER EIGHT

Through the Dark Valley,
1912–1945

A Japanese born with the turn of the century would have been old enough to remember quite clearly the national mourning which marked the death of the Meiji emperor in 1912. By the time that same Japanese had lived as long as the emperor had reigned – just over forty years – he or she would have seen the country gain acknowledged Great Power status, suffer the devastation of an earthquake of unprecedented magnitude, slide from constitutional government into miltarism, conquer and lose a vast Asian empire, endure the agony of atomic warfare and accept the humiliation of foreign occupation for the first time in its history.

End of an era

The funeral procession of the Emperor Meiji was rich in a symbolism which even Westerners could interpret. Mixed in with priests and courtiers wearing the costumes of centuries long vanished strode contingents of soldiers and sailors in the Western-style uniform which the emperor himself had invariably worn for the past forty years; keeping step with them marched an honour guard of 500 sailors from the British Royal Navy – a tribute to the closeness of the relationship between the two nations at that time. In 1913 the Meiji Jingu (shrine) was begun to honour the spirit of the departed ruler; surrounded by a large and leafy park it remains an oasis of calm in the noisy Tokyo of today.

NEW HORIZONS

Within two years of marching together in the funeral of an emperor

Japanese and British troops were engaged as allies in a world war. Japan's rapid conquest of the German treaty-ports of Kiaochow and Tsingtao on China's Shandong (Shantung) peninsula, and her seizure of German-controlled islands in the northern Pacific, were among the earliest victories on the Allied side.

Heartened by these successes Japan next sought to bolster its influence in a China still in turmoil from the fall of the Manchu dynasty in 1911. In January 1915 the Japanese government presented the infant Chinese Republic with a list of 'Twenty-One Demands' grouped in five categories. The first group related to Japan's new position in the Shandong peninsula, the second to her interests in Manchuria, the third to mining activities, the fourth to the undesirability of China offering concessions to other powers and the fifth to her 'wishes' that the Chinese authorities should accept the appointment of Japanese 'advisers' to assist key military and economic officials. Chinese resistance led to the dropping of the fifth group of demands and the modification of the others which, under British pressure, were grudgingly conceded.

At the end of the Great War Japan was accepted as one of the 'Big Five' at the Paris Peace Conference. Her possession of Germany's former Pacific islands was confirmed but under the proviso that they be held as mandated territory in trust from the League of Nations. Japanese attempts to insert a declaration of racial equality in the Charter of the League were frustrated by the USA, Britain and Australia, who feared its implications for immigration policy and insisted that citizenship status was an internal matter for each nation to determine. Japan was already smarting from the discrimination suffered by Japanese migrants in California and the failure to secure some form of international guarantee against such humiliations rankled deeply.

Nevertheless Japan remained committed at this stage to international co-operation. In 1918 Japanese troops were sent to join the Allied expeditionary force in Siberia which was confusedly attempting to stifle the Bolshevik revolution. (The Japanese contingent did not withdraw until 1922, after a futile and costly intervention which was deeply unpopular at home.) In 1921–2 Japan participated in the Washington Naval Conference which attempted to formulate a new security framework for the Pacific. Japan accepted a ratio of three capital ships to every five in the American and British navies; in return it was agreed that the western Pacific should be regarded as essentially an area of Japanese predominance, with Britain strengthening no bases nearer than Singapore, at the tip of the Malay peninsula, and the USA none nearer than Pearl Harbor in the Hawaiian Islands.

Although the new arrangements marked the ending of the Anglo-Japanese alliance after twenty years, the mutual desire for a continued close relationship was confirmed by an exchange of royal tourists. In 1921 Crown Prince Hirohito stayed as the personal guest of King George V at Buckingham Palace and was invested with the Order of the Garter. In 1922 the Prince of Wales undertook a reciprocal month-long tour in which he was 'carried across Japan on a wave of cheers'. The official account of this odyssey includes a photograph of the prince in the uniform of a Japanese general. Another picture shows him with his entourage, all dressed in kimono, the parting gift of Hirohito; the caption identifies a tall young man at the back as Lt L. Mountbatten – as commander of Allied Forces in South-East Asia he was, some twenty years later, to receive the surrender of Japanese forces in that region.

Taisho Democracy

The son and successor to the Meiji emperor took the reign-name *Taisho* ('Great Righteousness') and the period between his accession and the subversion of civilian rule some twenty years later is conventionally referred to as the era of 'Taisho democracy'. Taken at face-value the term is misleading; Japanese politics continued to be dominated by the traditional élites of imperial advisers, service chiefs and bureaucrats. Democratisation, in so far as it occurred, meant giving a higher priority to populist concerns on the political agenda and conceding that the leaders of the largest political parties had to be accommodated within the policy-making process. Taisho parliamentary politics were characterised by thuggery and mud-slinging at elections, undignified bickering in debate and corruption and back-stabbing in office.

The death of the old emperor had removed a figurehead who

represented at least stability and a paternalistic ideal of public service; his successor, crippled by hereditary mental illness, could not perform even this minimal function and in 1921 Crown Prince Hirohito (1901-89) became Regent in his place. (In 1926 he became ruler in his own right and took the well-intentioned reign-name *Showa* – 'Enlightened Harmony'.) At the same time the elder statesmen (*genro*) who had made the Meiji revolution and loyally guarded the regime ever since, were dying off year by year. With them departed much prudence. There-after, as Beasley has put it with characteristically dry understatement, 'a situation developed in which it was easier to keep order among the people than among those who ruled them'.

The prospects for a transition to a more participatory style of politics were unsettled by the domestic impact of the Great War. On the one hand Japan converted its long-standing trade-deficit into a surplus for the first time and benefited from the expansion of its industries, espe-cially chemicals and shipbuilding; but these changes were accompanied by rapid inflation which destabilised prices and led to nationwide 'Rice Riots' in 1918. In the same year the forceful and resourceful Hara Takashi became Japan's first commoner prime minister. The demo-cratic cause might gain encouragement from the victory of the democracies in the Great War – but it was also overshadowed by the spectre of Bolshevism. And, if the war boosted industry it also boosted industrial unrest. Whereas in the pre-war decade the number of strikes ran at an average of twenty a year, in 1919 there were just short of 500. In 1921 Hara was assassinated by a railway employee, 'punishing' him for corruption.

In 1922 a native Communist Party was established in Japan. Various types of radical, feminist and socialist, including Christian Socialist, groupings also emerged, adding to the ideological maelstrom. They remained small, dominated by the intellectual and the ineffectual, mutually antagonistic and out of touch with the fears and aspirations of ordinary peasants who were more genuinely represented by the tenants' movements which, in 1926, combined to create a leftist Japan Farmers' Party.

Given the profoundly conservative nature of the village societies in which most Japanese still lived, the government was probably taking fewer risks than it seemed when, in 1925, the vote was extended to all men over twenty-five. Laws providing for health insurance, dispute mediation and industrial safety were enacted to placate organised labour. The fact that these measures emerged from the Home Ministry's 'Social Problems Division' reveals the anxiety provoked in ruling circles by the growth of unionism among industrial workers and the popularity of Marxism among students and their professors.

A 'Peace Preservation Law', also passed in 1925, established a 'Special Higher Police' to combat such 'dangerous thoughts' and with extensive powers to harass suspected subversives. In the election year of 1928 alone some 1,600 suspected communists were rounded up. In the same year it became a capital crime to call for the abolition of private property or the restructuring of the constitution. (By 1941 another 74,000 'subversives' had been arrested, although only about 5,000 were actually imprisoned.) At the same time rural patriotic associations, led by service veterans and petty notables in public employment, such as headteachers and postmasters, recruited the young men of the villages to undergo a regimen of healthy paramilitary activities and improving talks. These clubs had the active encouragement and financial support of the army, whose senior officers were, no doubt, appalled at the appearance on the streets of Tokyo of the *mobo* ('modern boy') whose sole interests appeared to be bizarre western clothes, raucous western music and the pursuit of the indelicately clad *moga* (*modan gaaru* – modern girl). Not only did the rural patriotic associations provide employment for superannuated officers, they also represented a mechanism through which the military could influence the newly-enfranchised. As early as 1925, when so-called 'party government' was said to be in its heyday, the 'moderate' army minister, General Utagaki, confided to his diary the hope that:

> More than 200,000 troops in active service, more than 3,000,000 in the veterans' organisation, 500,000 or 600,000 middle and higher school students, and more than 800,000 trainees in local units: all of these will be controlled by the army, and their power will work as the central force aiding the Emperor in war and peace alike.

Ominously he added: ' The right of autonomous command over the

Emperor's army is, in a time of emergency, not limited to the command of troops, but contains the authority to control the people.'

CULTURAL COUNTER-CURRENTS

Social and political uncertainties were reflected by contrary tendencies in the arts. 'Engaged' writers rehearsed 'proletarian' or nationalist themes but much of the most significant literature of the period was politically detached. Shiga Naoya (1883–1971), one of the foremost exponents of the introspective ' "I" novel', came to public notice through his contributions to the avant-garde monthly *Shirakaba* ('White Birch'). Akutagawa Ryunosuke (1892–1927, *see p. 190*) proved himself a master of the bizarre and macabre before committing suicide at the age of thirty-five. His status was attested by the establishment of a literary prize named in his honour in 1935. One of Akutagawa's friends, the dramatist Kikuchi Kan (1888–1948), founded *Bungei Shunju*, one of Japan's most influential cultural journals; during the Pacific War he was to serve as chairman of the Japan Literary Patriotic Association.

The inter-war period is also notable for the appearance of two significant, though very different, women writers. Yosano Akiko (1878–1942) composed erotic poetry and produced an acclaimed version of *The Tale of Genji* (*see p. 47*). Waka Yamada (1879–1957) escaped a failed arranged marriage by turning to prostitution and exile in America and then escaped that through refuge in a Christian mission and marriage to a gifted but impoverished Japanese language-teacher. Returning to Japan Waka became a contributor to the feminist magazine *Seito* (Bluestocking), gained national fame through her women's advice column in the *Asahi Shimbun* and campaigned successfully for the enactment of 'Motherhood Care Legislation'.

In the plastic arts the most enduring development was the birth of the *mingei* (folk craft) movement, centred on Yanagi Soetsu (also known as Muneyoshi, 1889–1961), another of the founders of *Shirakaba* magazine. Yanagi's friendship with the English potter Bernard Leach introduced him to the work of the English engraver–mystic William Blake and of the designer William Morris. More local influences on his philosophy included an admiration for Korean craftsmanship and a renewed respect for Zen Buddhism, inspired by the writings of Suzuki Daisetsu. Other important figures in the *mingei* movement include the potter Hamada Shoji (1894–1978) and the woodcut-artist Munakata Shiko (1903–75). Painting, meanwhile, was dominated by the rivalry between *Nihonga* (Japanese-style painting) and *Yoga* (western-style painting), the latter much influenced by Impressionism. *Yoga* artists were naturally drawn to study in Paris. Fujita Tsuguhara (1886–1968) went there in 1913 – and died there as a French citizen, Leonard Foujita. His British counterpart was the charmingly eccentric water-colourist and illustrator Yoshio Markino (1869–1956) who lived in England from 1897 until his expulsion in 1942.

DESTABILISATION

If the Japanese economy was developing rapidly it was not doing so steadily. Almost inevitably some regions raced ahead while others lagged behind. The gap between city and country became increasingly more marked, not only in living-standards, but even more markedly in life-styles. Cheap imported rice from Korea and Taiwan undercut domestic producers. The brief post-war boom turned to recession in 1920. In 1921 a bitter dispute paralysed the nation's docks.

Then, in 1923, came the Great Kanto Earthquake which virtually wiped out Yokohama and much of Tokyo as well. The tremors and subsequent fires killed over 100,000 people and injured some 50,000 more. Three million homes were destroyed or seriously damaged across the Kanto plain. In the ensuing chaos it was rumoured that Korean immigrants were looting homes and robbing survivors, and perhaps as many as 6,000 Koreans died in pogroms provoked in the panic. Frank Lloyd Wright's handsome Imperial Hotel, opened the very day before the quake, was one of the few major buildings to survive virtually intact. It quickly became a combined hospital, field kitchen and relief headquarters as well as home to dozens of displaced diplomats and newsmen. (Ironically the Imperial, which also survived the Pacific War bombing, was demolished in 1967.) Although the disaster did bring various indirect benefits (the destruction of the tram system hastened the adoption of motorised transport) it also represented a huge setback

Destruction after the Great Kanto earthquake

to the economy. Budgetary retrenchment in 1924 meant that four divisions were cut from the army and 20,000 jobs axed from the civil service; this may have been no bad thing in itself, but it greatly irritated the military, already ruffled by the Siberian fiasco.

Just as the work of reconstruction seemed to be making headway, a major banking crisis in 1927 dealt a further blow to domestic business confidence. The panic brought down the government and thirty-seven banks. Then came the Wall Street Crash of 1929 and the resultant collapse of world trade which cut the price of raw silk by two-thirds in a single year, depriving rural communities of their major source of cash earnings. Unemployment rose to 3,000,000. An indisputable measure of the misery of the next decade is less the oft-quoted reference to farmers selling their daughters off to geisha-houses than the fact that some 40 per cent of deaths in the 1930s were due to preventable diseases.

SEEKING COMPROMISE

Against the background of these difficulties Japanese foreign policy, under the guidance of professional diplomat Shidehara Kijuro (1872–1951), still inclined towards seeking compromise with the western powers, notably in the tricky area of Chinese affairs. For Japan China represented a vast potential market and rich source of much-needed raw materials (e.g. ores for the state-run Yawata steelworks) – but it was plunged in political chaos as warlords, Nationalists and Communists battled for supremacy. America still supported the principle of the 'open door' which put all foreign powers on an equal footing. Japanese analysts increasingly resented this stance: for the United States economy foreign trade was of relatively marginal importance, for Japan vital; the strategic interests of the United States lay properly in the American hemisphere, of Japan on the neighbouring Asian mainland. Japan's population of 30,000,000 at the time of the Meiji Restoration had more than doubled; but restrictions strengthened by America in 1924 limited the possibilities of migration. The onset of depression brought protectionism which limited Japan's export opportunities. More and more Japanese nationalists, in the army, in right-wing patriotic organisations, in secret and not-so-secret societies and in the hard-pressed villages from which the army recruited the bulk of its soldiers and junior officers, called for 'stronger measures' to secure Japanese interests in Asia. The ideal of the frugal selfless samurai, pressing only for his country's advantage, could readily be invoked against the prevailing image of the sleazy politician and the selfish businessman.

In 1930 an international naval conference, convened in London, sought further reductions in armaments. Against the wishes of the service chiefs the Japanese delegation accepted concessions. In November of that year Prime Minister Hamaguchi was shot and fatally wounded by a youthful right-wing fanatic, though he lingered for months before death. The slide toward aggression had begun and the internationalists in Japan – well represented in the diplomatic corps, big business, the political parties and, to a considerable extent, the navy – revealed themselves increasingly powerless to halt it.

Empire and Expansionism

Japanese colonialism, like its western counterpart, was frequently jus-

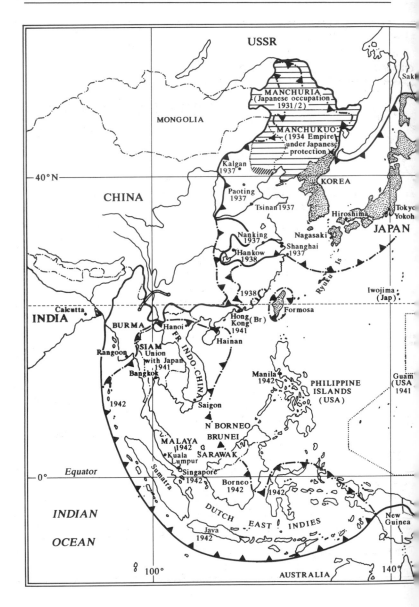

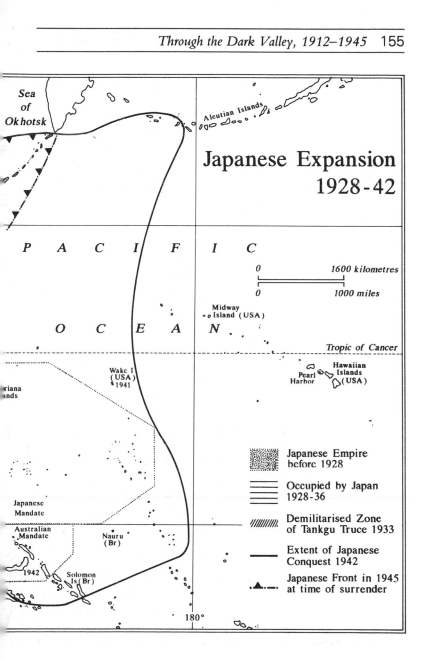

Sea of Okhotsk

Aleutian Islands

Japanese Expansion
1928-42

P   A   C   I   F   I   C

0   1600 kilometres

0   1000 miles

Midway
Island (USA)

O   C   E   A   N

Tropic of Cancer

Wake I
(USA)
1941

Hawaiian
Islands
(USA)

Pearl
Harbor

riana
nds

Japanese
Mandate

Australian
Mandate

Nauru
(Br)

1942

Solomon
Is (Br)

180°

Japanese Empire
before 1928

Occupied by Japan
1928-36

Demilitarised Zone
of Tankgu Truce 1933

Extent of Japanese
Conquest 1942

Japanese Front in 1945
at time of surrender

tified by the argument that, if it wasn't always benevolent in tone, it was beneficial in its effects. 'Development', as the colonialist conceived and defined it, would take place, whether the colonised co-operated willingly with the process or no.

The pressures behind Japanese expansionism were partly strategic, partly economic, partly demographic. The strategic impulse is, perhaps, the most immediately comprehensible. The military were an entrenched element in Japan's policy-making élite. As a latecomer to 'modernisation' Japan was only too aware of its continuing weaknesses vis-à-vis the other great powers with interests in the East Asia–Pacific region. And it was all too easy to slide from justifying the annexation of small, off-shore islands – to establish a 'line of security' – to arguing the necessity for occupying sizeable chunks of the mainland to create a 'line of advantage'.

The economic motive for imperialism related to both the supply and the demand side of Japan's productive potential. An overseas empire would, it was hoped, both provide Japan with vital raw materials and absorb the output of its growing industries and guarantee these benefits permanently by means of firm political control. The demographic argument rested on the 'need' to relocate Japan's 'surplus' population and the frustration of this need by the restrictions imposed on Japanese immigration by Pacific-rim powers such as the United States, Canada and Australia. As Hokkaido could scarcely be called overpopulated it is difficult to give much credence to this rationalisation. At bottom, perhaps, Japan's ambition to acquire an overseas empire was simply a manifestation of its desire to claim full equality with the Western powers; and it could at least claim that, unlike the others, it had a legitimate interest in the development of regions which were on its own doorstep and not in continents far distant from its homeland.

At its greatest extent Japan's overseas empire embraced territories almost as large as Japan itself and with a population of some twenty millions. The minor components consisted of foggy Sakhalin and sun-soaked Pacific islands, both relatively underpopulated and therefore thinly settled by the Japanese themselves; the major colonies were Korea and Taiwan, whose salient features and respective fates contrasted strongly with one another.

TAIWAN AND KOREA

Taiwan, a long-neglected former off-shore province of the declining Chinese empire, became a showcase of progressive experiment. Thanks to the energetic efforts of Japanese agronomists rice and sugar output rose so precipitously that a plentiful surplus was available for export to the home country. The health and educational standards of the local population rose with equally dramatic results. Even hostile, anti-colonialist observers, such as American missionaries, felt obliged to concede that Japanese rule had brought benefits. Positive relationships between colonisers and colonised are attested by the fact that at the time of the Pacific War almost two-thirds of the latter could speak Japanese.

Korea, a state and culture as old as Japan itself, put up a bitter resistance to its subjugation. In Taiwan the pacemakers of colonial policy were the engineers, doctors and teachers, in Korea the police and the military. Even the elementary schoolteachers wore swords. True, some Koreans bowed to fate and served the regime as a subservient sub-élite of collaborationists; but at the most their numbers are reckoned at not more than 5 per cent of the total. After thirty years of colonial rule less than 20 per cent of Koreans could understand Japanese. On the other hand the area of land under cultivation had virtually doubled and the output of local industry increased almost twenty-fold.

Renamed Chosen, Korea was to undergo even greater humiliations after the outbreak of the Pacific War. Its economy was further restructured to meet Japan's military needs. Korean people were obliged to take Japanese family names and, from 1942 onwards, Korean men were conscripted into the Japanese army or sent to Japan itself to work in factories and mines as virtual slave labour. Korea remained a resentful and embittered colony until August 1945. The legacy of a generation of brutal overlordship has cast its shadow over Japanese–Korean relations ever since.

The Guandong (Kwantung) army, which policed Japanese railway and mining interests in neighbouring Manchuria (still technically part of China), contained many expansionists who thought Japan should carve out a self-sufficient economic sphere within which it could shelter itself from the uncertainties of the depressed global trading system. Manchuria possessed huge reserves of coal, iron and other materials of strategic value to Japan. Looking back, the takeover of Manchuria appears to be a logical prelude to the attempted conquest of China itself. But the American historian, Robert M. Spaulding, has argued that the priorities of the day were quite different:

> Japanese army officers saw Manchukuo as a laboratory ... in which they could demonstrate the efficiency, the organisational innovations and the ideological purity which they found lacking in their own country ... they saw Manchukuo as a stepping-stone, not to control of China, but to reform of Japan.

In any case it was the Soviet Union, rather than China, that was perceived as the main sphere for military action. The Red army, huge and mechanised, posed far more of a threat to Japan's position in Manchuria.

THE DARK VALLEY

In 1931 officers of the Guandong army took the initiative into their own hands by faking a sabotage attack on the railway they were ostensibly guarding. This provided a pretext for attacking local Chinese troops and launching the outright conquest of the bleak but mineral-rich region which was subsequently proclaimed to be the 'independent' state of 'Manchukuo' under the (entirely nominal) rule of the last scion of China's deposed Manchu dynasty, P'u Yi. A million Japanese subjects came to constitute the effective ruling class. The Japanese government failed to disavow these actions, being severely shaken by the assassination in February 1932 of Finance Minister Inoue, in March of the head of the Mitsui conglomerate and in May of Prime Minister Inukai, the last party politician to head a government. Henceforth administrations would be dominated by service officers, bureaucrats and courtiers. An international investigation headed by Lord Lytton led the League of Nations to condemn Japanese actions in Manchuria as unjustified aggression. Japan rejected the findings and withdrew from the League in 1933.

The internal counterpart of increasing international isolation was a surge of what one might call nationalist fundamentalism, a fear-induced attempt to reaffirm a lost national consensus. This phenomenon took many forms, not least the effort to 'cleanse' Japanese culture and language of western 'corruption'. Linguistic purists sought to persuade drinkers in search of a beer to use an invented 'authentic' term – literally, 'barley brew' – instead of the loan-word *biru*. The urge to purge extended to individuals as well as terminology. When the distinguished (and highly conservative) legal scholar, Professor Minobe, had the temerity to refer to the emperor as 'an organ of the constitution' he found himself accused of *lèse-majesté* and stripped of his appointments. In its positive aspect ultra-nationalism promoted the revival of traditional cultural forms, especially combative pastimes such as sumo and kendo, and the propagation through the educational system of extremist propaganda via school texts lauding the unparalleled history of the 'god country' and the sacred solidarity of emperor and people, bound together in an indefinable *kokutai* ('national structure').

FASCISM?

Was 1930s Japan 'Fascist'? Insofar as fascism requires the inversion of classic liberalism it was not. Japan had never been very liberal and had less need to invert the liberal values represented by parliamentary government such as rational discussion, the search for compromise, the legitimacy of dissent, than simply to stifle their last gasps. Japanese ultra-nationalism does bear many similarities with European fascism: a romantic attachment to a national past conceived as heroic myth, an intoxication with the supposedly primal values of blood and soil, a longing for the passion of action rather than the tedium of negotiation. But Japan never spawned a charismatic leader to match Hitler or Mussolini. It mobilised the masses – but without the aid of a pseudo-revolutionary party. In the context of Japan neither were necessary. In the opinion of the doyen of Japanese political scientists, Professor Maruyama Masao, what Japan experienced was 'fascism from above'. And, while the hardliners might have locked up their opponents and the fanatics assassinated them, they never proscribed them, negated their human status or denied them the possibility of submission and re-acceptance.

One of the leading ideologues of the day was Kita Ikki (1883–1937), a former socialist and failed revolutionary. His *Outline Plan for the Reconstruction of Japan* was widely read by junior army officers. It called for the abolition of parties and peerages, nationalization of major industries, strict limits on personal wealth and a spearhead role for Japan in arousing Asian nationalists to throw off western rule.

OR MILITARISM?

If Japan wasn't in the European sense fascist it was certainly militarist. This meant at least two things – the assertion of military priorities in national policy-making and the extension of military influence throughout both economy and society. These processes were complicated by the long-standing rivalry between the navy and the army and the factional rivalries within the army itself; of the latter the most important was the antagonism between the *Kodoha* (Imperial Way) which favoured unswerving devotion to the emperor and 'spiritual training' and the *Toseiha* (Control Group) whose priorities inclined to greater mechanisation and economic mobilisation.

On 26 February 1936 junior officers of the *Kodoha* led 1,400 men of the crack 1st Division on to the snowy streets of Tokyo, surrounding the Imperial Palace itself in pursuit of a 'Showa Restoration'. Just what this might actually mean remained obscure: was it death to corrupt civilian politicians and the capitalists whose interests they served? relief for the suffering peasantry? a spiritual renewal of the nation? war against Communist Russia? Whatever it was it was to be achieved for the sake of the emperor. Actions taken from self-proclaimed motives of loyalty were held to be self-legitimating. The conspirators saw themselves as the high-principled heirs of the 'men of spirit' who had overthrown the feeble Tokugawa regime in the 1860s, opening the path to energetic national reconstruction. Three senior government leaders were murdered; Prime Minister Okada was saved only because the rebels shot his brother-in-law by mistake – an error appropriately emblematic of their confusion.

For once the emperor himself felt moved to state his own position unambiguously, disavowing any sympathy for the rebels. The attempted coup was soon snuffed out and its ringleaders tried in secret. Nineteen were shot and seventy imprisoned. One of the executed was

Kita Ikki. The suppression of the February coup attempt did not, however, amount to a reassertion of firm governmental control. The generals had long ago worked out that they could bring down any civilian administration not to their taste by simply refusing to provide serving officers to fill the posts of army and navy minister as the constitution required. Now they could claim that they themselves were under pressure from below and could only rein back their subordinates by leading them in the direction they wanted to go – a curious justification of leadership.

FOUNDING FORTUNES

Despite the volatility of the inter-war economy this period did see the establishment or significant development of a number of Japanese companies of enduring importance. Mazda, originally a producer of cork, then of machine-tools, produced its first vehicle, a three-wheeled truck, in 1931. In 1933 the Toyoda Automatic Loom Works, a company specialising in the manufacture of textile machinery, established a new division to make motor cars. Toyota Motor Corporation became an independent company in 1937. (It became Toyota because the company registrar's department made a mistake in writing the name of the Toyoda family who had founded it.) By 1941 Toyota was producing 2,000 cars a month. More important than its level of output, however, was the fact that it had already committed itself to a strategy of corporate development based on innovative research and production management based on the 'just in time' principle of parts delivery, which made huge economies in inventory costs. Nissan (literally meaning Daily Production Company) was also founded in 1933. By 1938 it was producing 8,000 cars a year.

The Fuji film company was established in 1934. In the same year the state-run Yawata Iron and Steel Works was re-established as the Nippon Steel Corporation.

Matsushita Electric, which began in 1917 as a backyard outfit making light-sockets, narrowly survived disaster in 1929 but by 1937 had become part of a group of nine companies making radios, light bulbs, batteries and heaters. All these companies are now household names with global operations.

The Path to War

In 1936 Japan joined Nazi Germany and Fascist Italy in an 'Anti-Comintern Pact', which was explicitly an anti-communist alliance and implicitly a pledge of mutual assistance in the event of a war involving the USA. In July 1937 a fabricated incident at the Marco Polo bridge on the Chinese border served as the pretext for an army-initiated invasion of China proper. By December Japanese forces had reached the Guomindang capital, Nanking, where large-scale atrocities were committed against disarmed Chinese forces and those civilians unable to take shelter in the international compound.

Governmental acceptance of a commitment to expansion by force was confirmed in April 1938 by the passage of a National General Mobilisation Law which geared the economy to military objectives. The direction of expansion was, however, partially determined by the Soviet Union. Incidents along the Manchurian border involving Soviet and Japanese troops in July 1938 and May 1939 resulted in bloody defeats for the Japanese; there would be no quick victories in Siberia. (Thanks to Germany Japan later secured a neutrality pact with the USSR which lasted until August 1945.)

The progress of war in Europe beckoned Japan south. The fall of France and the Netherlands and the seemingly imminent collapse of Britain in the summer of 1940 emboldened Japan to advance on their colonies in South-East Asia. Japan now proclaimed the establishment of a 'Greater East Asia Co-Prosperity Sphere', a new order in Asia under which enlightened, industrialised Japan would lead her less fortunate neighbours towards a higher plane of development while simultaneously freeing them from white, racist overlordship. The reality, under pressure of war, was to be a process of exploitation more vicious than anything white colonialism had inflicted. At home all political parties were declared abolished and merged into an 'Imperial Rule Assistance Association'.

Pacific Rivals

The USA expressed its displeasure with Japan by limiting exports of scrap steel, a vital strategic resource; then it embargoed oil. Japan had invested too much blood and treasure to retreat from China. Even after the American government froze Japanese assets in the USA both sides continued to negotiate, though what sort of compromise they might have found is difficult to imagine.

Confidential Japanese appreciations of America's war potential estimated it to be ten times as great as that of Japan. But Japanese 'thinking' on the subject of a trans-Pacific conflict, in so far as it justifies the term, was based on the premise that America, depraved by jazz and journalism, would not fight and, if deprived of its Pacific strike-force by a pre-emptive attack, could not fight, even if it wanted to. Given its strictly-limited reserves of oil the navy pressed for the offensive to be taken sooner rather than later – and delivered with all the advantage that surprise can give.

The fact that Japan's declaration of war was not delivered until after the attack on Pearl Harbor on 7 December 1941 is clearly attributable to the monumental incompetence of the Japanese embassy staff in Washington. The fact that the United States, despite much intelligence available to its diplomatic and military experts, was taken so completely unawares is less easy to explain. One of the fullest analyses says it all in its title – *At Dawn We Slept*.

Victories and Defeat

Tactically brilliant but strategically disastrous, the raid on Pearl Harbor enabled Roosevelt to unite an enraged nation for war. For a few months Japanese forces seemed unstoppable, conquering the Philippines and Indonesia, taking Singapore, bastion of British power in the East, and pressing through Burma to the borders of India itself. In retrospect it is clear that the turning-point came as early as June 1942 when Japan lost four aircraft-carriers in the battle of Midway.

Deprived of the heart of its naval strike-force Japan could not successfully oppose the island-hopping counter-offensive of the Allied forces. Nor could it look for much help elsewhere. Whereas the Allies fought with a genuinely co-ordinated strategy, the Axis constituted an alliance in name only. Germany helped Japan secure a neutrality pact with the USSR without ever informing Japan of her intended invasion. Japan likewise never informed Germany of the plan to attack Pearl Harbor. Both parties were inhibited from trust by their own racism. Among his intimates Hitler openly referred to the Japanese as 'yellow monkeys'; Japanese extremists, intoxicated by the vision of *hakko ichiu* ('all the eight corners of the world under one roof'), classified the Nazis as 'friendly enemies'.

With the capture of the Pacific island of Saipan in 1944 the Allies acquired a base from which Japan itself could be bombed into submission. In March 1945 Tokyo was subjected to three days of incendiary raids which killed 100,000 people. Okinawa, part of Japan's home territory, was invaded in April 1945 to provide a rescue-point for disabled bombers on their way home. Defending the island wiped out virtually the entire Japanese garrison of 110,000 as well as killing 150,000 civilians. By May 1945 13,000,000 Japanese had been rendered homeless.

The Potsdam Declaration of July 1945 called for the 'unconditional surrender' of Japan; although it added assurances that 'Japanese should not be enslaved as a race or destroyed as a nation' it gave no explicit

The bombed-out Trade Hall, Hiroshima

guarantee that the emperor-system would be allowed to survive. The Japanese cabinet ignored the call for surrender but attempted to seek mediation via the USSR. Taking Japan's failure to respond as a rejection, the United States decided to drop an atomic bomb on Hiroshima on 6 August 1945. On 8 August the USSR declared war on Japan, moving troops into Manchuria. Japan now faced the possibility that it might be partly occupied by the Soviets, which could have meant the permanent division of its home territory; if wholly occupied by the USSR it would certainly have meant the abolition of the imperial throne. On 9 August a second bomb was dropped on Nagasaki. Official pronouncements still spoke of resolutely pressing on with the war to a successful conclusion – but behind the scenes the government was deadlocked about whether or not to bow to the inevitable. Hardliners looked to the civilian population, half-starved and armed with bamboo spears, to fight a guerilla campaign of resistance, though might take 20,000,000 lives to preserve 'The Land of the Gods'. In the end it was the emperor himself who broke the impasse and opted for peace.

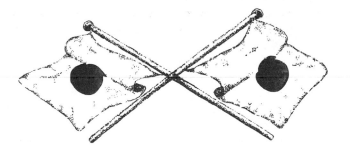

CHAPTER NINE

Reform, Recovery and Resurgence, 1945–1973

Nothing less than an occupation of the country will be necessary; not necessarily a very long one, but one long enough to make the fact of our victory and their defeat incontestable.... This then should be the programme: Defeat, Occupation, Demilitarisation, Opportunity. The period of occupation should be made to depend upon the ability of the Japanese to produce ... a government with liberal ideas that is willing and anxious to co-operate with the Allied Nations.... The chief task of the army of occupation would be to ensure that the new government is afforded protection and help while it is reorganising the administration.... Any attempt to discredit the emperor would, in my opinion, be disastrous. What we must do is convince the Japanese people that their emperor has been led astray by his military advisers. The whole-hearted co-operation of the emperor would be indispensable ... the goal of all our efforts will be to bring into being a peace-loving and contented Japan, an agreeable partner in international politics, a country that will contribute to a single unified world economy ... if we intend to demilitarise Japan ... we shall have to find an outlet for her economic energies....

These astonishingly prescient words were written in 1943 by John Morris, a former lecturer at Tokyo University who lived in Japan from 1938 to 1942. They foreshadow to a remarkable degree the history of the following decade.

Defeat

On 15 August 1945 the emperor broadcast to the Japanese people. It was the first time in history that an emperor had spoken directly to his subjects and the directness of his communication was obscured by the courtly manner of his speech. The word 'surrender' was never mentioned. Instead the Japanese were informed that the war situation had 'developed not necessarily to Japan's advantage' and that the time had come to 'pave the way for a grand peace for all the generations to come by enduring the unendurable and suffering the unsufferable'. Attempts to prevent the emperor's broadcast were successfully thwarted. After it some 500 army and navy officers committed suicide. Most civilians experienced shock, followed by relief, followed by fear. Japan had never been defeated, much less occupied, in its entire history. Would the occupying army inflict pillage and rape upon hapless and half-starved civilians?

While the nation hesitantly awaited the arrival of its conquerors there was time to make a preliminary estimation of the price of defeat. The war had cost Japan 1,855,000 dead and 678,000 wounded or missing. The loss of Taiwan, Sakhalin, Okinawa and various Pacific islands had reduced her national territory by almost half and the collapse of her overseas empire would bring the repatriation of its Japanese occupants, another 6,000,000 mouths to feed, at the very time when imported supplies of rice and soya beans would be denied her. Eighty per cent of the shipping fleet had been sunk. A third of all industrial machinery had been destroyed by bombing and a quarter of all buildings. Of the major cities only Kyoto, Nara and Kamakura had been spared devastation. When they landed at the end of August 1945 even the conquerors were stunned at the scale of the destruction. They had no wish to add to it. Their objective was not revenge but reform.

THE LAST SHOGUN

In theory the occupation of Japan was an Allied exercise; in practice it was almost entirely an American one. In Washington there was a Far Eastern Commission; but it was too far away from the scene of action to achieve more than vague supervision. In Tokyo there was an Allied Council for Japan; but that was soon paralysed by American–Soviet antagonism after Russian requests to occupy half of Hokkaido were rebuffed.

There were contingents of British and Australian troops in Japan, including many who were valued for their expertise in the Japanese language. But they represented token forces beside the Americans, who occupied most of the country's 2,800 military bases. Effective power was concentrated in the hands of one man – General Douglas MacArthur, designated SCAP – Supreme Commander of the Allied Powers. Vain but visionary, he had a strong, if romantic, sense of history and eagerly embraced the opportunity to combine the roles of crusading hero and the last of the shoguns. His position abounded in paradox. He would make the Japanese democratic by ordering them to be. They were defeated but if they chose not to co-operate, could frustrate the achievement of this primary objective. Censorship was to be abolished but SCAP HQ would zealously censor anything that smacked of militarism, from kendo to *kabuki*.

MacArthur's arrogant, theatrical style enabled him to appeal directly to ordinary Japanese and helped to compensate for the lack of Japanese-speaking staff available to him. But basically he had to operate through the existing machinery of state. He could 'purge' the military of 167, 035 office-holders and the political élite of another 34,892. In his view Japan did not need them and nor did he, but the number of officials who were purged was only 1,809 and businessmen 1,898. For the Occupation to work at all smoothly, let alone effect great changes, the co-operation of armies of Japanese clerks, policemen and postmen would be essential. To avert mass-unemployment and mass-starvation it would be necessary to harness the energies of businessmen, farmers and shopkeepers. All directives had to be passed down through a hierarchy of Japanese bureaucrats who could deliberately misunderstand or mis-translate their instructions – could, and did. An American Occupation could not help but be a very Japanese thing. And while the soldiers and the politicians lost their power, the power of the bureaucrats increased.

Fortunately the Japanese were eager to co-operate. One commentator cynically characterised the Occupation as an ideal relationship – the world's most self-confident teacher taking on the world's keenest student. Certainly the Japanese had lost neither their energy nor their enterprise. Less than a month after the signing of the surrender aboard the USS *Missouri* a publisher with abundant supplies of both those qualities brought out *A Handbook of English Conversation*. It became post-war Japan's first bestseller.

DEMILITARISATION

The Japanese had taken up arms at their emperor's bidding and at their emperor's bidding they laid them down. The demobilisation of the armed forces was substantially achieved by November 1945. (Most Japanese troops in Korea and Manchuria were seized by the Russians; many were indoctrinated, enslaved and never seen again.) By January 1946 the machinery of wartime censorship and repression had been dismantled. An Allied International Military Tribunal for the Far East was established to try twenty-five high-ranking Japanese officers and officials for war crimes against humanity. Seven, including ex-Prime Minister Tojo, were hanged and the rest imprisoned. (Most of those imprisoned had their sentences shortened later.) These proceedings were considered by most Japanese to be 'victor's justice', another part of the price of defeat, and having no proper foundation in pre-existing international law. The only international law specialist among the eleven judges representing the Allied nations was Radhabinod Pal of India; he found all the defendants not guilty. The indictments were lodged on the emperor's birthday in 1946. The executions were carried out on that of his son in 1948.

Democratisation

Western experts with first-hand experience of Japan soon persuaded MacArthur that any attempt to try the emperor as a war criminal would almost certainly lead to mass-resistance, obliging Occupation forces to devote all their efforts to maintaining order and wrecking any hope that constructive reform might be speedily achieved. MacArthur, having frightened the US government with the spectre of having to pay for 'a minimum of a million troops . . . for an indefinite number of years', was soon arguing that the emperor's endorsement of reform would be the best guarantee of its success and reassuring his distant masters that the emperor in fact had 'a more thorough grasp of the democratic concept than almost any Japanese'.

On New Year's Day 1946 an Imperial Rescript was issued denouncing 'the false idea that the emperor is divine and that the Japanese people are superior to other races and fated to rule the world...'. Instead it called upon the people 'to construct a new Japan through being thoroughly pacific, the officials and people alike obtaining rich culture and advancing the standard of living'. The Rescript did not, however, disavow the emperor's descent from the sun goddess or dissociate him from the performance of Shinto rites.

It can be argued that this 'renunciation of divinity' was as much for the benefit of Westerners as for the Japanese. True, schools had taught children that the emperor was an *arahitogami* – a *kami* manifest in a human being – but only a handful of nationalist ideologues believed that he was literally a god. To foreigners the announcement may well have conveyed the implication that the Japanese believed in his divinity so firmly that only an explicit disavowal by the 'god' himself could dissuade them from their error. What it actually meant was that the vast mass of Japanese no longer felt brow-beaten by a few fanatics to acknowledge as a literal truth something that manifestly was not. To equate 'god' and *kami* was, in any case, a gross error. To elevate a human being to the status of *kami* did not imply putting him on the same level as the creator of the universe. Japanese had traditionally given reverence to those who had rendered outstanding service to the nation by the quality of their lives or achievements; the scholar-poet Sugawara no Michizane (*see p. 36*), the national unifier Tokugawa Ieyasu (*see p. 74*) and the naval commander Togo Heihachiro (*see p. 144*) all came into this category and had shrines dedicated to them.

RULES OF THE GAME

On 6 March 1946 MacArthur announced that Japan was to have a new constitution. It was drawn up, not by an elected convention of Japanese representatives, but in English, by American lawyers serving in the Occupation forces. They took just over a week. Ironically the preamble to this new set of political ground-rules triumphantly proclaims that sovereignty resides in the people. But, like the 'feudalistic' 1889 constitution which it replaced, the 'Showa' constitution was also a gift from on high.

MacArthur's constitutional priorities were:
a) to entrench the destruction of aggressive militarism
b) to define the emperor's position as purely symbolic
c) to abolish the peerage and other legal inequalities.

The new constitution became operative on 3 May 1947. Significantly it devoted its first chapter not to the rights of the people but to the role of the emperor as 'the symbol of the state and of the unity of the people', with Article 4 reaffirming that '. . . he shall not have powers relating to government'.

The second chapter consisted solely of Article 9, a unique provision, to be found in no other constitution in the world:

> Aspiring sincerely to an international peace based on justice and order, the Japanese people forever renounce war as a sovereign right of the nation and the threat or use of force as a means of settling international disputes.
>
> In order to accomplish the aim of the preceding paragraph, land, sea and air forces, as well as other war potential, will never be maintained. The right of belligerency of the state will not be recognised.

Chapter III spelled out the 'Rights and Duties of the People' and was the longest. Echoing the American Declaration of Independence it affirmed in ringing tones 'Their right to life, liberty and the pursuit of happiness . . .' and, like the first ten amendments to the US constitution, guaranteed fundamental civil liberties. The affirmation in Article 13 that 'All of the people should be respected as individuals' amounted to an implicit abolition of the pre-existing legal code which gave unequal rights to husbands over wives and heads of households over family members. Article 20 not only proclaimed freedom of worship but also disestablished State Shinto by decreeing that ' no religious organisation shall receive any privileges from the State nor exercise any political authority' and banning the state from 'religious education or any other religious activity'.

Other chapters outlined the powers and functions of the various organs of government, stressing the supremacy of the legislature, the independence of the courts and the rights of local government against the centre.

DEMOCRACY WITHOUT ROOTS?

Could Japan be democratised by fiat? The new constitution was clearly an alien document, enshrining alien concepts and drafted in an alien language by a people long portrayed by Japanese propagandists as both demonic and immature. Raging inflation, near-starvation, a soaring crime-wave and a series of vicious and damaging strikes distracted the Japanese and depressed them with a profound sense of the dislocation of their society, whose very orderliness had for so long been a major source of national pride.

On the other hand there was a tradition of parliamentary government, flawed perhaps, but well understood. Illiteracy was virtually nil and the press well-developed. There were liberals and socialists who had endured persecution and might form the nucleus of a new political élite. Above all there was the fact that the disaster and disgrace of defeat had thoroughly discredited the militarists. In overseeing the implementation of his new dispensation MacArthur had, moreover, the advantage of undisputed authority; there was no need, as in Germany, to negotiate with partner Allies controlling separate zones. And Japan was effectively cut off from the rest of the world because the Occupation authorities themselves decided which foreigners could enter the country and which Japanese could leave it.

The journalist Yoshida Kenichi, son of post-war Prime Minister Yoshida Shigeru, summarised the political impact of the American victory and occupation thus:

> It has taken away . . . an army constructed on obsolescent principles with an obsolescent mentality to match. . . . It has called the Communists out into the open . . . and now we can fight them without fear of the police coming down on them and turning them into martyrs. . . . The Emperor has once more become the Emperor of the People . . . these changes . . . would never have been effected except for the war and, what is most important, if we had not lost the war. This is something we really and truly owe the Americans: that they defeated us in such a way as to leave no room for doubt as to who had won.

There was nothing inevitable about Japan's transition to democracy. That the new political framework preserved crucial elements of the past as well as setting the nation on a novel course is a tribute to the idealism and self-confidence of the Americans and the resilience and intelligence of the Japanese. The Showa constitution has never, since its adoption, been amended.

ROOTS OF THE MIRACLE

It was no part of MacArthur's brief to incubate an economic miracle. The official view was that 'the plight of Japan was the direct outcome of her own behaviour and the Allies will not undertake the burden of repairing the damage'. MacArthur's orders stressed that, 'You will not assume any responsibility for the economic rehabilitation of Japan or the strengthening of the Japanese economy.'

Initial thoughts tended towards 'de-industrialising' Japan with the aim of ensuring that it could never again produce anything more aggressive than a bicycle. Special attention was to be given to dismantling the 'big four' conglomerates which between them controlled a third of Japan's industry and half its finances: Mitsui, Mitsubishi, Sumitomo and Yasuda. The Occupation authorities took the view that, 'Whether or not individual *zaibatsu* were warmongers is relatively unimportant; what matters is that the *zaibatsu* system has provided a setting favourable to military aggression.' It was also believed that *zaibatsu* held down wages, stifled the growth of small businesses and were hostile to free trade unions. Their break-up would therefore be desirable in the interests of democratisation.

The immediate post-war years were dominated by shortages, soaring prices and a thriving black market. Many Japanese were literally living in the wreckage of defeat. Industrial output in 1946 was less than a third of what it had been ten years before. Food aid from America and Australia was essential to fend off famine. Rationing of staples did not end until after the Occupation. But, if the war had destroyed much, it also had its positive side. Army service had introduced millions of peasants to the mysteries of the motor-lorry, radio and telephone. Cameras and motor-cycles made for the military could be redesigned for the civilian market. Where factories and transport systems had been demolished by enemy action they could be replaced with new technology. Throughout history the Japanese had shown a remarkable tenacity in face of disaster, whether it be fire, earthquake or typhoon. Now, instead of rebuilding a village, they needed to rebuild a nation.

LAND REFORM

American attitudes to the Japanese economy were fundamentally shaped by its political implications. Partly to destroy what they regarded as 'feudal' oppression, partly to create a class with a vested interest in the new order and, *per se*, hostile to communism, they assigned a high priority to land reform. Half of the entire Japanese labour force consisted of peasant farmers and almost half the nation's land was worked by tenant sharecroppers who paid their rent in kind. Henceforth it was decreed that no one could own more than a hectare, unless they cultivated it personally, in which case the limit was three hectares. (In under-populated Hokkaido the limits were higher.)

All surplus land was bought by the government at 1939 prices and resold to farmers who bought it with vastly inflated 1947 currency. The losers might well have regarded this transfer of assets as virtual confiscation under cover of law. One landowner declined to take a last look at his estates on the grounds that the train fare would entirely swallow the compensation he had got for them. Some five million acres of arable land was redistributed to nearly as many tenants. Rents fell sharply, payment in kind virtually disappeared and in the end only about 10 per cent of the total was left to be worked by wage-labour. On the negative side the land reform froze the pattern of farming into small and scattered plots, which was wasteful of labour and hampered mechanisation. And, while it gave the farmer the incentive to raise yields, because the profits would be all his, it did little to give him the means of doing so.

EDUCATION

Educational reform was seen as another vital prop to the infant democracy. Ardent nationalists were sacked from the teaching profession; 100,000 were dismissed in all. Left-wingers acquired a hold on the teachers' unions they have never since lost and textbooks were rewritten to eliminate nationalist propaganda. The curriculum was revised to downgrade 'moral education' and upgrade science. The

English language was reintroduced. The old élite high schools were abolished and the American 6-3-3-4 structure substituted: six years of elementary school, followed by three years of junior high, three of senior high and four at university. Access was improved by raising the period of compulsory education from six years to nine and by establishing new universities so that every prefecture had at least one.

Changing the structure of education was one thing, changing its style quite another. Rote learning remained the dominant pedagogy. And the competitive pressure to pass written examinations now involved the mass of the population instead of being confined to its future élite.

Second Thoughts

As early as March 1947 MacArthur expressed the view that Japan's acceptance of reform had been so positive that an early end to the Occupation might be foreseen. The communists' rise to power in China favoured a re-evaluation of the position of Japan, which looked less and less like a defeated enemy to be treated with suspicion and disdain and more and more as a budding democracy to be fostered as a valued ally. American concerns to 'contain communism' favoured the appreciation of Japan as a strategic base, an 'unsinkable aircraft-carrier.'

SCAP became increasingly content to exercise an overall supervisory role and leave the initiation of policy to the Japanese. Industry was encouraged to rebuild and the break-up of the *zaibatsu* was abandoned. In 1948 the right to strike was limited by law; in 1950, the year in which communist forces invaded south Korea, a 'red purge' drove 12,000 alleged communists out of the Japanese trade union leadership. At the request of MacArthur Japan established a 75,000-strong National Police Reserve. By 1951 Prime Minister Yoshida was informing the Diet that 'large-scale armaments are something that defeated Japan cannot afford to undertake.'

NURTURING FRANKENSTEIN?

Looking back from the perspective of the 1990s many American commentators have seen the Occupation as a process whereby the United States created a Frankenstein's monster, destined to rival and then destroy the economy of its own creator. In his book *Remaking Japan*, Theodore Cohen, who drafted Japan's labour code, abjures the more paranoid analyses in favour of a muddle theory:

> ... economic democratisation, notably the liberation of the peasantry and the freedom of labour unions to bargain collectively, created for the first time in Japan's history, a domestic mass-consumer market in depth. It was the mainspring of subsequent Japanese economic development and all else that followed. American leaders ... were engrossed in preventing the resurgence of Japanese militarism and building democratic bulwarks against it. Nor did the Japanese see that far ahead at the time. They were happy to have their erstwhile domestic oppressors off their backs and a peaceful 'cultural Japan' in prospect.... The Americans got what they thought they wanted and so did the Japanese. What they got in addition was an 'economic miracle'.

Cohen might also have added that a disarmed Japan was by definition a Japan freed from the burden of arms-spending. By assuming the burden of Japan's defence (albeit with some contributions from the Japanese tax-payer) the United States released some 5 per cent of Japan's GNP for productive investment in industry. In addition to this, technical research was left entirely free to address itself to the needs of the market, rather than the military. Another unwittingly beneficial legacy of the Occupation was the battery of controls erected to manipulate industrial reconstruction through licensing, buying in technology, controlling foreign exchange etc. After 1949 these bureaucratic weapons were wielded by the Ministry of International Trade and Industry. Before that it had been called the Ministry of Commerce. Before that it was the Ministry of Munitions.

UNCLE SAM'S SHADOW

On 8 September 1951 Prime Minister Yoshida staked his political life by signing a 'majority peace' at San Francisco, burying the hatchet with the USA and its allies but leaving a settlement with the USSR and its satellites unresolved. Yoshida characteristically opted for practical politics rather than the unattainable 'overall peace' which, the Japanese opposition insisted, could alone guarantee security. With the outbreak of war in Korea the 'Cold War' was reaching a new height of tension. Japan had already been forced into the American camp by the fact of Occupation. Better to accept the alliance with enthusiasm, Yoshida reasoned, than try to wriggle out of it for no certain gain. 'Unarmed neutrality' might appeal to university pacifists but to an old diplomatic hand like Yoshida it looked like an open invitation for Japan to be bullied by its well-armed communist neighbours. Five hours after signing the San Francisco peace treaty Yoshida signed a Treaty of Mutual Co-Operation and Security with the United States. Its duration was open-ended. Its obligations were asymmetrical. The US was bound to defend Japan but not vice versa. The US was also to maintain bases on Japanese territory and to retain the right to intervene in the event of large-scale domestic unrest. Yoshida's decision carried the price of dividing Japanese opinion, a high cost in a nation psychologically driven to seek consensus. Relations with the USSR, moreover, remained tense. Japan continued to claim the Soviet-occupied Kurile Islands as national territory, the USSR reciprocated by vetoing Japanese membership of the UN. At the same time Japan was also bound to follow the American line of boy-cotting contact with the Communist People's Republic of China and supporting the nationalist regime on Taiwan.

The SCAP headquarters was disbanded on 28 April 1952, the day the San Francisco Peace Treaty took effect. Three days later left-wing protesters organised an anti-American rally outside the Imperial Palace. One student was killed, 1,000 people were arrested. Yoshida rode out his personal unpopularity inside and outside the Diet. In 1954 he established Japan's 'Self-Defence Forces', arguing that the right of self-defence was recognised as inherent in sovereign nations by the UN Charter and that, as Japan's new armed forces did not have the cap-ability for aggression, their existence did not breach Article IX of the Constitution.

Shortly afterwards Yoshida gave way to Hatoyama Ichiro who set himself the goal of re-establishing diplomatic relations with the USSR. This was achieved at the cost of side-stepping the Kurile issue. No formal peace treaty was signed – but Japan was admitted to the UN.

REVISION AND RIOT

The next prime minister, Kishi, set himself the goal of revising the US

National Diet Building, Tokyo

Security Treaty to establish a more equal partnership. The US should consult Japan before changing troop deployments or bringing nuclear weapons on to Japanese soil. It should renounce its right to intervene in Japanese affairs and to require payment for its bases. Japanese and US forces should co-operate in planning and training. And any renegotiated treaty should have a fixed duration of ten years.

Kishi found the US amenable to renegotiation but when he presented the agreed proposals to the National Diet it provoked violent protest both inside and outside. The vociferous left wing resented the continuing estrangement from Russia and China and feared that a partially rearmed Japan might easily become a fully-rearmed Japan. American commentator Paul F. Langer noted that anti-American feeling in Japan was fuelled by doubts about the reality of the communist bogey, doubts that US aid would materialise in the event of a threat, fears that if it did Japan would become a nuclear battlefield, resentment at the US military presence and horror at the contamination of Japanese fishing-grounds by fall-out from American atom-bomb tests. Kishi overrode all objections and made it clear that he would use his clear parliamentary majority to force through ratification. It was perfectly constitutional and very un-Japanese.

Socialist deputies boycotted the Diet while protesters besieged it. American President Eisenhower was obliged to cancel a long-scheduled 'goodwill visit'. Kishi pressed on regardless, secured the ratification and then resigned. The agitation died away. Japan and the United States moved forward to resolve a number of issues amicably. The last hundred war criminals were paroled. Japanese contributions to the costs of the Occupation were settled; in the event they were passed over to developing countries which both the US and Japan had interests in assisting. The erstwhile defensive alliance was evolving into a positive force for peace.

REVERSE COURSE?

The Occupation reforms which fitted in with what the Japanese themselves wanted proved most enduring. The democratic constitution and the land reform remained inviolable. But the American presumption in favour of decentralisation was thought by the Japanese to be wasteful and perverse. The Meiji reformers had seen local power centres as a threat to national stability and a cover for backwardness; central control became the guarantee of progress and quality. When the Americans decentralised control of the police the outcome was administrative confusion which was felt to benefit no one but criminals. From the 1950s onwards central powers over police, education and local government were gradually reasserted. This ' reverse course' did not, however, threaten the fundamental achievements of the Occupation. Although there was noisy talk in the Diet about the need for constitutional revision nothing came of it. And when the government attempted to curb labour radicalism by new legislation in 1958 it failed in the face of determined opposition from the Diet, the press and the general public. For many the new egalitarianism was strikingly symbolised by the marriage of Crown Prince Akihito in 1959. His bride, Shoda Michiko, was a commoner.

Opportunities and Ambitions

The outbreak of the Korean War in 1950 brought unexpected economic benefits to Japan in the form of 'special procurements' for US military forces needing supplies and provisions. By 1952 the income thus generated was sufficient to pay for half of Japan's imports. Additional cash came from US servicemen on leave and in hot pursuit of 'rest and recreation'; even after the Korean War ended spending by US troops stationed in Japan or on leave from other Asian postings amounted to $500,000,000 a year. In these circumstances the US decided to discontinue its direct aid, which by 1952 had amounted to $2,016,000,000. By 1954 Japanese average incomes were back where they had been in the mid-1930s, before the demands of war had distorted and ultimately shattered the economy. Already the fundamental principles of the nation's economic strategy had been determined. Given its lack of energy and other resources it would have been plausible to predict that Japan might reasonably aim to become what its ex-colony Taiwan did in fact become – an export-oriented producer of low-tech, light industrial products such as light bulbs, cutlery and sports goods. But, even before the Occupation had formally ended, the Japanese authorities had concluded that the only way for the nation's 70 million people to achieve a living-standard comparable to the West was to develop a comprehensive range of heavy, and eventually hi-tech, industries with steel and chemicals at the core. Plans were laid for a motor-vehicle industry and a flagship international airline. America was targeted not simply as the world's wealthiest market but as the key source of advanced technology. The US productivity specialist, W.Edwards Deming, pioneer of the application of statistical methods to quality control, had been brought in by MacArthur as an industrial consultant; among Japanese engineers he rapidly gained a following of devoted and enthusiastic followers. (The Deming Prize, funded by the royalties from one of his manuals, remains one of Japan's most prestigious industrial awards.) A National Productivity Centre was established to recruit teams of experts on an industry-by-industry basis and despatch them to scour the world to note and report on the latest advances in their field. In 1955 the Hatoyama Cabinet published a *Five*

Year Plan for Economic Self-Support which aimed to achieve 'a viable economy without reliance on special procurements' through five years of GNP growth at 5 per cent per annum.

CONFOUNDING THE CAUTIOUS

Between 1955 and 1960 the economy grew nearly twice as fast as had been hoped. Many export and modernisation targets were reached in two years rather than the envisaged five. By 1957 living-standards were already 27 per cent higher than they had been in 1954. By 1958 an official survey could proclaim recovery complete – though it warned that henceforth growth would be much less rapid.

Events continued to confound such cautious prophecies. Between 1956 and 1959 a whole new industry emerged as TV ownership rocketed from 165,000 sets to 3,290,000.

In 1960 Ikeda Hayato, a public finance wizard, took over as prime minister and unveiled a plan to double the national income in just ten years. Western commentators scoffed at such lunacy. He did it in seven. The detail of the Ikeda Plan, drawn up by future foreign minister, Okita Saburo, outlined five major priorities:
  a) improvement of infrastructure, such as roads, port facilities, water and sewage systems. Together with the construction of low-rent public housing this should stimulate the steel and materials industries, as well as removing bottlenecks to further growth
  b) encouragement of heavy industry, especially chemicals and machinery, whose progress was essential to a whole range of secondary industries with growth-potential, such as vehicle-building
  c) promotion of exports and expansion of links with developing countries, especially in resource-rich SE Asia
  d) up-grading of Japan's 'human resources' by increasing the output of science graduates, greater research spending and intensified vocational training
  e) narrowing the gaps between modernised and traditional industries and between rapidly prospering and more backward regions.

On 16 August 1945, the day after the emperor's 'surrender' broadcast, an informal think-tank calling itself the Committee on Post-War Problems had met in the bomb-scarred Tokyo headquarters of the South Manchurian Railway Company. Its secretary had been Okita Saburo.

LEFT BEHIND?

Rapid economic growth almost inevitably means uneven economic growth. Writing in 1961 rural sociologist, Fukutake Tadashi, drew attention to the lagging pace of change in the countryside. True, mechanisation was proceeding apace: in 1939 there had been only 90,000 units of electrically-powered machinery in use throughout the entire farm sector; twenty years later there were 2,500,000. Farmers' consumption levels rose by over a fifth between 1951 and 1956, but small farms could not provide adequate incomes for what was still 41 per cent of the total population. And whereas in 1952 the average farmer earned 83 per cent of what a town-based factory worker got, by 1956 the proportion was down to 67 per cent and falling. Fukutake warned ominously of the political implications of such a trend – 'people cannot develop democracy in their society while obliged to fight against poverty.' The only solution, he argued, was 'to reduce the chronic population pressure and make modern industries absorb those peasants who are engaged in outside jobs ... it is essential to provide more opportunities for economic independence of agrarian families.'

This is more or less what happened. The rural areas provided a pool of increasingly well-educated labour which rapidly-expanding new industries could draw on without having to offer higher wages to lure workers from existing industries. During the high-growth 1960s this was to prove a crucial asset in helping to keep costs under control while allowing output to rise unhindered. At the same time the farmers who stayed in farming benefited from generous subsidies which kept up the price of rice and other home-grown crops. The tax payer and the housewife in effect subsidised this. Looking back to the hungry days of defeat they probably thought it was worth it.

In 1950 one in two Japanese worked in farming, fishing or forestry; by 1960 the figure was one in three; by 1985 it would be one in ten.

MANAGING FOR GROWTH

The publication of the Ikeda Plan did not mean that Japan had become a communist-style 'command economy'. Government–industry relations rather resembled the French model of 'indicative planning' in which government technocrats drew up a 'vision' of the overall ways in which they expected the economy to develop and used such instruments as public investment programmes, 'tax holidays' and protective tariffs to 'assist' its realisation. Rather than 'command' the authorities 'suggested' – and reminded industry who was doing the suggesting.

The willingness of Japanese governments to arrange national priorities on the principles of 'economy first, production first, exports first' was not good news for the environment, but this became obvious only gradually. The drive for reconstruction had given way to growth as an end in itself and a means to acquire international prestige.

In the meantime Japan's astonishing success was acknowledged by its admission in 1964 to the 'club' of rich nations, the Organisation for Economic Co-Operation and Development. Japan's annual economic output was now as much as that of all the other Asian countries put together. In the same year Japan basked in the unaccustomed, but by no

The Shinkansen – symbol of re-birth

means unwelcome, attention of the world's news media as it hosted the Olympic Games with flair and efficiency and came fourth in the medals' table. Awestruck visitors shuttled between Tokyo and Kyoto aboard the 130 m.p.h. 'bullet-train', newly-inaugurated for the occasion. Few could deny that, having literally arisen from its own ashes, Japan was truly 'The Asian Phoenix'. To underline the point the Japanese chose nineteen-year-old Sakai Yoshinori to light the Olympic flame. He had been born in Hiroshima the day the bomb dropped.

SUPERGROWTH

From the autumn of 1965 to the summer of 1970 Japan passed through a period of uninterrupted economic boom, with an annual growth rate averaging a staggering 11 per cent. In 1955 Japan had produced the world's first transistorised portable radio. In 1965 it produced 454 million transistor radios, by 1970 1,813 million. Over the same period colour TV output rose from 98,000 units to 6,400,000 and motor-car production from 696,000 to 3,178,000. World trade was growing at around 8 per cent; but Japanese exports were growing twice as fast. In 1967 Japan surpassed West Germany to become the second largest economy in the non-Communist world. In 1968 Japan's balance of trade moved into surplus for the first time – and stayed there. In 1969 her foreign exchange reserves stood at $3.5 billion; by 1971 they were $15.2 billion. The structure of the nation's overseas trade changed markedly as exports of toys and textiles shrank into insignificance, to be replaced by ships, steel and vehicles; imports came to consist almost entirely of oil, minerals, wood pulp and, increasingly, foodstuffs like meat and soya beans. With wage-rates rising at 15 per cent per year and the population passing the 100 million mark in 1967 the massive home market was also fuelling growth and enabling manufacturers to achieve major economies of scale before launching their products on the export market.

Miracle Makers?

Every 'miracle' needs a little magic. The entrepreneurs who supplied it in Japan would have denied any supernatural gifts. Rather they preached the 'Victorian virtues' of effort, persistence and open-mind-edness. Mitsubishi Corporation boss Fujino Chijiro summarised the situation concisely: 'We, the industry and the country, have had the correct combination of labour, know-how, raw material available from abroad and sales ability. Drive is also very important. We work hard.'

Honda Soichiro went on record as saying that 'the single largest factor in both our company's success and Japan's success is our pioneer spirit.' Ibuka Nasuru, chairman of Sony, likewise endorsed the need to 'avoid following other firms.... New merchandise produces the markets and especially if others are not making what the world wants.' Ibuka learned about transistors on a study-visit to the US in 1952, when he told the Americans that he was going to use them to make radios they told him it was technically impossible. By 1958 he was exporting the 'impossible' radios to America.

HONDA

The epic success of Honda Soichiro (1906–91) illustrates how far, in an economy seemingly dominated by giant corporations and government ministries, the individual efforts of a single entrepreneur could still build a manufacturing giant. Honda, the son of a blacksmith, had gone into business for himself at the age of twenty-two, at first running a repair shop, then making piston rings for Toyota. During the war his company was obliged to supply the military, an experience which taught him to regard 'command economics' as a formula for failure – inflexible standards, set prices and an absence of competition removed every incentive for improvement.

The post-war shortage of private transport gave Honda his first new opportunity. Fitting small army-surplus motors to push-bikes he entered the motor-cycle industry. In 1951 he launched the lightweight, simple to operate, 146cc 'Dream'; he eventually sold 9,000,000 of them. In 1953 he introduced the C-100; by 1959 it was the biggest-selling motor-cycle in the world.

Honda knew that the ultimate key to success was to take on the best and beat it. He went to the British 'TT' races on the Isle of Man, a showplace occasion for motor-cycle technology. This decided him to make Honda a world-class competitor but his early entries were humiliated. He learned much by patient 'reverse engineering' – buying the latest British bikes and taking them apart with meticulous, white-gloved care. The lessons thus learned, and tested on the track – very expensive lessons – would later be incorporated into the production of everyday machines for everyday use. Racing gave Honda the edge by providing the most exacting standard of engineering excellence and at the same time giving the Honda name the status of a world-beater. At one point there were 300 Japanese motor-cycle manufacturers. In the end four survived. Honda was the biggest. Tohatsu, Honda's main rival, went bust in 1964. By the 1960s cars were next on the list, despite the hostility of the supposedly all-powerful Ministry of International Trade and Industry (MITI), which rated Toyota and Nissan as world-class producers and wanted to amalgamate all the other manufacturers into a single company. Honda declined to oblige and was later fond of saying 'the reason this company exists today is that I did the opposite of what MITI told me to do.' In 1972 Honda launched the fuel-stingy Civic – just in time for the 1973 energy crisis. Honda himself formally stepped down that year, to make way for 'fresh management built upon values that I would find bewildering.'

SECRETS OF SUCCESS?

In 1967 the Deputy Editor of *The Economist* of London compiled a report on 'The Risen Sun' in which he attempted to analyse the factors underlying Japan's success. The two elements he singled out for emphasis were close government–industry co-operation and the high average level of education. (His emphasis might, of course, have been biased by an awareness that these were two areas in which Britain was proving itself to be singularly inept.) Business-backed 'conservative' parties have ruled Japan, with the exception of a break of less than a year in 1948, ever since the end of the war. A realignment of the left in 1955 led the Tweedledum-Tweedledee Liberals and Democrats to put aside their squabbles and merge to form the Liberal Democratic Party (LDP) in the same year. It has remained in power ever since. Such continuity both strengthened business confidence in making long-term invest-ments and made government threats and promises that much more credible. As for education – by the late 1960s some 70 per cent of

Japanese children were staying on at school until the age of eighteen, over twice as high a proportion as in Britain. The disparity between the proportion of university graduates entering the labour force was even greater. Other major factors identified by Western analysts included:

a) the absence of lengthy strikes. The annual April 'spring offensive' (*shunto*) tended to consist of brief, ritualised stoppages, often lasting only a few hours. Long disputes which inflicted damage on a company's market-share were recognised by workers' leaders as advantageous only to their company's rivals. Between 1958 and 1974 Toyota, for example, lost not a single hour's production through strike action.

b) a savings ratio three times as high as Britain's, encouraged by tax and payments systems which encouraged savings and a banking structure which recycled them back to industry to fund long-term investment. (In time the Japanese Post Office was to become, in terms of cash deposits, the largest bank in the world.) By the 1960s Japanese annual capital formation was exceeding 30 per cent of GNP – about twice the US level.

c) a favourable international environment – low raw material and energy prices, expanding world trade and procurement benefits from the Vietnam conflict.

A tale of virtue rewarded? In part. But also a tale of ability to see opportunities and seize them with both hands and to capitalise on the arrogance of competitors who grossly underpriced new technologies because they totally underestimated the ability of Japanese to exploit and extend them.

Nor did the Japanese hesitate to protect their home market by every means available. At the end of the 1950s about 80 per cent of Japan's imports were subject to some sort of ban or quota. The rest were hedged about with dense thickets of documentation.

STANDARDS OF LIVING AND QUALITY OF LIFE

As the memory of war and hunger faded the simplicity of traditional life-styles gave way to a taste for gadgets and novelties. When a Japanese emperor is crowned he receives three treasures: a mirror, sword and jewel as symbols of his sacred office. By the 1950s Japanese consumers wanted their own three treasures: a television, a refrigerator and a washing-machine; by 1964 90 per cent could watch the Olympics on their own TV and more than half owned the other two items as well. By the late 1960s consumers were aiming at the '3 Cs' – car, colour (TV) and cooler (air-conditioning). The more covetous would in time aspire to the '3 Vs' – video, villa (by the sea) and vacations abroad.

During the student riots of 1968, when worldwide anti-Vietnam protests became a catalyst for more domestic discontents, the campus of élite Tokyo University came to resemble a battleground as undergraduates hurled petrol-bombs at police. The Japanese have tended to be very tolerant of youthful excess and some thoughtful social commentators generously interpreted this vandalism as a critique of the crass materialism of the age. On the other hand Japan appeared to many Western visitors to be refreshingly free from the social evils elsewhere regarded as almost inevitable accompaniments of 'affluence'. There was no drug problem to speak of. Street-crime was negligible. Graffiti were virtually unknown.

True, Japan had its *yakuza*, an 80,000-strong gangster class, five times as numerous as the American Mafia. Romanticised by the movies as modern-day embodiments of the samurai, they proclaimed their allegiance to an honour code which somehow combined a matter-of-fact willingness to run prostitutes and protection rackets with a keen sense of patriotism. (*Yakuza* have actually volunteered their services as plain-clothes back-up agents for the regular police to protect visiting foreign dignitaries from hostile demonstrators.) Organised in seven major networks, the *yakuza* have long enjoyed and exploited close links with high-ranking members of the political and business élite. Apart from terrorising reluctant vendors of strategically-located real estate or browbeating shareholders daring to ask awkward questions at company meetings, *yakuza* have invariably reserved their violence for each other, rather than venting it upon ordinary citizens. Deeply conservative in outlook, they were for decades a force for stability, if not virtue, in post-war Japan. (More recently *yakuza* infiltration of legitimate business, especially through 'property development', has become so significant that their previously cosy relationship with the forces of order has begun to look distinctly threatened.)

A report on *The Japanese and Their Society* issued by the Economic Planning Agency in 1972 drew a picture of a nation increasingly healthy but at the same time subject to stress and endangered by self-indulgence. On the positive side it was noted that Japanese now ranked with Swedes as having the longest life-span and lowest infant mortality in the world. Improved nutrition had increased the height, weight and strength of young people out of all recognition; Japan's young adults were, on average, some five inches taller than their grandparents would have been at their age. But while work was less likely to damage them from physical over-exertion it was no longer providing them with adequate exercise and 'their work is so intensive that accumulation of stress cannot easily be avoided by everyday sleep'. Stress-related fatigue was worsened by the fact that 'people do not take more than half of their paid holidays, which are substantially less than those in Western countries', and that 'people are not willing to take sick leave except when they are seriously ill . . . 40 per cent of those surveyed did not take sick leave while receiving medical care.'

HIGH LIFE AND LOW TASTES?

Japan's economic expansion and social progress in the decades after defeat were undeniable. Its cultural achievements were more patchy. Clubs and cabarets flourished on the expense accounts of senior *sararimen* (salarymen, i.e. managers), while teenagers and housewives flocked to patronise *pachinko* (pin-ball) parlours and *kissaten* (coffee-shops). The national appetite for soft-porn *manga* (comics) threatened to denude Japan of forests. But at the same time official sponsorship of 'Living National Treasures' kept alive the skills of outstanding craftsmen; and popular interest in such arts as flower-arranging and calligraphy promoted the proliferation of hundreds of academies and individual teachers. Prosperity democratised the traditional pastimes of the samurai élite.

One significant new development of the post-war period was a novel interest in Japanese culture in the West. The British potter Bernard Leach fired his contemporaries with admiration for Japanese ceramics, both traditional and avant-garde. The writer Alan Watts popularised the quirky philosophy of Zen. Enthusiastic groups of devotees began to meet to practise judo, kendo or *ikebana*. Other western cults developed around *koi* carp and *bonsai*.

The medium which first fed this new enthusiasm was probably the cinema. In 1951 Kurosawa's *Rashomon* won the Grand Prix at the Venice Film Festival. The chiefs at Toho, Japan's biggest studio, had almost failed to send it, fearing that it would be incomprehensible to foreigners (as it was to many Japanese). *Rashomon* tells, and more importantly retells, a medieval tale of robbery and rape from the point of view of the victims, the villain and an onlooker. To add to the potential confusion the story is told within another story about three eighteenth-century travellers finding shelter beneath the ruined Rasho gate (Rasho-Mon) in Kyoto during a thunderstorm. Kurosawa took his plot from the short story 'In a Grove' by the highly-talented Akutagawa Ryunusoke (1892–1927, *see p. 150*). Soon he was to find his plots being taken from him. *Seven Samurai* (1954) was relocated in Mexico to become *The Magnificent Seven*, while *Yojimbo* (1961) was caricatured by Sergio Leone to become *A Fistful of Dollars*, thus initiating a highly successful cycle of 'spaghetti Westerns'.

Japan's best-known post-war author proved not to be the lyrical Nobel Prize winner Kawabata Yasunari, who gassed himself in 1972, but the self-dramatising Mishima Yukio, who committed *seppuku* in 1970. A prolific writer of immense versatility, Mishima lived his own life as a work of art. Brought up in isolation by a tyrannical grandmother, he transformed himself from a shy weakling, too feeble to serve in the war, into a muscle-bound athlete of intense physicality. One of his best works, *The Temple of the Golden Pavilion* (1956) , tells the true story of how this ancient Kyoto treasure (*see p. 263*), having miraculously survived for more than five centuries, was deliberately burnt down by a deranged monk. Mishima was consistently fascinated by the macabre and bizarre and later wrote and starred in a film about the suicide of a young officer caught up in the 'incident' of February 1936 (*see p. 160*). Increasingly obsessed with what he saw as the moral decay of post-war Japan Mishima formed a paramilitary group, the Shield Society, dedicated to the spiritual regeneration of the nation. On the day he completed his last work, a four-part novel cycle entitled *The Sea of Fertility*, Mishima, accompanied by loyal members of the Shield

Society, attempted to launch a *coup d'état* in the name of the emperor at a barracks in suburban Tokyo. When the men of the garrison responded to his high-flown harangue with incredulity and derision he committed suicide in the traditional samurai manner.

Some Western experts on Japanese literature regret the undue prominence achieved by Mishima on the grounds that the publicity surrounding his life and work have overshadowed the fine achievements of other writers, such as Ooka Shohei's *Fires on the Plain* (1951), which recounts the horrors of wartime cannibalism in the Philippine jungles, Abe Kobo's claustrophobic *The Woman in the Dunes* (1962) and Endo Shusaku's *Silence*, which explores the persecution of Christians in sixteenth-century Japan. The 'grand old man' of post-war letters was Tanizaki Junichiro (1886–1965), whose first story had appeared in 1910. His masterpiece, translated as *The Makioka Sisters* (1943–8) is an evocation of middle-class life in pre-war days. His last novel *The Diary of a Mad Old Man* focuses on an old man who becomes sexually infatuated with his daughter-in-law's feet.

Comic and satirical novels by Japanese writers are rarely regarded as 'serious' enough to merit translation and Western readers are therefore easily left with the impression that Japanese literature is almost entirely melancholy, morbid or masochistic.

GENTLY DOES IT

During the Occupation the main aim of Japan's national policy was to regain the right to have one. During the 1950s Japan took few foreign policy initiatives, content to re-establish its involvement in the world of international organisations and to negotiate reparations agreements with formerly occupied countries. But in 1964, to coincide with the Tokyo Olympics, the complex regulations which had long restricted the overseas travel of private citizens were finally lifted, a small but significant symbol of Japan's emerging self-confidence as a player on the international scene. In 1965 Japan re-established diplomatic links with the Republic of Korea (South Korea), its former colony. Relations were scarcely cordial but opened the way to greater economic co-operation to mutual advantage.

The Japanese attitude to China was complex. Loyally following the

US line by recognising the Nationalist regime in Taiwan, Japan benefited from expanding trade with the rapidly developing island but at the same time maintained discreet, indirect contacts with mainland China through trading-houses ostensibly fronted by left-wing organisations sympathetic to the communist cause. By 1970 this accounted for 2 per cent of Japan's exports but 20 per cent of China's imports. Even right-wing Japanese continued to feel a grudging respect for China as a source of Japan's own cultural heritage, as a nuclear power and not least as a potentially vast future market.

Japanese attitudes towards the USSR remained profoundly negative. A 1971 opinion poll showed it to be even more heartily disliked than isolationist, militaristic North Korea. This was partly an expression of anti-Communism, partly in memory of the treatment of Japanese POWs at Russian hands and partly resentment at the continued Soviet occupation of the southern Kurile islands, which Japan stoutly maintained to be an integral part of her national territory. More than twenty years later the 'Northern Territories' issue remains unresolved and a barrier to economic and technological co-operation which could be of immense mutual benefit.

Deprived of military muscle, inexperienced in diplomacy, Japan felt most confident internationally dealing with matters of economy and technology. Much official effort therefore went into supporting 'Expo '70' at Osaka – an international exhibition to show the world just how far Japan had come in a quarter of a century. The events of 1971, however, were to jolt Japan into a painful realisation that it could ill afford self-congratulation. America, cornerstone of Japan's global policy, launched two initiatives which took the Japanese government completely by surprise – recognising 'Red China' and slapping a tariff on all imports, including Japanese ones. It was not so much that Japan could not accommodate itself to these major shifts in policy as the fact that their suddenness came as a shock, virtually an insult. The Americans subsequently smoothed things over by assuring the Japanese that they would reach no agreements with China prejudicial to Japanese interests and by allowing Okinawa finally to revert to Japanese sovereignty. Nevertheless Japan had been forcibly reminded that its 'special relationship' with the United States was still a very one-sided one.

THE DOWNSIDE

Economic 'miracles' are no exception to the rule that everything has its price. Water pollution by chemical and paper companies introduced toxins into the food chain which caused crippling deformities and premature deaths among farmers and fishermen. *Kogai* (pollution) soon became a familiar word to Japanese as they learned of the horrors associated with '*Minamata* disease' (mercury poisoning) and '*Yokkaichi* asthma'. Whereas once cities competed with one another to attract new factories now they began to band together to oppose them. By 1971 there were over 450 anti-pollution groups, with over a hundred in Tokyo alone. By this time the capital was experiencing a novel by-product of affluence – photo-chemical smog. In 1971 the Metropolitan Government officially declared that: 'The people of Tokyo today breathe polluted air. Their sources of water are contaminated. They are subjected to noise-levels that strain the nerves. The ground sinks under their feet. Animal, plant and sea life are threatened by industrial wastes.'

In that same year a full-blown Environment Agency was belatedly established, headed by a director with Cabinet rank. By 1973 the government was obliged to issue an official warning that no one should eat more than six prawns or a pound of tuna in any one week. Children and pregnant or nursing mothers were advised not to eat shell-fish at all.

Road construction was lagging far behind the expansion of car-ownership; in the thirty years after 1945 more people were killed on the roads in Japan than were killed at Hiroshima and Nagasaki added together. Cityscapes were dominated by grim, grey concrete blocks of offices and apartments. Forests and coastlines were despoiled. In 1973 the government admitted its failings in a fit of public breast-beating:

> The government has spent too large a proportion of public funds for pro-ductive investment, neglecting social services. It has failed to make adequate zoning plans to segregate the residential from industrial areas. It has done little to regulate the activities of polluting business except when the harm was obvious.

In the same year a Kyushu fisherman, arrested for demonstrating against the proposed construction of yet another petrochemical works, made much the same point but far more savagely:

Japan is an octopus eating its own legs. Our main wealth has always been in our oceans, rivers and good farmland and in the spirit of our people... In a race for more and more economic growth we are poisoning our soil, water and air, as well as ourselves. We are Number 3 in the world in Gross National Product, but we are Number 1 in Gross National Pollution.

A potential resolution of the crisis was soon to emerge from a quite unexpected quarter. The outbreak of war in the Middle East induced the Arabs to invoke 'oil sanctions' which quadrupled the price of Japan's largest single import item and threatened to bring her economy to its knees.

CHAPTER TEN

Internationalisation and Identity,
1973–1990s

The two decades since the 'oil *shokku*' of 1973 have witnessed major changes in the structure of the Japanese economy, as the energy-intensive heavy industries of the 'supergrowth' era, such as steel and chemicals, have given way to hi-tech manufacture focused on computers, mechatronics and biotechnology. Socially the long-term impact of ever-rising levels of affluence has given rise to concerns about the potential burdens of a rapidly-ageing population and the possible disaffection from traditional values of a youth generation so unlike its parents as to be dubbed *shinjinrui* – new human race. Politically the period could be characterised as one of unstable stability, with the LDP periodically shaken by scandals but retaining its hold on power and struggling vainly to free itself from the ties and pressures of special interest groups on whose goodwill, funds and votes it ultimately depends.

'Internationalisation' (*kokusaika*) has become a *ki-wado* (key word), an institutional imperative for businesses and universities. Everyone ought to do it; no one is quite sure what it should involve. Government itself has ardently promoted the concept as a desirable national priority. Conscious that the nation's economic clout impelled it towards a wider and more active international role, successive administrations have pledged Japan to respond more positively to global problems. But the Gulf crisis of 1990 provoked a reaction which was confused, half-hearted and flat-footed. The American statesman Dean Acheson once said of Britain that it had lost an empire but not yet found a role. Might the same be said of Japan – economic pacemaker, diplomatic onlooker?

Into Uncertainty

Japanese came to refer to the 1973 oil embargo not as a crisis but as a *shokku*. Political analyst Kosaka Masataka emphasised to his countrymen that this was not a situation in which Japan could stand on the side-lines. For the first time since 1945 the nation was squarely involved in a major and inescapable predicament. The entire history of the post-war era was thrown into a new light:

> Looking back . . . it must be admitted that Japan's fast economic growth . . . has been due not only to the capabilities of the Japanese people, but also to favourable international circumstances, especially the fact that she could almost endlessly expand her foreign trade and freely purchase resources. . . .

By the early 1970s oil accounted for three-quarters of Japan's energy needs and the vast bulk of oil imports were drawn from the politically volatile Middle East. Japan was using as much oil in a week as she had used in a year in 1941, when an oil embargo had prompted the attack on Pearl Harbor. Over the subsequent decades Japan had benefited immensely from international circumstances not of her own making; now that those circumstances had suddenly turned against her she was virtually powerless to affect them. As Kosaka cautiously put it, 'We all know Japan is now facing a trial. However, its nature is not necessarily very clear.' Apart from, somewhat belatedly, issuing soothing statements of sympathy for the Palestinian cause, the Japanese government was obliged to focus its efforts on disciplining the domestic situation.

In 1972 Prime Minister Tanaka had launched an ambitious plan for 'Remodelling the Japanese Archipelago'. This involved relocating industry away from the over-congested south and east and into the less-developed north and west. It assumed a continuation of 10 per cent annual economic growth for the next decade. The oil shock made that assumption absurd; the plan was abruptly junked. Instead, as industry scrambled for oil and housewives jostled for detergents and toilet-paper, a whole range of austerity measures was introduced to damp down inflation and reduce energy consumption. In government offices and schools strict curbs were placed on heating, lighting and air-conditioning. Hoarding fuel was treated as a criminal offence. The bright neon lights of the Ginza were dimmed – at least periodically.

1974 was an uncomfortable year. After a decade of unprecedented expansion the economy contracted. Profits fell and unemployment rose. The taboo on dismissing permanent, full-time staff limited outright redundancies but few recruits were taken on and many parttimers laid off. Managers took pay-cuts and workers accepted transfers and early retirements. An estimated one-third of the nation's industry stood idle, killing any prospect of revival through new investment. Industries which had come to depend on cheap oil were naturally hardest hit: chemicals most of all but also cement, lumber, paper, steel and shipbuilding. Salvation was achieved by belt-tightening and rationalisation. On the supply side, efforts were made to diversify sources of oil by increasing imports from Alaska, Mexico, Nigeria and other non-Arab producers; efforts were also made to develop non-oil supplies, such as coal, liquid natural gas and nuclear power. On the demand side the emphasis was on cutting back the energy-intensive industries and expanding those which required low inputs of energy and high inputs of skill, such as electronics. Spectacular increases in efficient use of labour, energy and raw materials raised productivity in Japanese industry by 8.4 per cent per year between 1975 and 1978 and thus restored the nation's international competitiveness. While investment at home marked time exports boomed again, rising from $56 billions in 1975 to over $80 billions in 1977, with 80 per cent of the increase coming from cars and electrical goods. By 1975 the balance of payments was back in surplus. By 1979 industry was operating at 90 per cent of its pre-shock level.

Then came the Iranian revolution and a second oil crisis, more than tripling the price of oil in less than two years. The lessons of 1973 now bore fruit. Inflation was reduced from 17.7 per cent in 1980 to 1.4 per cent in 1981. Oil imports actually fell by a quarter between 1979 and 1982. Japan would never again see the days of 10 per cent growth – but it had shown that it couldn't be crippled either.

Party Games

Although the 1960s had seen the establishment of a major new party, Komeito (*see p. 58*), and an increased vote for the communists, there had been no serious challenge to the dominance of the liberal democrats at national level. At municipal and prefectural level, left-wing parties could and did take power by campaigning on environmental issues; but the LDP eventually took the hint and headed off the threat by tackling quality of life issues more seriously. Meanwhile Prime Minister Sato Eisaku held power for almost eight years, retiring in 1972 to collect the Nobel Peace Prize for his opposition to nuclear weapons. In retrospect his period of office was to look like a golden age for the conservatives.

Sato's departure obliged the LDP to choose a new party president who would thereby – as leader of the majority party in the Diet – automatically become prime minister. There were four candidates, each the leader of a faction within the ruling party – Tanaka Kakuei, Miki Takeo, Fukuda Takeo and Ohira Masayoshi. Each was eventually to serve as prime minister in the course of the 1970s.

It was Tanaka who won out in 1972, sealing his triumph with a high-profile visit to Beijing to restore Japanese diplomatic relations with the People's Republic (*see p. 192*). Choosing as his motto in office the characteristically assertive slogan 'Decisiveness and Action', Tanaka was anything but a typical LDP machine politician. Most of Tanaka's colleagues were university men from well-to-do families, but he had come up the hard way, making his own fortune in the building-trade and acquiring on the way a very practical expertise in the matter of winning and placing public contracts. Initially Tanaka impressed the press and the public as a tough, shrewd go-getter, but his ambitious 'Remodelling' scheme kicked off an inflationary spiral as speculators rushed to buy sites thought likely to benefit from government-backed development. Then came the oil shock and an apparent lurch towards the abyss. Tanaka's efforts to shore up electoral support in the Upper House elections of July 1974 involved such blatant abuse of party funds that Miki and Fukuda left the Cabinet in protest. Then the prestigious monthly *Bungei Shunju* ran a detailed exposé of 'Tanaka Kakuei – His

Money and His Men'. The prime minister bowed to public outrage and resigned, but his carefully-cosseted constituency continued loyally to re-elect him to the Diet and he continued to remain a key manipulator of factional loyalties behind the scenes until rendered helpless by major illness.

A second scandal, also involving Tanaka, broke in February 1976. This time the charges involved bribery in connection with the purchase of aircraft from the Lockheed Corporation. Whether from principle or vindictiveness Miki declined to protect his predecessor, who was arrested. Miki himself was eventually forced from office as six LDP members ostentatiously dissociated themselves by forming the New Liberal Club, in effect yet another faction, but formally outside the framework of the party. In the general election of December 1976 the LDP failed to win 50 per cent of the vote for the first time since 1967. Miki, forced from office, was replaced by Fukuda, chosen by the narrowest of margins.

Fukuda used his tenure to inaugurate a new system requiring future LDP leaders to face re-election every two years. Ironically, in the first contest under the new system, Fukuda himself lost to Ohira. Virulent factional in-fighting brought LDP losses in the general election of October 1979 and the loss of a confidence motion in May 1980, forcing yet another election. After almost a decade of scandals and squabbling the prospects for the LDP looked uncertain indeed, but Ohira's sudden death mid way through the campaign jolted the party into a semblance of unity and prompted an unexpected wave of sympathy from the electorate. The result was a landslide victory, a stable majority and a compromise candidate for leader, Suzuki Zenko, who chose as his slogan 'Politics of Harmony'.

Japan entered the 1980s under a party which had been in power for a quarter of a century and seemed more firmly in control than ever. How could this be explained? One reason commentators volunteered was that, whatever its imperfections, the LDP gave the voters what they wanted – an ever-rising standard of living. Others opined that the voters lacked an alternative choice or rather were faced with too many alternatives in theory and none in practice. The largest opposition party, the Japan Socialist Party, was too limited in its appeal to win an election outright; its electoral base was grounded in the trade union movement which was not only limited but diminishing as heavy industry shrank in importance. Its leadership, moreover, was top-heavy with Marxist intellectuals and its policies consequently unrealistic. The only way the JSP could come to power would be by means of an electoral pact, but a move towards the left to secure communist support would alienate the centre parties it also needed – and vice versa. Which left the LDP, if not sitting pretty, at least still sitting.

Defence Dilemmas

The National Police Reserve of 75,000 established at MacArthur's behest in 1950 was soon upgraded to the status of a National Safety Force of 100,000. In 1954 it became the Self-Defence Force (SDF) with an estblishment of 146,000 divided into Ground, Air and Maritime units. In 1957 the Japanese government issued its first post-war statement on defence policy, pledging the nation to 'gradually improve its defence power to make it more efficient within the necessary limits of self-defence'. The stance was still ultra-cautious for the memory of defeat, poverty and humiliation was still strong. Left-wing parties were virulent in attacking any move that looked like a threat to Article 9 of the constitution (*see p. 171*). Many left-wingers favoured a totally 'unarmed neutrality' and even right-wingers saw that substantial rearmament would alarm Japan's neighbours and do more to destabilise east Asia than add to regional security. And everyone grasped that more spent on defence meant less to invest in industry; convention decreed that military expenditures remain within a ceiling of 1 per cent of GNP.

The Defence White Paper issued in 1970 reassured nation and neighbours alike that: 'Japan is a great power economically but it will not become a great power militarily. Rather it will become a new kind of state with social welfare and world peace as its goals.'

In the same year, however, the new Director-General of the Defence Agency, Nakasone Yasuhiro, called for a radical rethinking of the nation's military posture:

> If a part of town is left uninhabited, weeds spring up, snakes infest it and mosquitoes breed and it soon becomes a garbage dump. To create a military

vacuum is to create the maximum danger of inviting precisely such a situation. In this sense, it is the international duty and responsibility of every nation in today's world to establish and maintain a balance on its periphery with the minimum defence power necessary to deter other nations from entertaining aggressive ambitions and urges.

Where was Japan's 'periphery'? Nakasone argued that it lay far beyond 'the water's edge', in the Straits of Malacca through which the nation's vital oil supplies passed on their long journey from the Middle East. Himself a junior officer in the wartime navy, Nakasone called for a strengthening of Japan's naval and air capabilities to enable it to pursue a strategy of forward defence. If that meant revising the constitution, so be it.

Strong opposition in the Diet stifled action based on Nakasone's policy review. But the defence debate refused to go away. From 1973 onwards the US pulled its troops out of Vietnam, raising, however dimly, the spectre of isolationism. Would the 'American umbrella' be there when it was needed? Meanwhile the Soviet Union continued to build up its weaponry and not least its navy, a sizeable proportion of which was based at Vladivostok ('Rule the East') immediately north of Japan. In September 1976 the pilot of a Soviet MiG-25 landed out of the blue in Hokkaido, begging asylum. Japan's surveillance had, at one point, completely lost track of his craft. Once again a nagging sense of vulnerability was exposed.

In July 1978 the chairman of the Joint Staff Council, General Kirisu, remarked in a news interview that, in an emergency, front line SDF commanders might be obliged to take action before consulting their civilian political masters. Furore erupted as radicals raised the ghost of the 1930s with the military out of control again. Kurisu resigned. Prime Minister Fukuda ordered a review of the legal niceties involved.

If it was clear enough what the Japanese didn't want of their military, it was less certain what they did require. A 1978 *Asahi Shimbun* poll found that 57 per cent of the public favoured keeping the SDF at its current level – but 71 per cent were against changing the constitution to permit its upgrading. When asked what was Japan's best guarantee of security 42 per cent said a peaceful foreign policy and only 2 per cent put their confidence in the SDF. And while 54 per cent did not think

Japan would be attacked by a foreign power 56 per cent thought the US would not come to its aid if it was. Meanwhile the US alliance remained the cornerstone of national policy, the SDF had grown to an establishment of 240,000 men, 150 ships and 1,000 aircraft, and 'disarmed' Japan had become the ninth biggest military spender in the world.

The New Japanese

In May 1977 the Japanese government announced that more than 50 per cent of the population had been born since the war. This prompted information technology expert Masuda Yoneji to try to define the distinctive characteristics of these post-war Japanese and ultimately to conclude that:

> ...people of this generation are basically different from their predecessors ... they are westernised Japanese with a sense of individualism and a scientific outlook ... they know neither war nor hunger and, most important ... they are ignorant of the oppression of authority....

Masuda epitomised these 'semi-Americanised' thirty-somethings as the MEC generation: M meant motorisation, implying both mobility and affluence; E stood for English, being exposed to the language and culture of the English-speaking peoples; C invoked computing, meaning familiarity with hi-tech and the ability to think critically. Masuda saw them as more open, more optimistic and more flexible than their forebears; his major reservation was that they might ' lack the spiritual strength to weather the storms of a national crisis'.

A GENDER GULF?

Is the relationship between Japanese husbands and Japanese wives one of subordination? Or separation? Writing in 1979 marketing consultant, Abe Yoko, identified middle-aged women as Japan's new 'leisure-class'. A sample of less than thirty housewives in the 35–43 age-bracket revealed their pastimes to include mountaineering, tennis, riding, yoga, poetry, western and Japanese classical music, pottery, calligraphy, dancing, cooking and dress-making, not to mention their

A traditional Shinto wedding ceremony

involvement in correspondence-courses, driving-lessons, part-time jobs, throwing surprise parties and running their own businesses. Their husbands, however, confined themselves pretty much to gardening, board-games, listening to records and stroking the family pet. The conclusion was obvious:

> Men's leisure activities are indoor and retiring in nature, in dramatic contrast to the active and outgoing nature of their wives' interests.... The chief beneficiaries of Japan's high economic growth have been these housewives. Their husbands have sacrificed their holidays and relinquished their active participation in family affairs. And who has profited from this? The women.

Abe found that less than a third of husbands claimed to control the family purse-strings. Less than 5 per cent of men acknowledged prime responsibility for their children's education and discipline; over 40 per cent admitted that their wife took sole responsibility. When it came to meetings of the parent–teacher association four-fifths of wives were in attendance and at local community gatherings three-fifths. The comparable figure for men was less than one-fifth. Abe concluded bluntly:

> Overall, wives outweigh husbands in their control of the house, domestic affairs, the family, the children and civic matters.... Today's middle-aged men are no longer the heads of their households. Their wives, with their long experience as consumers, their abundant free time and their assets and income to look after, now stand at the helm as the managers of Japan's households.

GENERATION GAPS

What of the young? Surveys revealed a mixture of gains and losses. Between 1948 and 1978 the average height of fourteen-year-old boys increased by a staggering seventeen centimetres. They were certainly taller, and heavier, than their fathers had been; but tests showed they were actually less strong, supple and speedy. Teenagers were indisputably better off in terms of material possessions; 70 per cent of fourteen-year-olds had a watch and a radio or cassette-player, 30 per cent had a camera, 20 per cent some expensive hobby equipment such as a guitar, telescope or miscroscope. But were they better off in life-experience? Most lived in cities, regarding the countryside as simply a place to visit. Deprived of open play-space, they were dragooned at school during the day, passive in front of the television during the evenings. With the decline of small business, fewer and fewer grew up in homes which were also work-places; many children of commuters saw their fathers only at weekends. The trend to small families meant that most children had one brother or sister or none at all and increasing population mobility meant that most lived apart from their grandparents whom they saw only occasionally. Tradionally-minded social critics feared that the life-styles of affluence were breeding young Japanese sadly lacking in the qualities of resilience, realism and unselfishness in which previous generations had taken pride. A glance at the over-publicised punks of Harajuku, the centre of Tokyo's 'youth culture', no doubt confirmed these doomsters in their gloom.

If the situation of the nation's youth induced anxiety, the prospects for the elderly induced positive alarm. It was not that they were badly off, it was that every year there were so many more of them. In 1980 a 'Society of Families Supporting Senile Old People' was established. In the same year the prime minister's office, responding to public concern, conducted a comparative survey of the condition of the elderly in Japan, Britain and the USA. In terms of a general commitment to 'family values' the results were reassuring:

- in Japan only 6 per cent of the elderly lived alone, in Britain and the USA over 40 per cent did so;
- in Japan over half the elderly lived with their married children, in Britain and the USA less than 10 per cent did so;
- in Japan over 40 per cent of the respondents were still working, in the USA 24 per cent and in Britain 8 per cent;
- in Japan over 30 per cent of respondents received money regularly from their children, in the two Western countries virtually none did;
- in Japan 14 per cent considered themselves hard up, in Britain 18 per cent, in the USA 28 per cent.

The Japanese are aware, however, that there is no room for complacency. A smaller and smaller labour force of increasingly older workers will have to support an ever larger population of retired persons. Pension and medical costs will rise inexorably as a proportion of the nation's spending. Men whose life purpose was to work must learn to acquire a positive attitude to enforced leisure. Divorce in Japan is on the increase among over-60s whose lives, dedicated but essentially separate, did not prepare them to be constantly in each other's company. Positive retirement planning is one response to the situation. Others involve new business strategies to generate the future incomes needed to sustain current high standards of living such as investment in productive ventures overseas and the adoption of robotisation at home.

Technology...

In 1967 Japan imported its first robot from the USA and by 1970 Kawasaki Heavy Industries had produced the first domestic version. By

1979 Japan had 135 companies producing robots and eighty laboratory teams researching their development. An American survey conducted in the same year revealed that the USA had 3,000 industrial robots in operation, West Germany 6,000 and Japan 47,000. By 1980 Fujitsu had opened a factory where robots made robot parts although they were still assembled by humans. In 1979 a small workshop team of ten employees in Odawara City, near Tokyo, was achieving a daily output of 900,000 heads for disposable lighters. By 1984 two supervisors and a team of robots were turning out 4,000,000.

Businesswoman Umeshima Miyo, writing in 1983, argued that, while the advent of new technologies might be bad news for middle-aged men in industry, it was good news for women in offices. She found that women liked working with computers because:

> Unlike other occupations, there was no pressure on them to behave in certain pre-defined womanly ways. Their work was evaluated for what it was worth. One of the pleasures was the refusal of the computers themselves to discriminate between men and women.... Women who pride themselves on their brain-power and who thereby earn dislike at the normal company become well-adjusted workers in the computer business.

In making her analysis Umeshima took heart from the past:

> It was the vocational aptitude of women that supported the development of the textile industry ... and ... sustained the subsequent development of the electrical appliance industry. Now the tireless handwork of women is being put to use in another frontline industry.... In the past women brought ... patience, perseverance and perfectionism to their work. Given this favourable tradition, we can expect women to be put to even better use in work with computers.

More important still, Umeshima foresaw a growing congruence between professional ambitions and social responsibilities:

> As workplaces closer to home proliferate and arrangements for working at home take shape, women will not be forced to neglect their children or to skimp the care of elderly parents.... When I consider the inflexibility of Japan's male-dominated society, I feel hesitant in stating this so positively. But traditional patterns of dominance ... have little relevance in the computer world.

It is as well perhaps that Japanese women can look forward to working with gender-blind computers and robots. A 1988 *Japan Times* survey found that 70 per cent of Japanese men refused even to consider working for a woman.

. . .and Tradition

Many Japanese, especially of the older generations, have come to fear that new technologies and western influences will combine to make future generations careless of Japanese traditions. Writing in 1983 sociologist Kato Hidetoshi noted reassuringly that over 70,000,000 people had visited a shrine or temple on New Year's Day that year, a figure which had to include a goodly proportion of the nation's youth. Moreover, he suggested, thanks to increased leisure and the opportunities afforded by longer schooling and company-sponsored welfare schemes, there were far more women practising traditional arts than there would have been before the war:

> . . . tradition and modernisation are complementary, rather than contradictory . . . people now drive to shrines in their own cars and the women studying *ikebana* in factory classrooms assemble the most advanced electronic equipment at their work stations. . . . Japan is a country that permits the harmonious co-existence of old and new. Japan's very existence and functioning have built upon this harmony.

Examples of the persistence of tradition abound. Men wear western suits to the office but slip into a comfortable *yukata* at home. Executives may take a weekend in the country to meet clients over golf – and stay overnight in one of the country's 80,000 *ryokan* (traditional inns). Over 95 per cent of Japanese companies have word-processors and fax-machines but every year more than a million people take the official examinations for proficiency in the use of the *soroban* (Japanese abacus). Japan adopted the metric system over thirty years ago, but rooms are still measured in terms of the number of *tatami* (straw mats) they will hold. And there are still 30,000 traditional fortune-tellers in gainful self-employment.

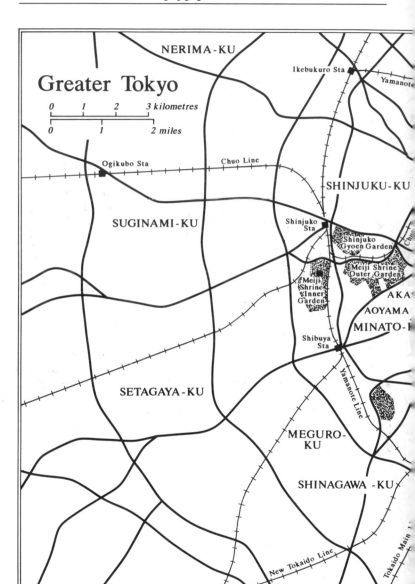

NERIMA-KU

Ikebukuro Sta

Yamanote

Greater Tokyo

| 0 | 1 | 2 | 3 kilometres |
| 0 | | 1 | 2 miles |

Ogikubo Sta   Chuo Line

SHINJUKU-KU

SUGINAMI-KU

Shinjuko
Sta

Shinjuko
Gyoen Garden

Meiji Shrine
Outer Garden

Meiji
Shrine
Inner
Garden

AKA

AOYAMA

MINATO-

Shibuya
Sta

Yamanote Line

SETAGAYA-KU

MEGURO-
KU

SHINAGAWA-KU

New Tokaido Line

Tokaido Main

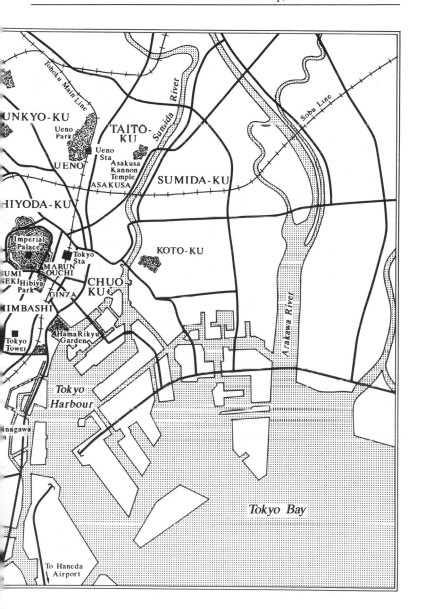

PARADOXES OF AFFLUENCE

In 1990 the English-language newspaper *The Japan Times* published a cartoon paperback by Leonard Koren, author of the thought-provoking *283 Useful Ideas from Japan*; this follow-up was entitled *Success Stories: How eleven of Japan's most interesting businesses came to be*. They are, indeed, an interesting selection, embracing not only such giants as the Mitsui group (*see p. 130*), Matsushita Electric (*see p. 161*), the Dentsu advertising agency and the Shiseido cosmetic empire, but also the Urasenke tea-ceremony foundation, Tokyo Disneyland, a bagel company, an agency specialising in western models, a real estate developer and the man who invented pre-packaged instant noodles. None of the triumphs chronicled has been more spectacular or intriguing, however, than that of the eleventh selection: Mujirushi Ryohin, MR for short.

By the 1970s Japanese social critics were berating consumers for their devotion to brand-names and logos. Kazume Yukiko, housewife and philosophy graduate of élite Keio University, attempted to explain to readers of the influential journal *Bungei Shunju* 'Why Japanese Women Buy Costly Imported Handbags'; likening consumer crazes to outbreaks of medieval religious fervour, she hinted darkly that 'instigators can be found in merchandising who know how to fan the flames of mass consumption before shoppers can establish their own identity'. The Japanese, it was being said, had acquired affluence, but not sophistication, their reliance on élite brands revealed a lack of self-confidence, informed taste and economic rationality. The reaction, when it came, took a distinctively Japanese form, abounding in paradox. Inspired by American achievements in mass-producing disposable goods for everyday use, it yet harked back to Japanese traditions of hand-crafted durability. Masterminded by a giant department-store chain, it was promoted as a 'small is beautiful' assertion of sound ecological values. Its *tour de force* was to launch a range of goods which was, in design terms, so anonymous that purchasing it was 'proof' of the consumer's resistance to the blandishments of style and therefore, paradoxically, a vindication of integrity, intelligence and individuality.

Mujirushi Ryohin ('No Brand, Good Product') was the creation of

Seiyu, a down-market division of the colossal Seibu Department Store empire (now Saison group). Seiyu's strategic planners were exhilarated by their 'discovery' of 'generics' – the basic everyday products sold by American supermarket chains in plain packaging at rock-bottom prices. In terms of Japanese traditional values this could be represented as a re-assertion of the Zen virtues of rustic simplicity and understatement (*see p. 59*). When developed, MR packaging said it all – and at some length. On brown, recycled paper each product bore not only its name, weight and price but also its cost per unit and a statement of why it represented excellent value.

MR's first range of forty products was launched in 1980 and it embraced some curious contradictions. Salmon heads (normally thrown away) were promoted as a cheap and highly nutritious food; the promotional slogan was a statement of the obvious with high-sounding ecological connotations – 'Salmon is the whole fish'. By offering its customers packets of broken mushroom pieces MR also offered them an implicit critique of the false perfectionism and wastefulness of consumers who insisted on whole mushrooms – which would only be broken up for cooking anyway. MR's highly successful freeze-dried coffee, however, scarcely represented a return to anything. From 1981 onwards MR poster campaigns asserted 'Love is Una-dorned' and proclaimed, tongue-in-cheek, the ever-widening range of 'Individual Mujirushi Ryohin' products such as unbleached socks and recycled memo pads.

In 1983 MR opened in downtown Tokyo's fashion conscious Aoyama district; the store, fitted out with recycled wood and tiles, was itself a statement of the MR philosophy. Its first-year sales-target was achieved within a month. By October of 1983 MR was releasing the seventh tranche of additions to a product range which now included 475 household items, 124 foodstuffs and 122 articles of clothing. Sales passed the $250,000,000 mark in 1985. In 1990 a 'Muji' store opened just off London's Regent Street. Within a decade this epic venture had come full circle – from the West, to the West. But in Japan itself consumers were complaining that MR goods were overpriced and of average, rather than superior quality. Having absorbed the nation's entire output of broken mushroom pieces MR was reduced to buying whole mushrooms in order to break them up to sustain the consumer idealism it had created to trade on. MR had become a prisoner of its own myth, a 'small is beautiful' victim of a runaway gigantic success which could no longer contain its own inherent contradictions.

Internationalisation

'The Japanese are a great people. They cannot and should not be satisfied with a world role which limits them to making better transistor radios and sewing machines and teaching other Asians how to grow rice.' This opinion, expressed by Singapore Prime Minister Lee Kwan Yew in 1965, was not widely shared. General de Gaulle is reported to have referred to a Japanese premier as 'that transistor salesman'. From Pakistan came the judgement that the Japanese were no more than 'economic animals'. A confidential EC report characterised them contemptuously as 'a nation of workaholics living in rabbit-hutches'. The funeral of the Showa emperor in 1989 was attended by heads of state and government from over a hundred countries; it was the largest such gathering in modern history and as such an implicit affirmation of Japan's world-standing. Yet the British tabloid press could not forbear to vilify the Duke of Edinburgh's cursory nod before the imperial coffin, a gesture of respect of finely calculated ambivalence towards a former enemy. Such incidents, much reported and discussed in Japan, confirmed many Japanese in the belief that foreigners were incapable of appreciating their virtues, strengths and achievements.

STILL THE CLOSED COUNTRY?

For a society so open to foreign ideas, so eager to buy foreign luxuries, Japan in the 1980s remained curiously closed to foreign people. A 'Survey on National Living Preferences', conducted by the Economic Planning Agency in 1986, confirmed that over 70 per cent of its sample of respondents favoured increasing the volume of news, mail, technology, telephone calls, visitors and students from overseas – but less than 30 per cent desired more permanent or intimate contact with foreigners as a result of allowing them to work in Japan or marry a Japanese national. Whatever Japanese may think about the matter, however, Japan has, as a by-product of its economic expansion, become more cosmopolitan. The annual number of foreign visitors rose eight-fold between 1965 and 1985; but at 2.3 million it was still only a sixth of the number passing through Britain each year. The number of registered aliens had increased almost five-fold over the same period; but 80 per cent of the 850,000 'aliens' were Koreans, mostly Japanese-born. The number of marriages between Japanese and non Japanese trebled between 1965 and 1985 to reach 1.7 per cent of the annual total. Between 1975 and 1985 the number of foreign students in Japan also trebled, amounting to 0.8 per cent of those enrolled in higher education, a tenth of the British figure. In 1982 official regulations were revised to allow state universities to offer permanent teaching posts to non-Japanese; by 1987 they had taken on fifty-two foreigners in a total staff strength of 40,000. On the other hand the JETS (Japan English Teaching Scheme) programme, which recruits young graduates in English-speaking countries and places them in Japanese schools, expanded from thirty places to 3,000 in a decade although the JETS' teachers are only on one-year contracts.

Japanese governments have repeatedly proclaimed their commitment to 'internationalisation' and have turned rhetoric into specific targets and programmes – doubling overseas aid donations in five years and doubling the number of Japanese tourists travelling abroad in four. But the reflexes of officialdom all too often recoil from the practical implications of opening up Japan. Japanese look with dismay at the problems other advanced industrial nations have with drug trafficking, AIDS and illegal immigrants. Japan's isolation has helped her contain these corrosive problems at a very low level. The implications are obvious.

WORKING IT OUT WITH UNCLE SAM

To a very great extent the issue of Japan's internationalisation has revolved around the nature of Japan's relations with the United States – its chief ally, major customer and most important source of foreign ideas and technology. When Nakasone Yasuhiro became Japan's first English-speaking prime minister in 1982 observers saw the possibility of a significant step forward in bilateral relations and Japanese journalists

Skyscrapers at Shinjuku, Tokyo

hailed the potential of a 'Ron–Yas dialogue' conducted face-to-face on first-name terms. But Japan's ever-growing trade surplus with the United States – $37 billion by 1984 – continued to sour the atmosphere. American politicians demanded tariff and quota protection against Japanese exports. Japanese manufacturers counter-charged that American corporations did not make the necessary effort to penetrate the difficult but immensely profitable Japanese market. Further disagreements arose over American participation in the Tokyo Stock Exchange, major construction projects and the development of Japan's privatised telecommunications system. As economic frictions exhibited a persistent tendency to worsen into diplomatic rows the Japanese authorities felt obliged to attempt gestures of appeasement. In 1985 Prime Minister Nakasone personally appeared on television to present an 'action programme' to boost imports. He appealed for every Japanese to buy at least $100-worth of foreign goods. The fact that his examples of suggested purchases included such paltry items as a non-stick frying pan and a set of pillow-cases unwittingly revealed what Japanese consumers thought about the quality and sophistication of foreign-made products. In 1986, the year in which Tokyo was hosting the annual summit of seven leading industrial democracies, the officially-sponsored Maekawa Report outlined a bold series of market-opening measures. Unfortunately, from the point of view of US–Japan relations, it was the manufacturers of Korea, Taiwan and Hong Kong who moved swiftly off the mark to benefit from this major initiative.

Outward-looking, internationalising, English-speaking Nakasone undid many of his own best efforts with an astounding gaffe when he suggested that, after all, Americans couldn't really be expected to compete effectively with the Japanese because the Japanese were so much better educated and more intelligent. The insult was further compounded by his attempted 'explanation' that Americans as such weren't actually less intelligent but that, having so many blacks, Hispanics and other ethnic minorities, the United States was intrinsically disadvantaged compared to homogeneous Japan. Japanese diplomats did what they could in terms of damage-limitation, but Nakasone's outburst undoubtedly struck a chord with many of his increasingly frustrated countrymen. The tetchy state of Japanese–American relations was clearly underlined by the runaway success in the early 1990s of a book entitled *The Japan that Can Say No!*.

Taking the Lead?

Between 1985 and 1987 the yen was revalued upwards by some 40 per cent. At the cost of driving hundreds of small export-based Japanese companies out of business this revision of relative parities did have some discernible impact on the trade surplus problem. But it also led some Japanese to wonder whether the entire relationship between Japan and the USA should not be re-examined. Economist Nakatani Iwao argued that America, architect, regulator and powerhouse of the post-war global trading system, was now visibly faltering. From being the world's largest creditor it had become the world's largest debtor, recklessly overspending on guns and butter. Japan, by contrast, was producing twice as much a year as West Germany; the mere annual increase in her national output was greater than the entire annual output of Belgium. All this out of 2.6 per cent of the world's population and 0.3 per cent of its land area. By 1986 Japan had seven of the world's ten biggest banks, by 1988 all ten of them. According to Nakatani the USA would become too absorbed in sorting out its own debt problems to provide the world economy with firm leadership. Japan would have to step in – but could it? Doing so would involve opening her own economy much more – at the cost of disturbing the cosy relationships which had long protected the interests of rice farmers, small shopkeepers, stock-brokers, building contractors and a host of other groups on whose support the ruling establishment depended. Japan, Nakatani concluded, faced a very painful choice – rise to the challenge of leadership or refuse to accept the pain of change and risk isolation, or worse.

AFFLUENCE AND INFLUENCE

Ironically the Japanese did not feel that well-off. While they could buy sophisticated cars and reliable gadgets at highly competitive prices it was quite a different matter when it came to goods and services that were not internationally traded, either because in their nature they could not be (transport services, houses or recreational facilities) or because they were protected by tariffs or quotas, like many foodstuffs. Increasing foreign travel also made it apparent to Japanese that when it came to public facilities like parks and libraries, or private enjoyments, like gardens, they were much worse off than nominally less 'successful' countries, like Britain. And they were still working six or seven hours a week longer than their European counterparts.

The ambivalence of Japanese towards their new international eminence is well illustrated in the 1985 ruminations of Takeuchi Hiroshi, the chief economist of the Long Term Credit Bank of Japan. Noting that the United States was still the largest single recipient of Japanese goods and capital, he concluded, with evident irritation, 'Ironically, we are aiding the growth of a country superior to ours in economic strength, technological resources and living standards. In return, we get bashed for our trade practices.' Accepting the rationality of relocating manufacture in a country where land costs 1 per cent of its Japanese price he conceded that:

> The spread of Japanese capital means the spread of Japanese culture, which is to be welcomed. Only by disseminating their culture and getting Westerners to recognise its value can Asians overcome their disadvantage in Western society.... In the United States today even the smaller cities have Japanese restaurants ... IBM's main office in New York has a Japanese-style garden.... Americans have begun to take Japanese-style baths.... Knowledge of the language has spread to the extent that it is no longer safe to insult someone in Japanese on the streets of New York. All this, of course, enhances Americans' understanding of Japanese culture and that is an excellent thing.

Where would this all lead? The conclusion he foresaw was not a happy one for a banker:

> Free of factories on its own soil and living graciously on high returns from its overseas investments, Japan will become a beautiful country ... then culture will truly flower. A flowering culture and a wilting economy: this is the direction in which Japan is headed.

Sociologist Hayashi Kenjiro, while accepting the general thrust of the arguments of Nakatani and Takeuchi, reformulated the task facing Japan in cultural rather than economic terms. By all means accept the burden of upholding free trade against protectionism, make the yen the major international currency and let Tokyo become the world's leading capital market. The real challenge would remain – to fashion 'a system of education designed to create first-class international citizens'. Hayashi's prescription has something of the air of a prediction:

> The twenty-first century will see Japan exporting culture and information to the rest of the world; at that point the process of Japan's internationalisation will be complete and the country will also have met the requirements for true leadership in the world community.

Japan's internationalisation is very far from completion. But every visitor, by virtue of their very presence in Japan, helps to advance it.

Shocks and Scandals

The last decade of the second millennium has started less than auspi-
ciously for Japan. In retrospect the decision – after much political
agonising – to send 1,800 troops (mostly engineers) to assist UN
reconstruction efforts in Cambodia for a limited period may one day
look like a small but significant turning-point on the road towards a
wider international role. At the time of writing it still seems overshadowed by the fact that Japan's contribution to the US-led anti-
Saddam alliance at the time of the 1991 Gulf War was limited to
defraying the costs. Tentative attempts to raise the possibility of
securing Japan a permanent seat on the UN Security Council have
been frustrated by continuing frictions with the USA and Russia and by
the ghosts of wartime horrors re-awakened by the fiftieth anniversary
of the ending of the Pacific War.

Japan–US relations continued to be aggravated by American
demands for better access to Japanese markets especially in relation to
politically sensitive sectors such as rice, auto-parts, telecommunications
and construction contracts, each of which involved potentially antag-
onizing well-organized Japanese domestic lobbies. Much 'megaphone
diplomacy' between officials and business spokesmen on both sides
ensued, punctuated by a 'get tough – back off' gavotte whenever
contacts were made at the highest level to find a way forward. Matters
were considerably worsened by the rape of a 12-year-old Okinawan
schoolgirl by three US sailors. Okinawan outrage was only marginally
assuaged by belated American efforts to manage their military presence
with greater sensitivity. Relations with Russia, initially warmed by the
hope that the post-Soviet regime offered real possibilities for resolving
old difficulties and creating new partnerships, were dashed by a continuing impasse over the status of the Kuril islands and Sakhalin and
further soured by clashes over fishing rights and Russian nuclear
dumping at sea.

Memories of the war proved especially problematic. In the course of
a state visit to China Emperor Akihito expressed regret for Japanese
atrocities not once but twice. Prime Minister Miyazawa courageously
did likewise on the anniversary of the war's ending. Neither gesture

succeeded in fully satisfying Japan's former enemies overseas, while both enraged right-wing elements at home. Worse still, two ministers were forced to resign – one for flatly denying that the 1937 'Rape of Nanking' (see p 162) had ever happened, the other for maintaining that Japan had never colonised Korea. Amidst all this a further issue arose – the hitherto unacknowledged tragedy of the 200,000 'comfort women', forcibly recruited in Korea, the Philippines and other Japanese-occupied territories to serve as unpaid prostitutes for the wartime army. To Japan's post-war generation the exposure of this outrage came as a revelation. Prime Minister Miyazawa mobilised the private sector to fund a bilion dollar 'atonement fund' to support documentation centres, scholarships and other goodwill gestures but emphatically rejected individual claims for personal compensation. A subsequent UN report not only republicised the whole issue but upheld the right of past victims to claim for compensation and called on Japan to chronicle the entire episode in its officially approved school textbooks.

Japan's capacity to manage external challenges was weakened by the distracted state of domestic politics and the all too visible faltering of a once dynamic and robust economy. The dizzy spiral of inflated land values and soaring stock prices which had characterised the late eighties came crashing down as the Nikkei index slumped from a peak of 38,000 in December 1989 to just 17,000 by March 1992. Nearly five years later it was still slipping below the 20,000 level. Lending policies which at the most charitable can be called unwise were cruelly exposed. An entire banking sub-sector – small credit institutions, known as *jusen*, which finance property loans for householders and small businesses – was wrecked, leaving the taxpayer to foot the bill. Governments fumbled with remedial budgets while rampant political opportunism devastated the once familiar landscape of parties and factions.

In 1993 Prime Minister Miyazawa resigned, confessing his personal inadequacy to the tasks confronting the nation. His successor, Hosokawa, leader of the recently formed Japan New Party, cobbled together a coalition which lasted less than a year, yielding to an administration headed by the Japan Renewal Party which lasted barely two months. In June 1994 the Social Democratic Party of Japan joined forces with its old enemy, the LDP, to participate in government for the first time since 1947 – immediately dumping its long-cherished rejection of the national anthem and flag, the SDF, the US alliance and economic deregulation. Against most predictions the unholy alliance lasted until January 1996, when leadership passed back to the LDP under Hashimoto Ryutaro. His decision to call an election in October, rather than wait until 1997, was not however rewarded with a majority. The dismal 59 per cent voter turn-out could be interpreted as disgust, apathy or plain weariness.

Certainly politics had no monopoly on provoking public disenchantment. At 5.46 a.m. on 17 January 1995 the port city of Kobe was shattered by an earthquake which killed an estimated 6,000 and rendered over 300,000 homeless. The response of the authorities proved to be woefully slow and inadequate. Victims compared official efforts unfavourably with the improvisations of local gangsters, cheerily distributing blankets and rice-balls. Two months later, during morning rush hour on 20 March, passengers on the Tokyo subway were assailed by the deliberate release of sarin nerve gas, manufactured by members of Aum Shinrikyo, an obscure religious sect. Twelve died and some 5,000 were injured by the attack, whose motives remained incomprehensible. Japanese learned with a shock that even their orderly society was not free from the random urban terrorism which had previously seemed to afflict only other and less happy lands. In the summer the scandal focus shifted from politics to business as one of the nation's leading banks, Daiwa ('Great Harmony'), was revealed to have concealed from the New York regulatory authorities undisclosed losses on bond dealings amounting to more than a billion dollars. A year later Sumitomo Corporation topped even that when copper trading losses amounting to $2,600,000,000 over a twelve-year period were exposed. In 1996 that particular disgrace competed with headlines proclaiming a cover-up over leakage at a nuclear power plant, an outbreak of mass food-poisoning caused by unhygienic school lunches and a scandal involving the treatment of hundreds of haemophiliacs with HIV-infected blood. The authorities meanwhile pressed ahead with plans – hastened by the Kobe catastrophe – to relocate the capital from Tokyo to some less vulnerable location by 2010. A new start for a new millennium?

The Japanese Language and Japanese Names

Differences

The Japanese language has a number of features which make it strikingly different from English:

- no gender distinction
- no distinctive singular/plural forms
  (plurals are understood from context or by use of special counting words)
- no definite ('the') or indefinite ('a') article
- there is no future tense, which is indicated by the use of adverbs
- adjectives and adverbs precede nouns and verbs
- the normal grammatical order is subject, object, verb
- words never end in consonants, except the nasalised 'n' sound
- there are no sounds for 'th' and 'l' and 'v' usually comes out as 'b'
- stress falls evenly on each syllable
- two consonants never come together in a single syllable.

LOAN WORDS

English loan-words, therefore, often require the insertion of additional vowels for Japanese to be able to pronounce them (e.g. 'strike' becomes *su-to-rai-ku*). The five vowels are pronounced as in modern Italian – A as 'ah'; E as in 'den'; I as in 'if' in the middle of a word and like the ee of 'see' at the end; O as 'oh'; and U as 'oo'. Doubled vowels are often indicated by a horizontal stroke (macron) above the vowel. Numerous words in Japanese have virtually the same pronunciation but quite different meanings, e.g. *hashi* – 'chopsticks' – can also mean 'bridge'. Words adopted from Western languages, mainly English, now account for about 20 per cent of the vocabulary in everyday use. Many are 'adapted' in the process – thus television becomes *terebi* and department store is *depato*. New words are coined by using parts of existing words – *pasacom* for personal computer, *remocon* for remote control. ('Walkman' was a pure invention by Morita Akio, Chairman of Sony.)

WRITING

Japanese is written with a combination of four script elements:

Kanji (Chinese characters). These convey major concepts. Simple *kanji* consist of two, three or four strokes, complex ones of a dozen or more. Strokes are written in a set sequence. By the time they are twelve Japanese children will have memorised about 900 *Kanji*; minimum literacy requires about double that number. (The illiteracy rate is 0.3 per cent.) Educated Japanese will recognise 5,000 *kanji* or more.

Hiragana is a cursive syllabary largely used for grammatical functions (i.e. where English would normally use prepositions and conjunctions).

Katakana is an angular syllabary mainly used for writing loan-words; also conventionally used for sending telegrams and telexes.

Romaji – Roman letters.

IMPLICATIONS

Given the complexity of Japanese writing, literacy and calligraphy (*shodo* – 'the way of the brush') have always been held in esteem in Japan. The expense of producing printed documents may also partly account for Japanese management's reliance on face-to-face meetings and hand-written notes and memos, as well as its eagerness to adopt photocopying and fax machines. The first Japanese typewriter (in effect a mini-press with a 3,000-symbol font) was not invented until 1915. The first Japanese-language word-processor was introduced by

Toshiba in 1978. In 1984 Brother introduced a word-processing typewriter capable of converting Romanised Japanese into a limited vocabulary of 2,965 Chinese characters. The Canon camera company pioneered the electronic *kanji* dictionary.

HONORIFICS *(KEIGO)*

Status and gender relationships are programmed into the language. Women's speech is distinguished from men's not only by tone but also by vocabulary and idiom. Speech directed towards older and superior persons is invariably self-deprecating.

Names

Japanese, even colleagues at work, do not usually use first names but use the family name followed by '-san' which can stand for Mr, Mrs, Ms or Miss. The suffix '-chan' may be used by close friends. It is incorrect to refer to oneself as '-san'.

Until the Meiji period peasants did not usually have surnames. Surnames have to be chosen from an approved list. Many contain elements relating to the landscape, e.g. *gawa* (river), *yama* (mountain), *mura* (village) or *bana* (tree). The most common Japanese names include Ito, Sato, Nakamura, Watanabe and Kobayashi.

For further information see:
Japanese: Language and People (BBC Books 1991)
The Japanese Language, Kindaichi Haruhiko (Tuttle)
Japanese in Action, Jack Seward (Weatherhill)
Japanese and the Japanese: Words in Culture, Suzuki Takao (Kodansha)

Buddhism

Its Importance

The history of Buddhism is even longer than that of Christianity and every bit as complicated in terms of its doctrinal disputes and sectarian sub-divisions. Like Christianity it has exerted a profound influence on the culture and customs of its adherents. Without some understanding of Buddhism it is difficult to comprehend much of Japan's artistic heritage in the general fields of sculpture and temple architecture, as well as peculiarly Japanese achievements in flower-arranging, garden-design, tea-ceremony, *Noh* drama and the martial arts – not to mention contemporary politics and social attitudes (e.g. preference for cremation).

ITS JAPANISATION

Buddhism originated in India in the sixth century BC and came to Japan over a thousand years later and via China. Japan encountered Buddhism, in other words, as a religion with a millennium of history behind it, established traditions of artistic expression and a huge body of learned commentary upon its fundamental teachings and scriptures. All this had to be appreciated largely through the medium of a foreign language, Chinese, or via the even more linguistically-remote sacred tongues of Pali and Sanskrit. Buddhist belief, behaviour and iconography then had to be accommodated to the existing religious traditions of Shinto and the ethical framework of Confucianism – an immense enterprise which absorbed some of the greatest intellects and aesthetic talents Japan has ever produced. The success attending these efforts was undoubtedly assisted by the close association of Buddhism with the advent of literacy and other major cultural advances in the arts and crafts.

In the course of this long and intensely complicated process Japan evolved forms of Buddhism which are now thought of as peculiarly Japanese, such as Nichiren and, to a lesser extent perhaps, Zen.

IS BUDDHISM A RELIGION?

Any effort to come to grips with Buddhism involves encountering a number of obstacles – apart from the aforementioned complexity – not least its extensive technical terminology. But the first, and in some ways most persistent, barrier that Westerners are likely to encounter is the fact that, coming from a Judaeo-Christian background, they impose upon it the perspectives and categories which provide the norms of their habitual thinking about religion, whether they are particularly 'religious' or not. It takes some time and reflection to come to terms with the style of a religion which, in some senses, dispenses with the notion of God altogether, conceives salvation as extinction rather than redemption and is, in many of its forms, indifferent to whether or not its followers adhere to another faith at the same time.

The Buddha

The term 'Buddha' is not a name but denotes the state of being of one who has a true knowledge of reality.

Buddhism originated in the teachings of Siddhartha Gautama, the scion of a house of warrior-rulers of a small state on the border of what is now India and Nepal. The details of his biography are overlaid with twenty-five centuries of often fanciful embellishment but its main outlines are clear enough. At the age of twenty-nine he renounced a life of pleasure and luxury and deserted his wife and child to seek a spiritual enlightenment which would give him insight into the nature of ultimate reality. (His renunciation is often symbolised in sculptures of the Buddha by extended ear-lobes, empty of their once elaborate ear-rings).

Accepting instruction in yogic practices and other mystical techniques from two eminent masters, he soon surpassed them and entered a six-year period of severe self-denial, accompanied by five other ascetics. These extremities brought him to the verge of death and a realisation that such behaviour was both self-destructive and self-deluding. Rejecting mortification he rebuilt his strength – at the cost of losing his disillusioned companions.

Gautama, honed by his ordeal to an acute self-awareness, turned to deep and extended solitary meditation and it was this that brought him to a state of enlightenment. Weeks of reflection enabled him to elaborate his fundamental insights into a coherent doctrine and practicable programme for living. An awareness that most of his fellow-creatures were blessed with but limited and varying abilities to comprehend his message induced him to hesitate before committing himself to a life of teaching. But eventually he rejoined his five former companions and induced them by his sincerity to listen to his first sermon, 'Setting in Motion the Wheel of Truth'.

The core of the Buddha's teaching is summarised in the Four Noble Truths:
– suffering and conflict are inseparable from human existence;
– they arise from egotism and its expression in desire, ambition etc.;
– liberation from endless reincarnation into non-existence is attainable;
– the means of attainment lies in the Noble Eightfold Path.

The Noble Eightfold Path, a 'middle way' between asceticism and hedonism, requires its follower to pursue:

right view, (i.e. of the Cosmos and the place of humans in it)
right purpose, (i.e. the essential moral energy to aspire to truth)
right speech, (i.e. avoiding false or defamatory speech)
right bodily action, (i.e. avoiding excessive sensuality, theft or aggression)
right livelihood, (i.e. occupations harmless to other living things)
right effort, (i.e. constant endeavour to cultivate virtue and avoid vice)
right sensitivity (i.e. constant self-awareness)
right concentration. (i.e. meditating to focus one's consciousness).

The congregation for the first sermon became the first five Buddhist monks, the core of the *sangha* (community) committed to living out and communicating his truth (in Sanskrit, *dharma*).

The Buddha devoted the rest of his life to teaching and died at eighty. (More strictly speaking he is regarded as having been finally released into nirvana from the round of rebirth.) After his cremation his relics were shared among the states and cities which had built monasteries to shelter members of the *sangha*.

BUDDHIST ICONOGRAPHY

Early Buddhism avoided representing the Buddha in human form, perhaps to avoid the implication of compromising his transcendence. Instead it focused its devotions on such devices as the *stupa* (monument built over a holy relic), the bodhi tree (under which Gautama received his enlightenment), the parasol (denoting kingly status and hence power) and the wheel (denoting the endless cycle of reincarnation through a multitude of existences). The conventions of Buddha imagery were probably established in second-century India and incorporate the thirty-two characteristics by which it was held a Buddha could be recognised – a mark on the forehead, a protuberant top-knot of hair, a sharply-curved nose, distinctive creases in the flesh of the throat etc. Buddha images are usually depicted making formalised hand-gestures (*mudras*) which symbolise events in his life or aspects of his nature.

The oldest Japanese image of Buddha is dated at 606. Buddha has been worshipped in Japan in various manifestations, depending on sectarian interpretations of the scriptures. Among the most common are:

Amida – Buddha of the Pure Land or Western Paradise

Yakushi – Amida's eastern, earthly counterpart, a healer

Miroku – Maitreya, the 'friendly one', Buddha of the Future

Dainichi Nyorai (Sanskrit Vairocana) – Great Illuminator Buddha

Kannon – (Chinese Guan Yin) – a bodhisattva of Amida, can take various forms (e.g. eleven-headed, thousand-armed) and in modern times has become feminised as a 'Goddess of Mercy'

Jizo – another bodhisattva, in the form of a shaven-headed monk; often represented as a group of six, representing the six levels of creation (angels, demons, humans, animals etc). A patron saint of those in need of comfort – children, travellers and pregnant women.

BUDDHIST ETHICS

Recognising the varying abilities of human beings to grasp the truth of its teachings Buddhism makes different demands on its followers, requiring more of monks, for example, than of lay followers. Laymen are normally expected to maintain an upright personal character (giving alms and avoiding viciousness, violence and mind-clouding stimulants), observe holy days and festivals and fulfil their obligations to society as a student, parent, worker, neighbour and friend. Monks were traditionally required to live by begging, wearing clothes made from discarded cloth and observing celibacy. Modern Japanese monks are often sophisticated men with sophisticated tastes.

National Holidays and Local Festivals

There are literally hundreds of local festivals (*matsuri*). Those listed below have been chosen either because they are particularly large or famous or because they have some unusual feature. (There are, for example, festivals which focus on igloos, phalluses, silkworms and seaweed, as well as special shrines for needles, dead children and the victims of car accidents). *Matsuri* usually originate in Shinto celebrations, often tied to the agricultural cycle of planting and harvesting. They may involve purification rituals, dances (*kagura*), feasts (*naorai*) and parades featuring floats or carts. Sacred objects, representing *kami*, are often carried in palanquin-style portable shrines (*o-mikoshi*). There may also be contests such as tug-of-war, horse-races, archery or kite-flying.

* denotes a National Holiday; when this falls on a Sunday, the following Monday is taken as the holiday. A day falling between two national holidays (e.g. 4 May) is also taken as a holiday.

Public transport becomes extremely crowded around three peak travel seasons as urban Japanese renew their rural roots, and it is customary to book weeks in advance; these are:

a) New Year – 27 December – 4 January and nearest weekends
b) 'Golden Week' – 29 April – 5 May and nearest weekends
c) 'O-Bon' festival of the Dead – celebrated in mid-July in some areas and mid-August in others

* 1 January New Year's Day (*Ganjitsu*)

The most important single festival in the entire calendar. Very few businesses will reopen before 4 January. More than 90 per cent of families will dress in their best clothes (kimono for ladies) and visit a shrine to pray for a year of health and happiness and buy amulets or fortune predictions. Meiji Shrine and Ise are particularly crowded. There are many customs related to ideas of purification and renewal. New Year's Eve was customarily marked by a thorough house-cleaning and settlement of outstanding debts and quarrels. Fathers take children kite-flying and girls still sometimes play a sort of shuttlecock game (*hanetsuki*) with elaborately-decorated paddle-shaped battledores (*hago-ita*). Children also receive gifts of money in special red envelopes (*otoshidama*). Older

228

Japanese relatives gather in cemeteries to honour their ancestors

people play traditional card-games (*karuta*) which involve matching flowers or verses. Mothers prepare *ozoni* – a rice-dumpling soup – and other dishes as 'New Year food' (*osechi-ryori*). New Year postcards (*nengajo*) are sent to relatives, clients, colleagues and old school friends; special arrangements are made by the post office to ensure that all cards are delivered on New Year's day by an army of students. On 2 January it is customary to practise calligraphy by writing appropriate poems or proverbs; many schools hold calligraphy competitions. The inner grounds of the Imperial Palace in Tokyo are open to the public. New Year decorations are taken down and burned on 7 or 11 January, depending on the region.

6 January *Dezomeshiki*
Since the Edo period Tokyo firemen have performed acrobatics on bamboo ladders to impress the public.

7 January Seven Herbs Festival
An ancient Chinese observance. Seven edible herbs are eaten in a rice gruel to ensure good health.

⋆ 15 January Coming-of-Age Day (*Seijin-no-hi*)
The local town hall holds a civic ceremony to honour those who have reached the voting age, twenty.

February
Snow Festival, held in Sapporo, capital of Hokkaido and host to the 1972
Winter Olympics. This features about 150 massive sculptures and carvings of ice
and draws some 2,000,000 visitors. Winter snow festivals (*yuki matsuri*) are
common throughout northern Japan. Snow-viewing became a general custom
in the Edo period and is often featured in literature.

February (third Saturday) *Hadaka Matsuri*
Saidaji temple, Okayama features a mob of nearly naked youths scrambling for
a pair of sacred wands.

3 February Bean-Scattering Festival (*Setsubun*)
This marks the last day of winter in the traditional lunar calendar. Roasted
soybeans are scattered around houses to drive away demons bringing illness or
bad luck. Celebrities such as actors or wrestlers born in the appropriate year of
the Chinese animal zodiac perform this ceremony at shrines, such as Asakusa
Kannon and Zojoji in Tokyo or Gion in Kyoto.

* 11 February National Foundation Day (*Kenkoko Kinen-no-hi*)
Abolished after 1945 this holiday was reinstated in 1967 and marks the supposed anniversary of the accession of the first emperor, Jimmu, in 660 BC.

14 February Valentine's Day
Custom decrees that women buy expensive chocolates for their senior male
office colleagues (who often give them straight back).

3 March Girls' Day (*Hina Matsuri*)
Sets of fifteen expensive dolls, representing the imperial court with attendants,
musicians, guards etc., are displayed in the *tokonoma* (focal alcove of the main
room). This day is also known as Peach Festival (*Momo-no-Sekku*) because peach
flowers represent gentleness and grace, the appropriate qualities for a girl.
Originally a festival for aristocrats only, this became a more general celebration
by the eighteenth century.

13 March *Kasuga Matsuri*
1,000-year-old dance staged at Kasuga shrine in Nara.

* 21 (or 20) March Vernal Equinox Day (*Shumbun-no-hi*)
Marks the coming of spring and is a traditionally important time in the Buddhist
calendar. Family graves are often visited.

April
Throughout the month parties (*hanami*) will be organised to view the cherry-
blossom (*sakura no hana*), a custom dating back to the reign of Emperor Saga
(809–23). Newspapers publish maps showing a cherry-blossom line (*sakura
zensen*) where the blooms can be seen at their best. Ueno Park in Tokyo is a
favourite venue for office or family picnics under the cherry-trees, often
accompanied by much drinking and a little dancing.

8 April Buddha's birthday (*Hana Matsuri*)
Celebrated in all Buddhist temples.

14–15 April *Takayama Matsuri*
Hie Shrine, Takayama features a parade of floats.

* 29 April 'Greenery Day'
This was formerly (i.e. in the reign of the Showa Emperor 1926–89) the Emperor's Birthday. Its retention relates to its convenience as marking the start of 'Golden Week' and its redesignation commemorates the former ruler's ecological interests. (He was an eminent marine biologist.) Citizens are encouraged to plant and cultivate natural vistas.

May (third weekend) *Sanja Matsuri*
Procession of over 100 *o-mikoshi* held near Asakusa Kannon temple, Tokyo.

May (third Sunday) *Mifune Matsuri*
Features ancient boats on the Oi river, Kyoto.

* 3 May Constitution Memorial Day (*Kempo Kinenbi***)**
Marks the promulgation of the 1947 'Showa' constitution (*see p. 170*).

3–4 May *Hakata Dontaku*
Fukuoka features a parade of legendary gods on horseback

3–5 May *Odako-age*
Kite-flying festival at Hamamatsu

* 5 May Children's Day (*Kodomo-no-hi***)**
This was formerly Boys' Day. It was customary to fly wind-sock type streamers painted like carp; the carp swims against the stream to spawn and is therefore a symbol of determination, which is thought to be a highly appropriate male virtue.

11 May to 15 October
Cormorant fishing on the Nagara river, Gifu.

15 May Hollyhock Festival (*Aoi Matsuri***)**
Dating from the fifteenth century and organised by Kamigamo and Shimo-gamo shrines in Kyoto. The main feature is a procession featuring an ox-cart, an imperial messenger on a fine horse and a portable shrine (*o-mikoshi*) representing the goddess Saioh, all accompanied by hundreds of attendants wearing costumes in the style of the Heian court. In obedience to an ancient oracle shrine buildings are decked with hollyhocks to ward off earthquakes. The ceremonies also include traditional music and dance.

17–18 May Spring Festival
At the Toshogu Shrine, Nikko features a 1,200-strong procession clad in samurai costume.

1-14 June *Sanno Matsuri*
Hie shrine, Tokyo; involves parading *o-mikoshi* through the Akasaka District.

14 June Rice-Planting Festival
Sumiyoshi shrine, Osaka features girls in traditional costume transplanting seedlings.

7 July Star Festival (*Tanabata***)**
Celebrated nationwide and especially at Sendai. A Chinese legend tells that on

this day alone the separated star lovers, Altair (a cowherd) and Vega (a weaver princess), can meet across the Milky Way on a bridge of magpies.

13–15 July (in some areas 13–15 August) *O-Bon*

Buddhist festival observed nationwide to honour the memory of the dead. Only New Year outranks this observance in importance and as an occasion for gift-giving. Ancestral graves are cleaned and offerings of food and flowers placed before the family altar at home. Ceremonies involving bonfires or paper lanterns are organised to welcome back the souls of the dead. Many city-dwellers return to their ancestral village to visit graves or take part in dances (*odori*).

14 July *Nachi Himatsuri*

The Nachi shrine, Nachi-Katsuura features white-robed priests carrying twelve giant torches.

17 July Gion Festival

Associated with the Yasaka shrine, this began in 869 to drive an epidemic out of Kyoto. It is now marked by a huge procession of floats and musicians.

20 (and 27) July *Sagi-mai* festival

Tsuwano in Shimane Prefecture features a unique 'heron dance'.

24–5 July *Tenjin Matsuri*

Organised by the Temmangu shrine, Osaka; features floating shrines on the Dojima river.

August

A favourite month for moon-viewing (*tsukimi*) – traditionally accompanied by poetry and sake.

1–7 August *Neputa Matsuri* in Hirosaki and *Nebuta Matsuri* (2–7 August) in Aomori

Feature parades of outsize papier-mâché figures.

5–7 August *Kanto Matsuri*

Akita City features a parade of lighted paper lanterns on ten-metre poles.

12–15 August *Awa Odori* festival

Tokushima, featuring folk dances.

16 August *Daimonji* bonfire

On the hills overlooking Kyoto.

9 September Chrysanthemum Festival

A court celebration revived in the Meiji era. The sixteen-petalled chrysanthemum is the heraldic crest (*mon*) of the Imperial family and is used on stamps and coins. From mid-October to mid-November displays of chrysanthemums are exhibited at Meiji shrine, Yasukuni shrine and Shinjuku Imperial gardens.

* 15 September Respect-the-Aged Day (*Keiro-no-hi*)

This was established as a national holiday in 1963 but ceremonies honouring the aged date back to the Edo period. The official retirement age was set at sixty by law in 1986.

16 September Demonstrations of *Yabusame* **(archery from horseback)**
Tsurugaoka Hachimangu shrine in Kamakura.
★ 23 (or 24) September Autumn Equinox Day (*Shubun-no-hi***)**
Marks the coming of autumn and was traditionally important in the Buddhist calendar. Family graves are often visited.
October (mid) Nagoya City Festival
Features a giant parade of impersonations of historical figures. All the deities of Japan are said to gather at Izumo Taisha near Matsue, Shimane Prefecture, around this time.
7-9 October *Okunchi* **festival**
The Suwa shrine, Nagasaki features a Chinese dragon dance.
★ 10 October Health-Sports Day
Commemorates the 1964 Tokyo Olympics. Many schools and companies hold sports meetings.
11–13 October *Oeshiki*
Hommonji temple, Tokyo commemorates Nichiren (*see p. 57*).
17 October Autumn Festival
Toshogu shrine, Nikko features samurai in full regalia.
22 October Festival of the Ages (*Jidai Matsuri***)**
Organised by the Heian Shrine (Heian Jingu) in Kyoto since 1895, this features a procession of 1,700 participants representing historical figures dating back to the foundation of the shrine in 794. A torchlight procession takes place on the same date at the Yuki shrine in Sakyo-ku, Kyoto.
★ 3 November Culture Day (*Bunka-no-hi***)**
Redesignated in 1948, this was formerly the birthday of Emperor Meiji. The traditionally-minded may still visit the Meiji Shrine. The Emperor awards Cultural Orders of Merit (*Bunka Kunsho*) to outstanding artists, writers etc. On the same day the Daimyo Gyoretsu in Hakone re-creates the passage of a feudal lord and his entourage.
15 November (Seven-Five-Three Festival) *Shichi-go-san*
Girls aged three and seven and boys aged five are taken to Shinto shrines to give thanks for their health and pray for its continuation (a reminder of the traditionally high rates of infant mortality in pre-modern times). Girls invariably wear kimono and elaborate hair ornaments and are much photographed.
★ 23 November Labour Thanksgiving Day (*Kinro-Kansha-no-hi***)**
This was formerly a Shinto festival (*Niiname-sai*) to celebrate the harvest but now recognises the contribution of all who work. The emperor still offers newly-fermented sake to the gods.
December (mid-onwards)
'*Bonenkai***'** (forget-the-year) parties are hosted by companies for staff and clients.
17-19 December *Toshi-no-ichi*
Fairs are held to sell traditional New Year battledores (*see* 1 January).

* 23 December Emperor's Birthday (*Tenno Tanjobi*)

The inner grounds of the Imperial Palace are opened to the public. The emperor appears (on a bullet-proof glassed-in balcony) to acknowledge the cheers of well-wishers.

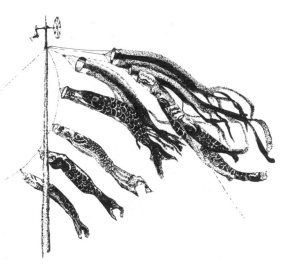

Food and Drink

In Meiji times Western visitors to Japan were generally enchanted by the landscape and appalled by the food. Sir Rutherford Alcock, Britain's first permanent diplomatic representative in Japan, was a hearty and normally ebullient ex-Army surgeon, but even he was driven close to gastronomic despair:

> Pork and tough fowls for meat, and rice for vegetables, eggs for milk (butter and milk being both unknown luxuries here), with an occasional pigeon for entremet, may support life even under the barbarous handling of a Japanese ... cook ... but I am satisfied there must be a limit somewhere.... The total deprivation of beef and mutton must in time be a serious detriment to the English constitution.

The *Handbook for Travellers in Japan* published by John Murray in the 1890s advised visitors to anticipate deprivation of all normal culinary comforts outside the treaty-ports and contained such helpful hints as the suggestion that soy sauce should be liberally added to watery soups to add zest and curry powder sprinkled over virtually everything else to add flavour.

A century later Japanese food has taken its place among the world's great cuisines, though the principles and practices which make it distinctive are still not widely understood. The emphasis is on freshness and simplicity, a light touch in seasoning, skilful use of the knife and elegance of presentation. As cookery expert Lesley Downer has neatly put it, 'the stars of the show are the ingredients themselves'. Japanese cuisine is low in fats and high in minerals; if it has a fault, it is erring on the salty side.

The Range of Choice

Kaiseki is Japanese haute cuisine. Originating as the accompaniment to a tea ceremony, a *kaiseki* banquet consists of a succession of as many as a dozen or more dishes, each artfully arranged, though often consisting of no more than a mouthful. The influence of this tradition on nouvelle cuisine is obvious. *Kaiseki* is served in the classiest restaurants (*ryotei*). Many restaurants (*ya*) specialise in a specific type of dish:

Sushi-ya – serve *sashimi*, slices of raw fish, eaten with soy sauce or *wasabi* (horseradish), and *sushi*, patties of vinegared rice topped with varieties of raw fish.

Tempura-ya – serve fresh vegetables, prawns etc. flash-fried in a crisp light batter.

Soba-ya – serve noodles, usually made on the premises.

Okonomiyaki-ya – serve a type of pancake filled with small pieces of meat or vegetables.

Yakitori-ya – serve bite-sized chicken 'kebabs'.

Some restaurants concentrate on the preparation of one particular type of ingredient such as eels or mushrooms. There are also *robatayaki-ya*, farmhouse-style restaurants which specialise in grilled foods, Buddhist temples which serve vegetarian dishes, usually based on *tofu* (bean curd), and 'red lantern' street-stalls and road-side bars (*nomiya*) which offer simple snack-food to peckish passers-by. At *teppanyaki* restaurants the food (usually steak) is cooked on steel griddles which are part of the table guests sit at. Chinese and Korean restaurants are also commonplace. That awareness of the changing seasons which is such a pervasive feature of Japanese culture extends to food as well. Winter is the time for thick, warming stews, summer for iced noodles, spring for fresh, young root-crops and autumn for raw fish at its best.

A BALANCED DIET

Rice boiled, plain and glutinous (easier to eat with chopsticks [*hashi*]) is served with every meal. Indeed, the traditional term for breakfast literally means 'first rice'. It is not 'done' to pep up plain rice by pouring soy sauce over it (green tea or raw egg are OK), though it may be topped with toasted *nori* (seaweed), *natto* (fermented soybeans) or *uni* (sea-urchin).

Vegetables are chosen for maximum freshness; most Japanese housewives still shop every day. Vegetables are eaten raw and pickled as well as boiled or steamed and include plants such as ferns, water-lilies and burdock (*gobo*) which are not generally eaten in the West. Pickles include such unfamiliar items as plums, ginger and giant radish (*daikon*).

Fish is still the main source of protein and features in almost every meal. Sea-foods include not only shellfish but also sea-weed and algae. The basic soup-stock and seasoning, *dashi*, is made from dried bonito and kelp.

A BALANCED MEAL

Instead of 'meat and two veg' a typical Japanese meal consists of 'soup and three (dishes)', each of which is cooked by a different process, i.e. grilled, simmered, fried, steamed, boiled or raw.

DRINK

Tea is served both with meals and throughout the day. It is made with green (i.e. dried, rather than fermented) leaves and hot, rather than boiling, water and is drunk immediately, rather than being left to draw.

Sake is usually drunk hot in winter and enjoyed 'on the rocks' in summer; it is least satisfactory at room temperature. There are no vintages but connoisseurs would stick to dry-tasting *junmaishu* (sake unmixed with added alcohol or sugar) rather than the sweeter varieties (*amakuchi*) usually served in restaurants. (As a rough guide it usually follows that the shorter the list of ingredients on a bottle the better the quality of its contents.) Sake is graded as *tokkyu* (special), *ikkyu* (first grade) or *nikyu* (second grade) and is best consumed within three months of bottling. There are 2,500 sake breweries in Japan; Nada, Fushimi, Akita and Hiroshima are particularly famed for the quality of their products.

Whisky is invariably drunk with crushed ice and a high (1:6) dilution of water (*mizuwari*). Japanese domestic whisky is therefore often strongly flavoured to take account of this and can be correspondingly unpalatable if taken 'straight'.

Beer – Japanese *biru* is a lager-type, based on German models. Inhabitants of Sapporo are proud to emphasise that their famed breweries are on the same latitude as Munich and Milwaukee. Beer accounts for 70 per cent of national alcohol consumption. Streetside vending-machines serve it ice-cold.

Shochu is a colourless, virtually flavourless spirit made from rice or sweet potatoes; originally the working-man's hooch but now increasingly fashionable among the young when drunk with a mixer.

Etiquette – when drinking in bars there is invariably a hostess to keep your glass topped up; otherwise the rule is to top up your companions' glasses and wait for one of them to keep yours similarly full. The normal toast is *Kampai!* If you wish to stop drinking just leave your glass full.

ENTERTAINING

It is normal to entertain guests and clients at a restaurant (Tokyo has about 80,000) rather than inviting them home. (Japanese homes are usually cramped and often a long commute from the city centre.) Lunch is usually eaten at a brisk pace at any time from noon onwards. (Set lunches cost a fraction of what may be charged for the same meal in the evening.)

Leisurely and lavish entertaining is usually confined to the evenings, beginning immediately after work. In provincial cities restaurants are often closed by 9.00 p.m. Entertaining in hotels is therefore quite common as is the use of private dining rooms.

READING

Lesley Downer's *The Taste of Japan* (BBC Books 1991) is a simple-to-follow introduction for western novices. See also the same author's *Step by Step Japanese Cooking* and *Japanese Vegetarian Cookery*.

Chronology of Major Events

BC

8000	Approximate beginning of Jomon period
660	Traditional date for accession of Emperor Jimmu
300	Approximate ending of Jomon period

AD

300	Approximate ending of Yayoi period
400	Approximate date for emergence of Yamato dynasty; Kofun period begins
538 (or 552)	Traditional dates for the introduction of Buddhism
577–622	Prince Shotoku
587	Soga clan achieves ascendancy at court
604	Prince Shotoku's 'Seventeen Article Constitution'; adoption of Chinese calendar
607	First official mission to China; foundation of Horyuji
645	Taika reforms introduce Chinese-style administration
663	Loss of Japanese foothold in Korea
701–2	Taiho law code
710	Establishment of capital at Heijo, later known as Nara
712	Publication of *Kojiki* (*Record of Ancient Matters*)
720	Publication of *Nihon Shoki* (*Chronicle of Japan*)
724–49	Emperor Shomu
741	Provinces ordered to build Buddhist monasteries
749–58	Empress Koken (and 764–70)
752	Dedication of the Great Buddha at Nara
ca 760	*Man'yoshu* poetry anthology compiled
794	Establishment of capital at Kyoto
858	Fujiwara clan achieves ascendancy at court
ca 1000	Composition of Sei Shonagon's *Pillow Book* and *Tale of Genji*
1185	Battle of Dannoura ends Heike/Gempe wars
1192	Shogunate established at Kamakura

1232	Samurai legal code issued
1274	First Mongol invasion
1281	Second Mongol invasion
1333–8	Restoration of imperial rule by Go-Daigo
1338–1573	Ashikaga shogunate
1392	Reunification of northern and southern courts
1467–77	Onin wars
1543	Portuguese land at Tanegashima
1549	Arrival of St Francis Xavier
1573	End of Ashikaga shogunate
1582	Death of Oda Nobunaga; Toyotomi Hideyoshi takes over drive for national reunification
1588	'Sword hunt' separates warriors from peasants
1590	Hideyoshi completes reunification of Japan
1592 & 1597	Japanese invasions of Korea
1597	Martyrdom of twenty-six Christians at Nagasaki
1600	Battle of Sekigahara; William Adams arrives in Japan
1603	Tokugawa Ieyasu adopts title of shogun
1614–15	Siege of Osaka Castle; suicide of Hideyori
1636–9	Japan closed to foreign contacts;
1637	Shimabara rising
1688–1704	Genroku period
1701–2	Forty-Seven Ronin affair
1707	Last eruption of Mount Fuji
1722	Partial lifting of ban on importation of Western books
1781–8	Major famines, risings and riots
1837	Popular uprising in Osaka
1839–42	'Opium War' in China
1853	Commodore Perry's 'Black Ships' 'open' Japan
1854	Treaty of Kanagawa signed with USA
1858	'Unequal treaties' signed
1867	Fall of Tokugawa shogunate
1868	'Meiji Restoration'; Tokyo becomes the capital
1872	Tokyo-Yokohama railway opened
1877	Satsuma rebellion crushed
1889	Adoption of Meiji constitution
1894–5	Sino-Japanese war
1896	First demonstration of cinema in Tokyo
1902	Anglo-Japanese Alliance
1904–5	Russo-Japanese war
1910	Annexation of Korea
1911	Japan regains tariff autonomy
1912	Death of Meiji Emperor

1915	'Twenty One Demands' submitted to China
1918	Hara forms first party cabinet; 'Rice Riots'
1921	Crown Prince Hirohito visits London; assassination of Hara
1921–2	Washington Naval Conference
1922	Prince of Wales tours Japan
1923	Great Kanto earthquake
1925	Males over 25 given the vote
1926	Death of Taisho Emperor
1927	Banking crisis leads to fall of government
1930	London Naval Conference; Prime Minister Hamaguchi shot
1931	'Manchurian Incident'
1932	'Manchukuo' puppet-state established in Manchuria
1933	Japan withdraws from League of Nations
1936	Attempted *coup d'état* by junior officers; Japan joins Anti-Comintern Pact
1937	Marco Polo bridge incident
1941	Attack on Pearl Harbor
1942	Battle of Midway; conquest of Singapore, Philippines and Indonesia
1945	Invasion of Okinawa (April); Potsdam Declaration (July); bombing of Hiroshima (6 August) and Nagasaki (9 August); formal surrender of Japan (15 August) followed by Allied Occcupation under General Douglas MacArthur
1947	Democratic constitution comes into force
1948	General Tojo and other war-leaders hanged
1951	Japan signs San Francisco Peace Treaty
1952	End of Occupation
1953	TV broadcasting begins
1954	Self-Defence Forces established
1955	Liberal Democratic Party established
1956	Japan admitted to United Nations
1958	Japan launches world's largest oil-tanker
1959	Crown Prince Akihito marries a commoner
1960	Riots accompany revision of US Security Treaty
1964	Tokyo hosts Olympic games; Japan joins OECD; 'bullet train' begins
1967	Population passes 100,000,000
1970	Suicide of Mishima Yukio; Expo '70 at Osaka; first industrial robot
1972	Okinawa reverts to Japanese sovereignty; Sapporo hosts Winter Olympics; restoration of diplomatic relations with China

1973	First 'oil shock'
1976	Lockheed bribery scandal
1978	Narita airport opened
1979	Second 'oil shock'
1985	Yen revalued 40 per cent against the dollar
1986	Maekawa Report calls for opening of Japanese economy to imports and inward investment
1988	Japan becomes world's largest creditor nation and aid donor; Seikan tunnel links Honshu and Hokkaido
1989	Death of Showa Emperor (Hirohito); scandals force resignation of Prime Ministers Takeshita and Uno; Kaifu Toshiki succeeds as prime minister
1991	Miyazawa succeeds Kaifu as prime minister
1992	New law allows up to 2,000 Japanese troops to perform humanitarian tasks overseas under United Nations command
1993	Marriage of Crown Prince Naruhito to Miss Owada Masako, a commoner and career diplomat
1994	Oe Kenzaburo is awarded the Nobel Prize for Literature; Socialists participate in government for the first time since 1947; Reformist opposition parties unite to form Shinshinto bloc
1995	Kobe earthquake – death-toll estimated at 6,000; Aum Shinrikyo religious sect launches nerve-gas attack on Tokyo underground killing 12 and injuring 5,000; Emperor Akihito and Prime Minister Maruyama issue public expressions of regret for Japan's wartime conduct
1996	Scandals relating to nuclear power accidents, infected blood, copper trading and food poisoning; Low general election poll turnout indicates widespread public disenchantment with the current political climate

List of Emperors and Empresses

Reign dates for the first twenty-eight sovereigns are taken from the *Nihon shoki* (*Chronicles of Japan*). The first fourteen sovereigns are considered legendary; and while the next fourteen are known to have existed, their exact reign dates have not been verified historically. When the years of actual accession and formal coronation are different, the latter is shown in brackets after the former. If only the coronation year is known it is in brackets. Antoku's reign (1180–85) overlaps that of Go-Toba since the latter was placed on the throne by the Minamoto clan after the rival Taira clan had fled Kyoto with Antoku.

Jimmu *(660)–585 BC*	Yuryaku *456–479*
Suizei *(581)–549 BC*	Seinei *(480)–484*
Annei *549–511 BC*	Kenzo *(485)–487*
Itoku *(510)–477 BC*	Ninken *(488)–498*
Kosho *(475)–393 BC*	Buretsu *498–506*
Koan *(392)–291 BC*	Keitai *(507)–531*
Korei *(290)–215 BC*	Ankan *531(534)–535*
Kogen *(214)–158 BC*	Senka *535–539*
Kaika *158–98 BC*	Kimmei *539–571*
Sujin *(97)–30 BC*	Bidatsu *(572)–585*
Suinin *(29 BC)–AD 70*	Yomei *585–587*
Keiko *(71)–130*	Sushun *587–592*
Seimu *(131)–190*	Suiko (empress regnant) *593–628*
Chuai *(192)–200*	Jomei *(629)–641*
Jingu Kogo (regent) *201–269*	Kogyoku (empress regnant) *(642)–645*
Ojin *(270)–310*	
Nintoku *(313)–399*	Kotoku *645–654*
Richu *(400)–405*	Saimei (empress regnant Kogyoku rethroned) *(655)–661*
Hanzei *(406)–410*	
Ingyo *(412)–453*	Tenji *661(668)–672*
Anko *453–456*	Kobun *672*

Temmu   *672(673)–686*
Jito (empress regnant)
   686(690)–697
Mommu   *697–707*
Gemmei (empress regnant)
   707–715
Gensho (empress regnant)   *715–724*
Shomu   *724–749*
Koken (empress regnant)   *749–758*
Junnin   *758–764*
Shotoku (empress regnant Koken
   rethroned)   *764(765)–770*
Konin   *770–781*
Kammu   *781–806*
Heizei   *806–809*
Saga   *809–823*
Junna   *823–833*
Nimmyo   *833–850*
Montoku   *850–858*
Seiwa   *858–876*
Yozei   *876(877)–884*
Koko   *884–887*
Uda   *887–897*
Daigo   *897–930*
Suzaku   *930–946*
Murakami   *946–967*
Reizei   *967–969*
En'yu   *969–984*
Kazan   *984–986*
Ichijo   *986–1011*
Sanjo   *1011–16*
Go-Ichijo   *1016–36*
Go-Suzaku   *1036–45*
Go-Reizei   *1045–68*
Go-Sanjo   *1068–72*
Shirakawa   *1072–86*
Horikawa   *1086–1107*
Toba   *1107–23*
Sutoku   *1123–41*
Konoe   *1141–55*
Go-Shirakawa   *1155–58*
Nijo   *1158–65*
Rokujo   *1165–68*

Takakura   *1168–80*
Antoku   *1180–85*
Go-Toba   *1183(1184)–98*
Tsuchimikado   *1198–1210*
Juntoku   *1210(1211)–21*
Chukyo   *1221*
Goshirakawa   *1221(1222)–32*
Shijo   *1232(1233)–42*
Go-Saga   *1242–46*
Go-Fukakusa   *1246–59/60*
Kameyama   *1259/60–74*
Gouda   *1274–87*
Fushimi   *1287(1288) 98*
Go-Fushimi   *1298–1301*
Go-Nijo   *1301–08*
Hanazono   *1308–18*
Go-Daigo   *1318–39*
Go-Murakami   *1339–68*
Chokei   *1368–83*
Go-Kameyama   *1383–92*

The Northern Court
   Kogon   *1331(1332)–33*
   Komyo   *1336(1337/38)–48*
   Suko   *1348(1349/50)–51*
   Go-Kogon   *1351(1353/54)–71*
   Go-Enyu   *1371(1374/75)–82*
   Go-Komatsu   *1382–92*

Go-Komatsu   *1392–1412*
Shoko   *1412(1414)–28*
Go-Hanazono
   1428(1429/30)–64
Go-Tsuchimikado
   1464(1465/66)–1500
Go-Kashiwabara   *1500(1521)–26*
Go-Nara   *1526(1536)–57*
Ogimachi   *1557(1560)–86*
Go-Yozei   *1586(1587)–1611*
Go-Mizunoo   *1611–29*
Meisho (empress regnant)
   1629(1630)–43
Go-Komyo   *1643–54*

Go-Sai   *1654/55(1656)–63*
Reigen   *1663–87*
Higashiyama   *1687–1709*
Nakamikado   *1709(1710)–35*
Sakuramachi   *1735–47*
Momozono   *1747–62*
Go-Sakuramachi (empress regnant)
   1762(1763)–71
Go-Momozono   *1771–79*
Kokaku   *1780–1817*

Ninko   *1817–46*
Komei   *1846(1847)–66*
Meiji, personal name Mutsuhito, era
   name Meiji   *1867(1868)–1912*
Taisho, personal name Yoshihito, era
   name Taisho   *1912(1915)–26*
Kinjo, personal name Hirohito, era
   name Showa   *1926(1928)–89*
Akihito, personal name,
   era name Heisei   *1989(1990)–*

List of Prime Ministers

Name	Party	Term
Ito Hirobumi (*1st time*)		*1885–88*
Kuroda Kiyotaka		*1888–89*
Yamagata Aritomo (*1st time*)		*1889–91*
Matsukata Masayoshi (*1st time*)		*1891–92*
Ito Hirobumi (*2nd time*)		*1892–96*
Matsukata Masayoshi (*2nd time*)		*1896–98*
Ito Hirobumi (*3rd time*)		*1898*
Okuma Shigenobu (*1st time*)	Kenseito	*1898*
Yamagata Aritomo (*2nd time*)		*1898–1900*
Ito Hirobumi (*4th time*)	Seiyukai	*1900–01*
Katsura Taro (*1st time*)		*1901–06*
Saionji Kimmochi (*1st time*)	Seiyukai	*1906–08*
Katsura Taro		*1908–11*
Saionji Kimmochi (*2nd time*)	Seiyukai	*1911–12*
Katsura Taro (*3rd time*)		*1912–13*
Yamamoto Gonnohyoe (*1st time*)		*1913–14*
Okuma Shigenobu (*2nd time*)		*1914–16*
Terauchi Masatake		*1916–18*
Hara Takashi	Seiyukai	*1918–21*
Takahashi Korekiyo	Seiyukai	*1921–22*
Kato Tomosaburo		*1922–23*
Yamamoto Gonnohyoe (*2nd time*)		*1923–24*
Kiyoura Keigo		*1924*
Kato Takaaki	Kenseito	*1924–26*
Wakatsuki Reijiro (*1st time*)	Kenseito	*1926–27*
Tanaka Giichi	Seiyukai	*1927–29*
Hamaguchi Osachi	Minseito	*1929–31*
Wakatsuki Reijiro (*2nd time*)	Minseito	*1931*
Inuki Tsuyoshi	Seiyukai	*1931–32*

Saito Makoto		*1932–34*
Okada Keisuke		*1934–36*
Hirota Koki		*1936–37*
Hayashi Senjuro		*1937*
Konoe Fumimaro (*1st time*)		*1937–39*
Hiranuma Kiichiro		*1939*
Abe Nobuyuki		*1940*
Yonai Mitsumasa		*1940*
Konoe Fumimaro (*2nd time*		*1940–41*
Konoe Fumimaro (*3rd time*)		*1941*
Tojo Hideki		*1941–44*
Koiso Kuniaki		*1944–45*
Suzuki Kantaro		*1945*
Higashikuni Naruhiko		*1945*
Shidehara Kijuro		*1945–46*
Yoshida Shigeru (*1st time*)	Jiyuto	*1946–47*
Katayama Tetsu	Shakaito	1947–48
Ashida Hitoshi	Minshuto	*1948*
Yoshida Shigeru (*2nd time*)	Jiyuto	*1948–49*
Yoshida Shigeru (*3rd time*)	Jiyuto	*1949–52*
Yoshida Shigeru (*4th time*)	Jiyuto	*1952–53*
Yoshida Shigeru (*5th time*	Jiyuto	*1953–54*
Hatoyama Ichiro (*1st time*)	Minshuto	*1954–55*
Hatoyama Ichiro (*2nd time*)	Minshuto	*1955*
Hatoyama Ichiro (*3rd time*)	Jiyu-Minshuto	*1955–56*
Ishibashi Tanzan	Jiyu-Minshuto	*1956–57*
Kishi Nobusuke (*1st time*)	Jiyu-Minshuto	*1957–58*
Kishi Nobusuke (*2nd time*)	Jiyu-Minshuto	*1958–60*
Ikeda Hayato (*1st time*)	Jiyu-Minshuto	*1960*
Ikeda Hayato (*2nd time*)	Jiyu-Minshuto	*1960–63*
Ikeda Hayato (*3rd time*)	Jiyu-Minshuto	*1963–64*
Sato Eisaku (*1st time*)	Jiyu-Minshuto	*1964–67*
Sato Eisaku (*2nd time*)	Jiyu-Minshuto	*1967–70*
Sato Eisaku (*3rd time*)	Jiyu-Minshuto	*1970–72*
Tanaka Kakuei (*1st time*)	Jiyu-Minshuto	*1972*
Tanaka Kakuei (*2nd time*)	Jiyu-Minshuto	*1972–74*
Miki Takeo	Jiyu-Minshuto	*1974–76*
Fukuda Takeo	Jiyu-Minshuto	*1976–78*
Ohira Masayoshi (*1st time*)	Jiyu-Minshuto	*1978–79*
Ohira Masayoshi (*2nd time*)	Jiyu-Minshuto	*1979–80*
Suzuki Zenko	Jiyu-Minshuto	*1980–82*
Nakasone Yasuhiro	Jiyu-Minshuto	*1982–1987*
Takeshita Noboru	Jiyu-Minshuto	*1987–89*

Uno Sosuke	Jiyu-Minshuto	1989–1989
		(2 mths only)
Kaifu Toshiki	Jiyu-Minshuto	*1989–1991*
Miyazawa Kenji	Jiyu-Minshuto	*1991–1993*
Hosokawa Morihiro	Japan New Party	*1993–1994*
Hata Tsutomo	Shinseito (Japan	
	Renewal Party)	*1994*
Murayama Tomiichi	Nippon Shakaito	
	(Social Democratic	
	Party of Japan)	*1994–1996*
Hashimoto Ryutaro	Jiyu-Minshuto	*1996–*

Further Reading and Reference

Guidebooks

Among the many excellent guidebooks on Japan the following are recommended:

Kanno Eiji and Constance O'Keefe, *New Japan Solo* (Kodansha 1988)

Ian McQueen, *Japan: A Travel Survival Kit* (Lonely Planet 1989)

James K. Weatherley, *Japan Unescorted* (Kodansha 1986)

Jim Rickman's *Japan for the Impoverished* (Borgnan 1995) describes itself in its own title as does Harry Guest's *Traveller's Literary Companion: Japan* (In Print 1994)

Publishers and Authors

The English-language publishing houses with the strongest lists on Japan are Kodansha, Weatherhill and Tuttle. Specialist British houses include The Athlone Press, In Print and The Japan Library.

A number of authors manage to be both expert on their subject and enjoyable to read; these include the diplomats Sir George Sansom and Sir Hugh Cortazzi (history); academics W.G.Beasley (history), R.P.Dore (sociology), Donald Keene (literature and the arts) and Oliver Statler (history); businessmen Boye de Mente, George Fields and Peter Tasker (business/consumer behaviour); and resident *gaijin* journalists Jean Pearce, Paul Meredith Smith and Rick Kennedy.

Reference

The standard English-language reference work is the 8-volume *Kodansha Encyclopedia of Japan* (Kodansha 1983, supplement 1986).

Basil Hall Chamberlain's witty and erudite pocket encyclopaedia *Things Japanese* rapidly went through half a dozen editions after it was first published in 1894. Since 1971 it has been available as a Tuttle paperback reprint and the fact that by 1990 it had reached its 18th reprinting confirms it has lost none of its appeal.

Dorothy Perkins' *Encyclopedia of Japan: Japanese History and Culture, from Abacus to Zori* (Roundtable Press 1991) is a large-format dictionary-style ready reference work, particularly strong on traditional culture.

Boye de Mente's *Everything Japanese* (Harrap 1989) is in the same format but more contemporary and business-related in its orientation.

The most recent single volume reference work is *The Cambridge Encyclopedia of Japan* (Cambridge University Press 1993), edited by Richard Bowring and Peter Kornicki.

The *Cultural Atlas of Japan* (Phaidon 1988) compiled by Martin Collcutt, Marius Jansen and Isao Kumakura is in fact a general outline of Japanese history superbly illustrated with colour photographs and some maps.

Richard Perren's *Japanese Studies from pre-history to 1990: A bibliographical guide* (Manchester University Press 1992) lists and briefly evaluates virtually every single academic work in English of significance.

Boye de Mente's *Japan Encyclopaedia* (Passport Books 1995) is a useful desk-top companion.

General Accounts

HISTORICAL

Sir Hugh Cortazzi's *The Japanese Achievement* (Sidgwick and Jackson 1990) crisply synthesises recent historical scholarship and is notable for paying much attention to literature and the arts; the glossary and bibliography are especially full.

Sir George Sansom's *Japan: A Short Cultural History* (1931), now available in a 1987 'Cresset Library' paperback edition, is naturally outdated in many particulars and ends with the Edo period but it remains a great pleasure to read. It can be complemented by W.G. Beasley's *The Rise of Modern Japan* (Weidenfeld and Nicolson 1990) which is far more readable than its status as a standard undergraduate text might imply.

Conrad Totman's *Japan before Perry: A Short History* (California University Press 1981) covers the same ground as Sansom.

Janet Hunter's *The Emergence of Modern Japan: An Introductory History Since 1853* (Longman 1989) offers an unusual perspective by tackling its subject-matter thematically, with separate chapters on urbanisation, women, religion, the military etc.

Oliver Statler's *Japanese Inn* (Random House 1961 and many subsequent paperback editions – Pyramid, Picador etc.) is a charming, informal evocation of Japan from the 1590s to the 1950s as told through the comings and goings at a *ryokan* on the Tokaido.

Sir Sidney Giffard's *Japan Among the Powers 1890–1990* (Yale University Press 1994) is a concise and elegant survey by a former British ambassador.

Showa: The Japan of Hirohito edited by Carol R. Gluck and Stephen R. Graubard (W.W. Norton 1992) is a wide-ranging survey of the years 1926–89.

CONTEMPORARY

Ardath W.Burks' *Japan: A Postindustrial Power* (Westview Press 3rd ed 1991) is concise and contains much historical background, as does Edwin O. Reischauer's rather longer *The Japanese Today* (Belknap/Harvard 1988). Roger Buckley's *Japan Today* (Cambridge University Press 2nd ed. 1990) is also concise. Louis D. Hayes' *Introduction to Japanese Politics* (Paragon House 1992) is broader than its title suggests. Thomas Crump's acclaimed *The Death of an Emperor* (Oxford University Press 1991) likewise goes far beyond its point of departure. Peter Tasker's *Inside Japan: Wealth, Work and Power in the new Japanese Empire* (Penguin 1989) is a fast-paced account by an English banker. Ezra Vogel's *Japan as No. 1: Lessons for America* (Tuttle 1980) argues that Japan's low-crime, high-productivity society is worth looking at with care; it was a bestseller – in Japan.

Intercultural Studies

Sir George Sansom's pioneer work *The Western World and Japan: A Study in the Interaction of European and Asiatic Cultures* (Knopf 1950) remains a classic. *Japan versus the West* (Penguin 1991) by Endymion Wilkinson, an EC official, reviews current frictions in the light of four centuries of encounters. Marie Conte-Helm's *Japan and the North-East of England: From 1862 to the Present Day* (Athlone Press 1989) is an unusually enlightening case-study. *The United States and Japan* (Knopf 3rd ed. 1981) is the work of an eminently qualified author, Edwin O. Reischauer, former US Ambassador to Japan. Not to be outdone Mrs Haru Matsukata Reischauer has produced a fascinating dual biography of her two grandfathers, one of whom was a Meiji-period official, the other a pioneer of the silk trade with America – *Samurai and Silk: A Japanese and American Heritage* (Tuttle 1987).

Aspects of Society and Lifestyles

Paul Meredith Smith's *Nihonsense* (The Japan Times 1987) offers a hundred short, good-humoured essays on such puzzling phenomena as why the Japanese have strawberry sandwiches, still use the abacus, salute trains, fingerprint foreign residents and wear panties in bed.

Jo Eastwood's *100% Japanese* (The Japan Times 1989) covers much the same ground statistically (viz. 79.4 per cent of housewives say they take their neighbours gifts when they are sick; 93 per cent of men who go to public baths like to sit in the corner nearest the door). The fact that the book was an instant bestseller in Japan itself says much about Japanese anxieties to conform to social norms. (N.B. 96.5 per cent of Japanese pay their parking fines.) Cherry Kittredge's *Womansword* (Kodansha 1987) explores the female perspective through the idioms used by and about women.

Market researcher George Fields' droll observations on Japanese consumerism have been published as *From Bonsai to Levis* (Macmillan 1983) and *Gucci on the Ginza: Japan's New Consumer Generation* (Kodansha 1988). Joseph J. Tobin's *Re-Made in Japan: Everyday Life and Consumer Taste in a Changing Society* (Yale University Press 1992) offers a dozen case-studies of such phenomena as shopping, restaurants, drinking, baths and Disneyland.

American anthropologist, Ruth Benedict, originally wrote *The Chrysanthemum and the Sword: Patterns of Japanese Culture* (Secker & Warburg 1947) as a guide for the Occupation authorities and without the benefit of ever actually having visited Japan; it emphasises radical paradoxes in Japanese behaviour, posits the existence of a 'non-principled' 'situational ethic' and remains a classic study, reprinted many times. Doi Takeo's *The Anatomy of Dependence* (Kodansha 1973) is a psychiatrist's interpretation of the origins of Japanese 'groupism', while Nakane Chie's *Japanese Society* (Penguin 1973) emphasises the 'verticality' of relationships Joy Hendry's *Understanding Japanese Society* (Croom Helm 1987) synthesises much recent analysis, while her *Becoming Japanese: The World of the Pre-School Child* (Manchester University Press 1986) is a non-technical account based on her own involvement in a playgroup while doing field-work in Japan. The same author's *Wrapping Culture: Politeness, Presentation and Power in Japan and Other Societies* (Oxford University Press 1993) argues that architecture, language and society itself in Japan can be better understood in terms of 'packaging'.

Nicholas Bornoff's *Pink Samurai: An Erotic Exploration of Japanese Society* (Grafton 1992) focuses on the sex industry. Ian Buruma's *A Japanese Mirror: Heroes and Villains of Japanese Culture* (Penguin 1986) combines erudition and wit to relate sexual archetypes to long-term cultural trends and their representation in literature, drama and cinema. R. P. Dore's *Shinohata: A Portrait of a Japanese Village* (Pantheon 1978) offers sociology without jargon. Dr Junichi Saga's prize-winning *Memories of Silk and Straw: A Self-Portrait of Small-Town Japan* (Kodansha 1990) is based on recorded interviews. O-Young Lee's *The Compact Culture* (Kodansha 1984) explores the significance of miniaturisation in traditional culture and modern industry.

Ann Waswo's *Modern Japanese Society 1868–1994* (Oxford University Press 1996) is a helpful synthesis of modern scholarly research.

On specific Japanese cultural phenomena see:

Rand Castile, *The Way of Tea* (Weatherhill 1979)

Peter Grilli and Dana Levy, *Furo: The Japanese Bath* (Kodansha 1985)

Hiroshi Kondo, *Sake: A Drinker's Guide* (Kodansha 1984)

Jill Lidell, *The Story of the Kimono* (E.P.Dutton 1989)

Omae Kinjiro and Tachibana Yuzuru, *The Book of Sushi* (Kodansha 1982)
Donald Richie, *The Japanese Movie* (Kodansha revised ed.1982)
F.L.Schodt, *Manga Manga: The World of Japanese Comics* (Kodansha 1983)
L.Sharnoff, *Grand Sumo: The Living Sport and Tradition* (Weatherhill 1989)

Places and Encounters

Paul Waley's *Tokyo: City of Stories* (Weatherhill 1991) uncovers some of the
hidden depths of the nation's capital. Edward Seidensticker's *Low City: High
City* (Knopf 1983) covers the rapid development of Tokyo from 1867 to 1923;
the same author's *Tokyo Rising* (Knopf 1990) continues the story. Philip Ward's
Japanese Capitals (Oleander Press 1985) is a guide to the major sights of Tokyo,
Kyoto and Nara. Lesley Downer's *On the Narrow Road to the Deep North*
(Sceptre 1990) retraces the famous literary odyssey of the *haiku* poet Basho.
(Alan Booth's *The Roads to Sata*) recounts an even more ambitious trek, from
one end of Japan to the other. Lisa Martineau's *Caught in a Mirror, Reflections of
Japan* (Macmillan 1993) mixes travelogue, history and shrewd observation.
    Other personal accounts include:
Fosco Maraini, *Meeting with Japan* (Hutchinson 1959)
Pearl S.Buck, *The People of Japan* (Robert Hale 1966)
George Mikes, *Land of the Rising Yen* (André Deutsch 1970)
Charles A.Fisher, *Three Times a Guest* (Cassell 1979)
John David Morley, *Pictures from the Water Trade* (André Deutsch 1985)
David Scott, *Samurai and Cherry Blossom: A Journey to Modern Japan and Along the
Ancient Tokaido* (Century 1987)
Jo Stewart Smith, *In the Shadow of Fuji-san: Japan and its Wildlife* (Viking/
Rainbird 1987)
    Anyone attempting to go beyond the confines of a conducted tour would be
well-advised to read Boye De Mente's *Japan Made Easy: All You Need to Know to
Enjoy Japan* (Passport Books 1990) which is a mine of information and sensible
advice on the practicalities of travel, eating and sightseeing. Helmut Morsbach's
pocket-sized *Simple Etiquette in Japan* (Paul Norbury Publications 1984) should
prove a prudent investment for the uninitiated. For greater depth consult
Donald Richie's *A Taste of Japan: Customs and Etiquette* (Kodansha 1985).
Coping with Japan (Basil Blackwell 1985) by John Randle and Mariko Watanabe
is full of useful information and advice for those intending to settle; readers are
advised to acquire the most recent edition.

Arts and Crafts

Joan Stanley Baker's *Japanese Art* (Thames & Hudson 1984) and Hugo Munsterberg's *The Arts of Japan: An Illustrated History* (Tuttle 1973) provide concise

overviews. John Reeve's *Living Arts of Japan* (British Museum Publications 1990) is a user-friendly, beautifully-illustrated and surprisingly inexpensive introduction. Siegfried Wichmann's *Japonisme* (Thames & Hudson 1981) explores in depth the impact of Japanese art on the West. On specific aspects see the 31-volume *Heibonsha Survey of Japanese Art* published by Weatherhill.

Biographies of specific figures in the arts include:

Henry Scott Stokes, *The Life and Death of Yukio Mishima* (Tuttle 1975)

Kurosawa Akira, *Something Like an Autobiography* (Knopf 1982)

Bernard Leach, *Hamada, Potter* (Kodansha 1975)

Barbara Adachi's *The Living Treasures of Japan* (Kodansha 1973) illustrates the talents of master-craftsmen in action.

On specific crafts see:

Timothy Barrett, *Japanese Papermaking* (Weatherhill 1983)

Raymond Bushell, *The Inro Handbook* (Weatherhill 1979)

W.H.Coaldrake, *The Way of the Carpenter* (Weatherhill 1990)

Sukey Hughes, *Washi: The World of Japanese Paper* (Kodansha 1978)

Lorraine Kuck, *The World of the Japanese Garden* (Weatherhill 1968)

Seike Kiyosi, *The Art of Japanese Joinery* (Weatherhill 1977)

Business

The prolific Boye De Mente's *How to do Business with the Japanese: A Complete Guide to Japanese Customs and Business Practices* (NTC Business Books 1989) pretty well lives up to its ambitious title. *The Economist Business Traveller's Guide: Japan* (The Economist Publications 2nd ed. 1991) offers terse, self-confident summaries of the business landscape plus advice on specific hotels, restaurants, travel arrangements and other practicalities; it is essential to have the most recent edition. For an off-beat overview see Ishinomari Shotaro's *Japan Inc. (The Comic Book): An Introduction to Japanese Economics*, published by Japan's equivalent of the *Wall Street Journal* (Nihon Keizai Shimbun Inc. 1988). James V. Reilly's *Everything You Ever Wanted to Know about Business Otsukiai: A Guide to Japanese Business Protocol* (NTT Mediascope 1990) deals with the subtle ins and outs of introductions, networking, gifts, entertaining etc. Mitsubishi Corporation's bilingual *Japanese Business Glossary* (Toyo-Keizai-Shinposha) comes in two handy, pocket-size volumes. Robert M. March's *The Honourable Customer: Marketing and Selling to the Japanese in the 1990s* (Pitman 1990) is a systematic analysis based on the author's wide reading and practical experience.

Classic studies of business organisation include *Kaisha: The Japanese Corporation* by James C. Abegglen and George Stalk (Harper & Row 1986), Rodney Clark's *The Japanese Company* (Yale University Press 1979) and R. P. Dore's intriguing comparative case-study of the electrical goods industry *British Factory: Japanese Factory* (Allen & Unwin 1973). Chalmers Johnson's *MITI and the Japanese Miracle: The Growth of Industrial Policy 1925–75* (Tuttle 1986) is a definitive study of the allegedly all-powerful Ministry of International Trade and Industry. *The Development of Japanese Business 1600–1973* by J. Hirschmeier and T. Yui (Allen & Unwin 1979) is a lengthy synthesis of academic researches. R. S. Milward's *Japan: The Past in the Present* (Paul Norbury Publications 1979) is an attempt to summarise the historical background much more concisely for the benefit of businessmen. For futurology see F. L. Schodt's *Inside the Robot Kingdom: Japan, Mechatronics and the Coming Robotopia* (Kodansha 1988). *The New Masters: Can the West Match Japan?* (Business Books Ltd 1991) by Phillip Oppenheim MP is an attempt at an overview embracing both past and present, with a discussion of policy options for business and government.

Ito Takatoshi's *The Japanese Economy* (MIT Press 1992) is a comprehensive university textbook description. Katayama Osamu's *Japanese Business into the 21st Century: Strategies for Success* (The Athlone Press 1996) presents corporate case studies drawn from different sectors of the economy.

EARLY HISTORY (CHAPTERS 1, 2 AND 3)

Ancient Japan (Phaidon 1977) by J.E.Kidder and *The Heian Civilization of Japan* (Phaidon 1983) by Rose Hempel offer well-illustrated general surveys. Ivan Morris' *The World of the Shining Prince* (Penguin l964) is a fascinating account of life at the Heian court. Oliver Statler's *Japanese Pilgrimage* (Tuttle l984) is remarkable study of the sage Kukai (Kobo Daishi), his enduring appeal and the phenomenon of pilgrimage.

THE WARRIOR AGE (CHAPTER 4)

Louis Frederic's *Daily Life at the time of the Samurai 1185–1603* (Tuttle 1973) is a broad general treatment. Stephen Turnbull's *Samurai Warriors* (Blandford Press 1987) and *The Samurai: A Military History* (George Philip l987) offer meticulously-illustrated, detailed accounts of battles and personalities by an expert enthusiast. For broader treatments see Richard Storry's *The Way of the Samurai* (Putnam l978) and Shimizu Yoshiaki's *Japan: The Shaping of Daimyo Culture 1185–1868* (George Braziller Inc.1989).

THE CHRISTIAN CENTURY (CHAPTER 5)

Charles Boxer's classic *The Christian Century in Japan* (Cambridge University Press 1951) remains a pleasure to read but has been superseded by Derek Massarella's *A World Elsewhere: Europe's Encounter with Japan in the 16th & 17th centuries* (Yale University Press 1990).

Michael Cooper's *They Came to Japan: An Anthology of European Reports on Japan 1543–1640* (California University Press 1981) is a cabinet of delights. *Rodrigues the Interpreter* (Weatherhill 1974), by the same author, is a biography of a leading Jesuit.

The true story behind Clavell's *Shogun* is revealed in A. L. Sadler's biography

The Maker of Modern Japan: The Life of Shogun Tokugawa Ieyasu (first published in 1937, republished by Tuttle 1978) and Richard Tames' biography of William Adams, *Servant of the Shogun* (Paul Norbury Publications 1981/St Martin's Press 1983).

THE EDO PERIOD (CHAPTER 6)

Charles Dunn's *Everyday Life in Traditional Japan* (Batsford 1969) is a lively general account. Stephen and Ethel Longstreet's *Yoshiwara: The Pleasure Quarters of Old Tokyo* (Yenbooks 1988) focuses on the 'floating world'. R. P. Dore's *Education in Tokugawa Japan* (Athlone Press 1981) explains much more than the title suggests, as does Donald Keene's *World Within Walls* (Grove Press 1978) which is a general survey of the literature of the period. The same author has also written major works on *Bunraku: The Art of the Japanese Puppet Theatre* (Kodansha 1965), *Major plays of Chikamatsu* (Columbia University Press 1964) and *Rangaku – The Japanese Discovery of Europe* (Kegan Paul 1952). There are dozens of books on woodblock prints and the work of individual artists; *The Floating World* (Random House 1954) by the novelist James Michener is a popular account which relates the art to its historical background, as does Hugo Munsterberg's *The Japanese Print: A Historical Guide* (Weatherhill 1982).

THE MEIJI PERIOD (CHAPTER 7)

Two delightful books by Pat Barr recount from contemporary sources the tribulations of Westerners during the Meiji period: *The Coming of the Barbarians* (Macmillan 1967) which covers the period 1853–70, and *The Deer Cry Pavilion* (Macmillan 1968) which covers 1868–1905. Jean Pierre Lehmann's *The Image of Japan: From Feudal Isolation to World Power 1850–1905* (Allen & Unwin 1978) analyses Western reactions to Japanese modernisation.

Sir Hugh Cortazzi's anthology *Victorians in Japan* (Athlone Press 1987) focuses on the treaty ports. The *yatoi* phenomenon is analysed in Hazel Jones' *Live Machines: Hired Foreigners and Meiji Japan* (Paul Norbury Publications 1980). Richard Tames' *Encounters with Japan* (Alan Sutton 1991) offers an anecdotal account based on the writings and experiences of British and American visitors, lavishly illustrated with contemporary photographs. Robert A. Rosenstone's *Mirror in the Shrine: American Encounters with Meiji Japan* (Harvard University Press 1988) focuses more narrowly on the experiences of W. E. Griffis, E. S. Morse and Lafcadio Hearn.

For biographies of individuals see:
Pat Barr, *A Curious Life for a Lady: the story of Isabella Bird* (Macmillan 1970)
Carmen Blacker, *The Japanese Enlightenment: A Study of the Writings of Fukuzawa Yukichi* (Cambridge University Press 1964)
Hugh Cortazzi, *Dr Willis in Japan 1862–1877: British Medical Pioneer* (Athlone Press 1985)

Hugh Cortazzi & George Webb, *Kipling's Japan: Collected Writings* (Athlone Press 1988)

L. K. Herbert-Gustar and P. A. Nott, *John Milne, Father of Modern Seismology* (Paul Norbury Publications 1980)

Victoria Manthorpe (ed.), *The Japan Diaries of Richard Gordon Smith* (Viking/Rainbird 1986)

Kenneth Strong, *Ox Against the Storm: Tanaka Shozo, Japan's Pioneer Conservationist* (Paul Norbury Publications 1977)

EMPIRE AND WAR (CHAPTER 8)

W.G.Beasley's *Japanese Imperialism 1894–1945* (Oxford University Press 1987) offers a judicious summation. Richard Storry's *The Double Patriots* (Greenwood Press 1973) is the classic study of ultra-nationalist extremism. Stephen Howarth's *Morning Glory* (Hamish Hamilton 1983) is a history of the Imperial Japanese navy. *Fifty Years of Light and Dark – The Hirohito Era*, published by the *Mainichi Daily News* in 1975, and the more recent *Hirohito and his Times* (Kodansha 1990) by Kawahara Toshiaki have much interest for a western reader in offering a Japanese perspective on events. The same can be said for Akira Iriye's *The Origins of the Second World War in Asia and the Pacific* (Longman 1987), the same author's *Power and Culture: The Japanese-American War 1941–5* (Princeton University Press 1981), and the Pacific War Research Society's *Japan's Longest Day* (Kodansha 1968) which chronicles the ending of the war. Robert J. C. Butow's *Tojo and the Coming of the War* (Stanford University Press 1961) examines the role of a crucial personality. John Toland's *The Rising Sun: The Decline and Fall of the Japanese Empire 1936–45* (Random House 1970) and John Costello's *The Pacific War* (Rawson,Wade 1982) offer broad general accounts. The most recent review of the era and its aftermath is *Emperor Hirohito and Showa Japan: A Political Biography* (Routledge 1993) by Stephen S. Large. W. J. Macpherson's *The Economic Development of Japan ca 1868–1941* (Macmillan 1987) presents a highly-compressed account of the modernisation of the economy.

THE POST-WAR ERA (CHAPTERS 9 AND 10)

Nippon, New Superpower: Japan Since 1945 (BBC 1990) is a well-paced overview jointly authored by William Horsley and Roger Buckley, the BBC's former Tokyo correspondent and a lecturer at International Christian University.

John Hersey's classic, first-hand reportage *Hiroshima* is available in reprint (Penguin 1986). Theodore Cohen's *Remaking Japan: The American Occupation as New Deal* (Free Press 1987) is written by the man who drafted the post-war code of industrial relations. R. P. Dore's *Land Reform in Japan* (Athlone Press 1984) analyses the impact of change in the countryside. John Dower's biography *Empire and Aftermath: Yoshida Shigeru and the Japanese Experience 1878–1954* (Harvard University Press 1979) illuminates the role of a crucial personality.

Yoshida's memoirs are available in an edition published by Greenwood Press (1973). Hirano Kyoko's *Mr Smith Goes to Tokyo: Japanese Cinema under the American Occupation 1945–52* (Smithsonian Institution Press 1993) has wider implications than its title might at first sight suggest.

Toyoda Eiji's *Toyota – Fifty Years in Motion* (Kodansha 1987) is a celebratory history of the world's second largest motor manufacturer. Kamata Satoshi's *Japan in the Passing Lane* (Unwin Paperbacks 1984) is an exposé of the harsher side of the automobile industry. For a more up-beat view of Japanese industry see *Made in Japan* (Weatherhill 1987), the autobiography of Morita Akio, the founder of Sony Corporation. Shunsuke Tsurumi's *A Cultural History of Postwar Japan 1945–80* (Kegan Paul International 1987) is less comprehensive than its title suggests, offering case-studies of such essentially ephemeral phenomena as comic books, popular songs, guidebooks and vaudeville artists. Dutch journalist Karel van Wolferen's *The Enigma of Japanese Power* (Macmillan 1989) has attracted comment and acclaim with its provocative (and extensively documented) argument that basically no one is in charge of the country. Brian Reading's *Japan: The Coming Collapse* (Weidenfeld & Nicolson 1992) is a prolific economist's apocalyptic vision of the near-future. Tsuru Shigeto's *Japan's Capitalism: Creative Defeat and Beyond* (Cambridge University Press 1993) is a crisp survey of the post-war Japanese economy.

Regions of Japan

Convention, based on a combination of geography and history, divides Japan into eight regions which have been used since 1905 as basic units for description and comparison. From north to south they are:

Hokkaido

Japan's northernmost island accounts for 22 per cent of the nation's land area but only 5 per cent of the population. Hokkaido constitutes a single prefecture with Sapporo as its capital. Only formally part of Japan since 1868, it is relatively underpopulated and still heavily forested. Major economic activities include agriculture (especially dairying), fishing, paper and pulp, beer and tourism (based on skiing, the Ainu, Noboribetsu hot springs and Japan's largest National Park). Major cities: Sapporo, Hakodate, Kushiro.

Tohoku

The northernmost six prefectures of the main island, Honshu-Aomori, Akita, Iwate, Yamagata, Miyagi and Fukushima. Historically the snowy climate has made this a poor, backward region (*Michinoku* – the end of the road) until the development of cold-resistant strains of rice a century ago. Now it produces a quarter of Japan's rice and 70 per cent of its apples. Fishing, horse-breeding and handicrafts are also important. With almost 18 per cent of the national territory, Tohoku still holds less than 9 per cent of the population. Major cities: Sendai, Akita, Morioka, Aomori, Hachinohe, Fukushima, Yamagata.

Kanto

This region, consisting of Japan's largest plain and the mountains to its north-west, comprises the prefectures of Ibaraki, Tochigi, Gunma, Saitama, Chiba, Kanagawa and Tokyo. Here some 30 per cent of the population are crowded into less than 9 per cent of the national territory. All major industries (except

258

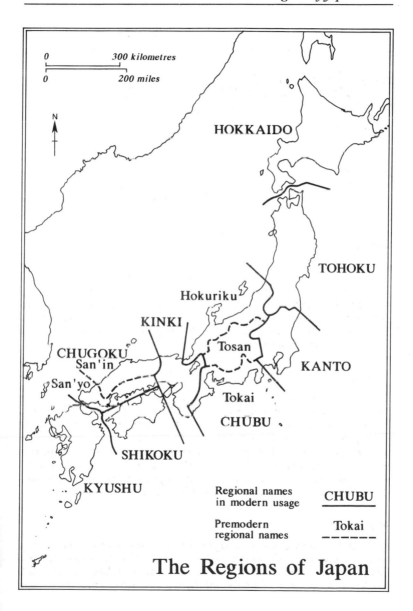

The Regions of Japan

textiles) are important here but so also are farming and fishing. Major cities: Tokyo, Yokohama, Kawasaki, Chiba, Hachioji, Ichikawa, Funabashi, Urawa, Omiya.

Chubu

The nation's crossroads comprises nine prefectures: Shizuoka, Yamanashi, Nagano, Niigata, Toyama, Ishikawa, Fukui, Gifu and Aichi. Seventeen per cent of the population live on just over 17 per cent of the land area. Sprawling across the 'waist' of Honshu, the region is conventionally divided into a southern, Pacific half (Tokai), centred on the Nobi plain, and a cooler, northern Japan Sea half (Hokuriku), separated by a ridge of central highlands rising to over 3,000 metres. Rice and lumber are major products but Shizuoka specialises in tea, mandarins and eels and Yamanashi in grapes. Major industries include textiles (Nagoya), oil-refining (Yokkaichi), vehicles (Toyota), musical instruments (Yamaha at Hamamatsu) and precision machinery (Suwa). Major cities: Nagoya, Hamamatsu, Shizuoka, Gifu, Shimizu, Yokkaichi, Toyota, Niigata.

Kinki

The cradle of Japanese civilisation is home to Kyoto, Osaka and Kobe and Lake Biwa, Japan's largest lake. The region consists of the prefectures of Mie, Shiga, Kyoto, Nara, Osaka, Hyogo and Wakayama. Here 18 per cent of the population live on less than 9 per cent of the land. The Osaka–Kobe sprawl (Hanshin) is Japan's second largest industrial complex but fishing and farming (tea, oranges) are also important. Major cities: Osaka, Kyoto, Kobe, Sakai, Amagasaki, Himeji.

Chugoku

Mountainous Chugoku, comprising the prefectures of Tottori, Okayama, Shimane, Hiroshima and Yamaguchi, has just over 8 per cent of the land and 6 per cent of the population. Divided by a massive mountain ridge it falls, like Chubu, into a northern (San'in) half (noted for sand dunes) and a southern half (San'yo). Fishing, farming (rice, peaches and pears) and traditional handicrafts are still important, though the pollution of the Inland Sea by chemical plants has diminished the fishing catch. Major cities: Hiroshima, Shimonoseki, Fukuyama, Okayama, Kurashiki, Kure.

Shikoku

The smallest of the four major islands is divided into the prefectures of Ehime, Kochi, Tokushima and Kagawa, each representing an ancient feudal domain.

Here under 4 per cent of the population live on 5 per cent of the national territory. Major economic activities include fishing and the production of chemicals, paper and vegetables. Major cities: Kochi, Tokushima, Matsuyama, Takamatsu.

Kyushu

Half the size of Hokkaido, the island of Kyushu has just under 12 per cent of Japan's land area and just over 12 per cent of its population. It is divided into the prefectures of Fukuoka, Oita, Saga, Nagasaki, Kumamoto, Miyazaki and Kagoshima. The mild climate favours a diversified economy, with fishing, farming (sweet potatoes, tobacco, oranges, wheat, rice, dairying), tourism (Beppu hot springs), crafts and modern industry (coal, steel, rubber, ships, semi-conductors) all well represented. Major cities: Kita-Kyushu, Fukuoka, Nagasaki, Oita, Sasebo, Kurume, Kagoshima, Miyazaki.

Historical Gazetteer

Aizu-Wakamatsu This castle-town of the Matsudaira clan, renowned for such traditional industries as sake-brewing and lacquerware, was badly burned in the fighting which accompanied the Meiji Restoration (*see p. 114ff*) but narrow winding streets and mud-walled warehouses still recall the past. Byakkotai Memorial Museum recounts the story of the civil war, while Aizu Buke-Yashiki chronicles the city's history and includes reconstructions of samurai houses. Tsurugajo Castle, destroyed in 1874, was restored in 1965. Nearby Kitakata has over 2,000 traditional mud-walled houses.

Aomori An art museum celebrates the creativity of a local man, the modern print artist Munakata Shiko (*see p. 151*).

Atami Atami literally means 'Hot Sea' and this major spa resort is perched on the remains of a volcano which half collapsed into the ocean. At nearby Ito a memorial and shrine are dedicated to the memory of William Adams (*see p. 78*) and his shipbuilding efforts. There is also a valedictory poem to read by Edmund

Blunden, sculpted on stone.

Beppu This hot-spring resort relies on its 'hell ponds' of boiling mud and 3,795 hot springs to draw 13,000,000 visitors a year. The timorous may prefer the imposing Meiji-period Takegawara public baths. Beppu's Great Buddha (1927) has been called 'the most unpleasant large statue in the world'. For a more uplifting sculptural experience go to Usa, to the north, where Tokoji temple has a 'Grove of 500 Disciples of Buddha' (Gohyaku Rakan), each statue bearing a different expression.

Chiba The reconstructed castle houses a museum detailing the city's life. The nearby Kasori Shellmound Site and museum chronicles the secrets of an important prehistoric settlement.

Echigo-Yuzawa A hot spring (*onsen*) resort for 800 years, this was the setting for *Snow Country*, the most famous novel of Nobel prize-winner Kawabata Yasunari (1899–1972).

Fukuoka Nowadays a sprawling (99 square miles) industrial city which has absorbed (1889) the ancient port of Hakata (famed for its distinctive pottery dolls) where, in Higashi Park, a monument records the attempted Mongol invasions (*see p. 55*). Important local shrines include Hakozaki Hachiman (923); Sumiyoshi (dedicated to the god of seamen); and Temmangen (established 950, oldest buildings from 1590) at Dazaifu, 9 miles south, the ancient capital of Kyushu. There are also the temples of Shofuku (1195 – considered the oldest Zen temple in Japan), Kinryu and Kanzeon. The remains of Fukuoka castle (1601) can be seen in Ohori Koen park. Fukuoka may have been the site of the disputed kingdom of Yamatai (*see p. 14*).

Hakodate The city takes its name (Box Castle) from the fifteenth-century stronghold of the Kono clan. It was designated as a coaling station for foreign ships in 1855 and in 1859 became one of the first five ports opened for trade. The chief historical attraction of this gateway to Hokkaido is a star-shaped fortress called Goryokaku; built in 1864, it was Japan's first western-style fortification.

Hakone A famous hot-spring resort, set in a National Park. The Old Hakone Check-Point (established in 1619, replica built 1965) recalls the elaborate security arrangements involved in 'alternate attendance' at the shogun's court during the Edo period (*see p. 89*). The local shrine, founded in 757, is designated an 'Important Cultural Property' and an avenue of 420 cryptomerias planted in 1618 to shade this section of the Tokaido highway (*see p. 98*) is protected as a 'Natural Treasure'. It is also possible to see surviving sections of this historic route, laid out in 1619

and stone-paved in 1862. Overlooking Lake Ashi is the Hakone Detached Palace, built as a villa for the Imperial household in 1887; the gardens have been open to the public since 1946. Soun-ji was established as a family temple for the Hojo clan in 1521; the picture of 'The Dragon and the Tiger' painted on the sliding doors of the main sanctuary is scheduled as an 'Important Cultural Property'. Five generations of Hojos rest in a family mausoleum in the district.

Hamamatsu City The donjon reared by Ieyasu was restored in 1958. In the mountains to the north is Ryotan-ji temple, famed for its Edo-period garden.

Hiraizumi Modelled on Kyoto, this town was closely associated with the Fujiwara (*see p. 35*). At the Chuson-ji temple, built in 1109, is found the fabulous Konjikido, a mausoleum, covered in pure gold, where three mummified Fujiwara lie. The garden of the nearby ruined Motsu-ji temple (founded 850) is a good example of the 'paradise style' favoured in the Heian period.

Hiroshima Hiroshima (Broad Island) is the home of the Mazda, Japan's third largest car manufacturer, and of Kirin beer, one of the nation's four big brands. The events of 6 August 1945 are recorded in detail in a 'Peace Memorial Museum'. The city is now twice as large as it was then. There is a restored castle (1593 and 1958) and Shukkeien garden, first laid out by tea-master Ueda Munetsutsu in 1620.

Ise Shinto's most important shrine

complex (*see p. 29*) is set in a National Park. The distance between the Outer (Geku) and Inner (Naiku) Shrines is 6 kilometres. The Inner Shrine houses the sacred mirror which is one of the three sacred imperial treasures.

Itsukushima Shrine Located on sacred Miyajima island, which is officially designated as both a 'Special Historic Site' and 'Special Place of Scenic Beauty', the shrine complex juts out into the sea, appearing to float at high tide. Until 1868 neither births nor deaths were allowed to 'pollute' the island; burials are still forbidden

Joetsu City Takada Park's 3,000 cherry trees make it one of the nation's three most famed sites for blossom-viewing in the spring; the moats of the former castle of the Matsudaira clan are also clearly visible. To the north of the city stand the ruins of Kasugayama castle, the stronghold of sixteenth-century warlord Uesugi Kenshin. Records and belongings of the Uesugi can be seen at Kasugayama shrine and the nearby Rinsenji temple.

Kagoshima Japan's contact with the West began with Portuguese castaways on the off-shore island of Tanegashima (*see pp. 74–5*). In 1863 this capital of the Shimazu clan was bombarded by the British navy (*see p. 120*). In 1877 it was the base for the Satsuma rebellion (*see p. 123*). During the Second World War it was a kamikaze base. Nanshu Shrine in Shiroyama Park is the last resting-place of Saigo Takamori (*see p. 123*) and 2,023 of his comrades in arms; a nearby museum records his stormy

life. At the bottom of Shiroyama hill the Terukuni shrine memorialises Nariakira Shimazu (d. 1858), lord of Satsuma and pioneer of that Japanese national obsession – photography. The Shoko Shuseikan museum holds a portrait of the man himself, Japan's earliest photograph (1857); another picture shows eight samurai prior to their departure for study in London in 1865 (*see p. 120*). St Francis Xavier's Memorial church was built in 1949 to mark the 400th anniversary of his landfall. Nearby tranquil Chiran is a peaceful Edo-period village with period homes, six of which open their gardens to visitors; ironically it was the last HQ of the kamikaze and has a museum which exhibits the last letters they wrote to their families.

Kamakura This ancient seat of shogunal government (*see Chapter 4*) is an hour's train ride from Tokyo. Part commuter-town, part resort, it attracts tourists and Tokyoites alike. The most famous sights are the 122-ton, 11.4 m. Daibutsu and the Tsurugaoka Hachimangu shrine (founded 1191; present building 1828), which holds displays of *yabusame* (archery from horseback) every September.

Engaku-ji temple, ranked second of the Five Great Zen Temples (*see p. 67*), has a Hall of Holy Relics of Buddha which, dating from 1282, is the oldest Chinese-style building in Japan. Kencho-ji, the foremost of the Five, has the city's second oldest bell (1255) and a fine sandalwood statue of the Hojo regent who founded the temple in 1253.

Hase Kannon temple is the oldest; its 9.3-metre image of the Goddess of

Mercy, the tallest wooden statue in Japan, is believed to have been carved in 721. Tokei-ji temple, founded in 1285, was a traditional place of refuge for battered wives in feudal times; three years residence brought auto-matic divorce. It is surrounded by hundreds of small statues of Jizo, the guardian deity of children.

Kanazawa A peaceful castle town whose Kenrokuen Park (1822) is rated as one of the three most beau-tiful in Japan. The *Noh* (*see p. 67*) theatre is nationally renowned. The local five-colour glazed *kutani* pottery is displayed in the municipal Art Museum. Oyama shrine, built by a Dutchman in 1875, has unusual Western touches, such as stained-glass.

Kobe This hilly port developed rapidly in the Meiji period, now has the world's largest container-handling capacity and is building the world's largest artificial island. It suffered a devastating earthquake in 1995. The Kitanocho district still has many for-mer foreign residences. The lasting impact of foreign influences can be seen in the fact that Kobe is famed for its fine beef, had Japan's first golf course and has its only sizeable Indian community as well as a 'Chinatown'. The Kobe City museum appro-priately includes a special collection of *namban* art (*see p. 75*). More tradi-tionally historical attractions include the Minatogawa shrine, dedicated to Kusunoki Masashige (*see p. 64*) and the Kanteibyo temple, long revered by Chinese residents. Kobe is the home of Japan's confectionery industry and in mid-August hosts the

All Japan High School Baseball Tournament, possibly the most emotion-laden event in the national sporting calendar.

At Nada to the east of the city can be seen old sake breweries and museums devoted to the history of brewing. Nearby Arima is Japan's oldest hot-spring resort.

The coastal resort of Takarazuka is the home of the ultra-glamorous all-female Takarazaka Revue, founded in 1914 to provide wholesome entertainment to women and chil-dren from genteel families. Along the coast, at Himeji, the castle (1581–1624 and known as Hakuro Jo - White Egret) is rated as one of the most beautiful in Japan. Unlike most modern reconstructions which are of ferro-concrete, Himeji has been carefully restored using original materials. Its labyrinthine fortifica-tions have been much admired by military engineers for their ingenuity. Many of the scenes for Clavell's *Sho-gun* (*see p. 79*) were shot here. Inspired perhaps by the name of its castle the city is twinned with Phoe-nix, Arizona.

Kumamoto The castle (restored 1960) was the focus of a ferocious siege during the Satsuma rebellion of 1877 (*see p. 123*) and now houses a fine military museum. Seventeenth-century Suizen-ji park reproduces in miniature all the surviving landscape features of the Tokaido highway, including Mt Fuji.

Kurashiki Almost the only town on the Inland Sea to have survived war-time bombing. The old merchant's quarter still has tile-roofed houses, black brick granaries and willow-fringed canals. There is a folkcraft museum and a pottery museum with works by Hamada Shoji (*see p. 151*).

Kyonamachi A fine modern museum celebrates the achievements of this town's most famous son, the print artist Moronobu (*see p. 96*)

Kyoto The treasures of the ancient capital are too numerous even to list comprehensively. Among the most important are:

Byodo-in: Buddhist temple built in 1053 (*see pp. 43–5*).

Chion-in temple: one of the largest in Japan and headquarters of the Jodo sect (*see pp. 42–3*); founded in 1234, the present buildings date from 1619–41; it has a statue of the founder, Honen (*see p. 42*), carved by himself.

Chishakuin temple: garden by Sen-no-Rikyu.

Daitoku-ji temple: a Chinese-style complex of temples and 22 affiliated monasteries, built between the fourteenth and seventeenth centuries; Zen architecture and gardens on the grand scale by master-landscaper Kobori Enshu; of particular importance are the Daisen-in ('Zen Temple Without Equal') with Kano School panel-paintings and richly symbolic gardens, the Juko-in monastery, last resting-place of Sen-no-Rikyu (*see p. 81*), and the Zuiho-in monastery, founded by Zen warlord Ohtomo Sorin who converted to Christianity and sent the first Japanese mission to Europe (*see p. 77*).

Ginkakuji (Silver Pavilion): the elegant retreat of Ashikaga shogun Yoshimasa, built in 1489; it was never actually covered in silver-leaf as ori-ginally intended; garden designed by Soami.

Gion: the entertainment district; *kabuki* (*see pp. 108–10*) is featured at Minamiza theatre; Gion Corner offers a crash-course in traditional arts which compresses demonstrations of tea-ceremony, *ikebana*, *bunraku* (*see pp. 107–8*), *kyogen* (*see p. 68*) and dance into a single hour.

Heian Jingu (shrine): a scaled-down reproduction (1895) of the Heian period (794) original.

Higashi-Honganji temple: the largest wooden structure in the city (founded 1602; present buildings 1895).

Imperial Palace: this particular incarnation dates from 1855 and is where the enthronement of emperors takes place; foreign visitors (with passports) are admitted to twice-daily tours (10 a.m./2 p.m.), normally taking priority before Japanese.

Jakko-in temple: burial place of Empress Dowager Kenrei-mon-in who became a nun here (1185) after the drowning of her son Antoku (*see p. 51*).

Katsura Imperial villa: a master-piece of understated elegance, considered one of the greatest masterpieces of traditional Japanese architecture. The interior wall panels were decorated by masters of the Kano school (*see p. 100*). The villa and gardens were designed by Kobori Enshu at the behest of Hideyoshi (*see p. 71*); the artist stipulated that there should be no interference from his patron and no limit on the time or budget available to him. Hideyoshi died without ever seeing it.

Kinkakuji (Golden Pavilion): probably the single most photographed building in Kyoto, built in 1394, rebuilt 1955 (*see p. 65*).

Kitano Temmangu shrine: founded 947 in honour of the persecuted scholar Michizane Sugawara (*see p. 36*).

Kiyomizu temple: a wonder of woodwork, clinging to a mountainside, with panoramic views over the city; founded 798, with present buildings dating from 1633, it is approached up a steep slope, lined with souvenir shops, which nineteenth-century tourists dubbed 'Teapot Lane'.

Koryu-ji temple: founded in 622 for Prince Shotoku (*see p. 18*); its lecture hall (1165) is the second oldest building in Kyoto; its modern Reihokan museum houses an outstanding collection of medieval sculptures.

Kyoto National Museum: superb collection of sculptures and paintings, e.g. landscapes by Sesshu (*see p. 67*).

Mount Hiei: site of Enryaku-ji temple, founded in 788 (*see p. 38*) and set in a deep cedar forest; the present buildings date from the seventeenth century.

Museum of Traditional Industry: displays and demonstrations of the luxury crafts for which the city is famed – textiles, porcelain, lacquerware, fan-making etc.

Nanzen-ji temple: originally an imperial palace, this became the headquarters of the Rinzai sect (*see pp. 59, 67*) in 1293; the 'Leaping Tiger Garden' is by Kobori Enshu and the Shohojo ('Superior's Quarters') has a screen painting of the same subject by Kano Tanyu (*see p. 101*) ; the 30-metre Sammon gate (1628) gives a fine view of Mt Hiei.

Nijo Castle: built for the Tokugawa shoguns after 1603. Its unusual features include an elaborate Chinese gateway and a squeaking 'nightingale floor', designed to give warning of unwanted intruders.

Nishi-Honganji: one of the finest examples of Buddhist architecture in Kyoto; founded in 1272 and moved to its present site in 1591; a leading centre of the Jodo sect (*see pp. 42–3*); the buildings incorporate many splendid fittings and Kano school paintings from Hideyoshi's Fushimi castle (dismantled 1632).

Nishijin Textile Centre: displays and demonstrations of traditional silk-weaving, a speciality of this fashion-conscious city.

Ryoan-ji: Zen temple famed for its walled garden of raked sand and 15 rocks, designed by Soami in 1473.

Saiho-ji temple: famed for its moss garden (*see p. 59*).

Sanjusangendo ('Hall of Thirty-Three Bays'): founded in 1164 and rebuilt in 1266, this temple has 1,001 gilded wooden statues of Kannon, Goddess of Mercy; the main image was carved by the master Tankei (*see p. 62*) when he was 82. A traditional archery contest is held here annually.

Sanzenin temple: famed for its maple leaves in November.

Shimogamo shrine: famed for the Hollyhock festival, it long predates the city itself.

Shinsen-en garden: one of the

city's oldest, it originally surrounded a Heian palace.

Shisendo temple: renowned for its tiny but exquisite garden.

Shokoku-ji: founded in 1392; one of the Five Great Temples.

Shoren-in temple: traditional residence of the abbots of the Tendai sect (*see p. 37*); founded in 1194, the present buildings date from 1895. The garden, designed by Soami and Enshu Kobori, is considered one of Kyoto's finest.

Shugakuin Imperial Villa: seventeenth-century three-villa retreat for an ex-emperor, set in Kyoto's largest garden.

Tenryu-ji temple: one of the Great Five Zen Temples of Kyoto; medieval garden and nineteenth-century buildings.

Toei Uzumasa Movie Land: cinema sets of houses and streets used in making feudal-period films by Japan's biggest studio; complemented by a history of the Japanese film industry.

Tofuku-ji temple: Zen architecture and a variety of famed gardens.

Toji temple: founded 796; has a five-storey pagoda (rebuilt 1644), the tallest in Japan (184 feet).

Yasaka shrine: features one of the tallest entrance arches (*torii*) in Japan, built in 1666.

Yuzen Cultural Hall: displays and demonstrations relating to dyed silks.

Mashiko   A pottery town, home of twentieth-century master Hamada Shoji (*see p. 151*).

Matsue   Matsue has a castle and the Lafcadio Hearn Memorial Museum

(*see p. 137*). Nearby Izumo Taisha shrine is one of the oldest in Japan and dedicated to the god of marriage; over seventy festivals are held there throughout the year.

Matsumoto   The donjon of Matsumoto castle, built by the Ishikawa clan between 1592 and 1614, is the oldest surviving example in Japan. The Folklore Museum just outside the castle walls has major collections of dolls and clocks. Matsumoto's unusual historical survivals include the nation's oldest wooden courthouse (now a police museum) and two Meiji period schoolhouses. There are also museums of prehistoric archaeology, *mingei* (*see p. 150*) and *ukiyo-e* (*see p. 95*).

Gofuku-ji, a Shingon (*see p. 38*) temple, has a fine setting on Mount Hachibuse and houses eight precious ancient statues.

Genkoji is a Jodo (*see p. 42*) temple, surrounded by peonies. Tsukama Jinja shrine has buildings dating from the Edo period.

Matsushima   This scenic bay, dotted with over 250 islets, has for centuries been regarded as one of the three most beautiful places in Japan. The Zuiganji temple dates back to 828, though the present buildings date from 1609.

Matsuyama   Shikoku's largest city has a well-preserved castle.

Miyazaki   Miyazaki has a collection of *haniwa* (*see p. 12*) housed in a garden.

Mount Fuji   Rising 3,776 metres (12,388 feet) high, the nation's sacred volcano last erupted in 1707. It is open to climbers from 1 July to 31

August and 400,000 make the ascent each year. Tradition decrees the costume of pilgrimage – all-white dress and the wearing of straw sandals over one's climbing shoes. (Until 1868 women were not allowed on the mountain.) Most climbers now come by bus from Tokyo to the fifth of the ten stations which punctuate the north face route (there are five others); from there the ascent to the summit takes 5–9 hours, the descent 3–5.

Mount Kiyosumiyama Kiyosumi-dera temple (also known as Seicho-ji) stands near the summit and is where Nichiren (*see p. 57*) entered the Buddhist priesthood in 1233. Down below, on the coast of Chiba prefecture, is where he was born at Tai-no-Ura beach; Tanjo-ji temple was founded there in 1276 to mark the fact. The red sea bream found offshore were long held to contain his spirit and were considered sacred; they are now protected as a 'Special Natural Monument'.

Mount Koya The Shingon monastery founded here in 816 by Kukai (*see p. 39*) now consists of 120 temples, over fifty of which offer lodgings and (vegetarian) food to a million visitors each year.

Mount Nokogiriyama Nihonji temple is home to the largest Buddha in Japan, a stone monster 31 metres high; 1,533 figures of his disciples are ranged on the surrounding mountainside.

Nagasaki The Monument of the 26 Christian martyrs (*see p. 78*) attracts many pilgrims. In 1615 Christians were boiled alive in the nearby

Unzen springs. Oura Catholic church, built in Gothic style, is Japan's oldest wooden church.

The island of Dejima, where Dutch traders were once confined (*see p. 80*) is now part of the mainland. A museum has relics of the community and Hollander Slope has some houses of Dutch residents of a later period.

Kofuku-ji temple was built in the Ming style in 1620 to serve local Chinese merchants. In 1634 the abbot built stone double-arched Meganebashi bridge, the oldest of its kind in Japan.

Sofuku-ji temple (1629) is another example of Ming architecture.

The Glover Mansion is the century-old residence of a British arms-dealer; the owner's liaison with a local Japanese girl may have indirectly inspired Puccini's *Madame Butterfly* which is set against the background of the port.

A modest Peace Park marks the epicentre of the atomic bombing of 9 August 1945. (It was actually aimed at the Mitsubishi shipyard, now the largest privately-owned yard in the world.) A single arch of the old Urakami Catholic church, the only structure to survive the full force of the blast, provides a fitting complement to the memorial statues.

Nagoya Japan's fourth largest city grew up around a castle, burned down in the war. A reproduction stands on its site.

The Tokugawa Art Museum houses some 10,000 art objects associated with the most illustrious dynasty of shoguns (*see Chapter 6*).

Atsuta shrine, rebuilt in 1935, ranks

second only to Ise in the hierarchy of Shinto and houses one of the three legendary articles of the imperial regalia, the 'Grass–Mowing Sword' (*see p. 14*).

Nearby Inuyama boasts Japan's oldest extant fortress.

Meiji Mura is an outdoor museum featuring fifty western–style buildings constructed since Meiji times, including the lobby of Frank Lloyd Wright's famed Imperial Hotel.

Naha The capital of Okinawa is home to the Naminoue shrine, dedicated to the heavenly ancestors of the Imperial family, and Sogen–ji temple, mausoleum of the local royal dynasty. There is also a park filled with monuments commemorating the 200,000 casualties of 1945 (*see p. 164*), including hundreds of school-children who died in mass–suicides. Naha was the setting for *Tea House of the August Moon*, starring Marlon Brando, a gentle Hollywood satire on the naivety of the American Occupation (*see Chapter 9*).

Nara The city's most famed attractions are the eighth–century Daibutsu (*see p. 23*) and the even older Horyu–ji complex (*see p. 23*) of forty-five temple buildings, which includes the oldest of all, a five-storied pagoda (607). The Nara National Museum contains a comprehensive collection of Buddhist art of all periods.

Chugu–ji temple: contains a frag-ment of the oldest embroidery in Japan.

Kasuga Grand Shrine, founded in 768, is one of the 'Three Great Shinto Shrines of Japan'. Its vermilion-lac-quered buildings (rebuilt 57 times) are hung with 1,000 metal lanterns and the surrounding gardens have 1,800 more stone ones.

Kofuku–ji temple: founded in 710; once there were 175 buildings here; of the six that survive, four are National Treasures.

Todai–ji temple: has been one of Japan's most important temples ever since its foundation in the eighth-century. It houses the Daibutsu (last repaired 1692) in the largest wooden hall in the world (rebuilt 1709) and the Shoso–in treasure house (*see p. 24*). The great Nandaimon gate is flanked by guardian deities carved by Unkei and Tankei (*see p. 62*).

Toshodai–ji temple: founded in 759 by the blind Chinese priest Ganjin.

Yakushi–ji temple: founded in 680, with an exquisite pagoda (730).

Narita North-west of Tokyo's new international airport can be found the Fudoki-no-Oka museum which preserves over a hundred 1,300-year-old *kofun* (burial mounds) (*see p. 12*) as well as old farmhouses and other protected buildings. The nearby Boso-no-Mura museum recreates the lifestyle of 200 years ago.

The castle town of Sakura, to the west of Narita, houses Japan's first private hospital, built in 1843, and, perhaps surprisingly, the superb National Museum of Japanese His-tory, which presents 70,000 exhibits, grouped in 13 historical and 6 folk-loric themes.

At Shibayama, south of Narita, is a museum devoted to *haniwa* (*see p. 12*) and the Shibayama Nioson temple. Appropriately near to Narita itself is the Museum of Aeronautical Sciences.

Nikko The exuberantly-decorated Toshogu shrine (1634–6) mixes Shinto and Buddhist elements and houses the mausoleum of Tokugawa Ieyasu (*see p. 74*). It is approached through an avenue of 13,000 cedars planted three centuries ago (originally there were 40,000). The work employed 15,000 of the nation's top craftsmen and absorbed 2,489,000 sheets of gold-leaf. The most striking single feature is the fantastically carved and embellished Yomeimon Gate.

The nearby Futarasan shrine is even older, dating from 1617. Near that is found the Daiyuin mausoleum, housing the remains of shogun Iemitsu (*see p. 80*).

Okayama Eighteenth-century Korakuen garden is one of the three most famous in Japan.

Osaka The commercial heart of the nation is birthplace of such business empires as Marubeni, Sanwa, Daiwa and Sumitomo and of two of the nation's three major newspapers – the *Asahi Shimbun* and *Mainichi Shimbun*. It is also the home of Japanese pharmaceuticals and the leading centre of biotechnology research. Almost half of Japan's exports pass through Osaka.

The city is criss-crossed by canals and dominated by a reproduction (1931) of the core of the great castle built by Hideyoshi in 1586. The museum inside the castle documents the history of his family (*see p. 71*).

In Nakanoshima Park stands Temmangu shrine, allegedly founded in 949 and dedicated to Michizane Sugawara (*see p. 36*).

Hidden away in the Sonezaki amusement district is the Ohatsu Tenjin shrine, the setting for Chikamatsu's famous drama about double-suicide (*see p. 108*).

The Dotombori entertainment area focuses on a canal completed in 1615; *bunraku* (*see p. 107*) can still be seen here, where it was born, at Asahiza theatre.

At Nakanoshima, the city's administrative centre, are grouped a library, bank and public hall dating from the Meiji and Taisho eras.

A mint founded in 1871 can be seen at Sakuranomiya; a nearby museum illustrates the history of Japan's coinage.

Shitenno-ji temple, founded in 593, is claimed to be the oldest in Japan, though the actual buildings have been reconstructed many times. On 22 April, the anniversary of the death of Shotoku Taishi (*see p. 18*), ancient court dances (*bugaku*) are performed here in his honour.

Sumiyoshi Taisha shrine claims an even more ancient foundation – in the early third century by Empress Jingu – but its present structure dates from 1808–10; it is designated as a National Treasure.

Osaka's 30,000 factories produce a quarter of Japan's manufacturing output; many visitors therefore take an Industrial Tour.

Sado Island Japan's largest offshore island (857 sq kms/331 sq mi) was once a major centre of goldmining; museums recreate the history of the industry and art of refining.

At Ogi Japan's last surviving traditional sailing vessel, *Saiwai Maru*, is housed.

The Myosen-ji temple is dedicated to Nichiren (*see p. 57*) while the Chokoku-ji, founded in 807 by Kukai (*see p. 39*), possesses three images of eleven-faced Kannon ranked as National Treasures.

Sapporo The Clock Tower Building (1878) houses a museum illustrating the settlement and development of Hokkaido (*see p. 141*). The Historical Museum also records pioneering days. The Batchelor Museum in the Botanical gardens records the career of a lifelong friend of the Ainu (*see p. 137*).

Throughout Hokkaido western visitors are struck by the 'Mid-West' style barns built under the influence of Meiji-period American agricultural advisers. But it was a German who founded the local brewing industry; locals will inform you with pride that Sapporo lies on the same latitude as Munich and Milwaukee. A local man, who married a Scottish girl, founded the Nikka (Japan's No.2 brand) whisky distillery here because he thought Hokkaido the part of Japan most closely resembling Scotland.

Maruyama Primeval Forest is a designated National Treasure.

Sendai The largest city in Tohoku (northern Honshu) was the stronghold of the Date clan, whose power is attested by the site of ruined Aobajo castle (1602) and the recently reconstructed Zuihoden Hall, their sixteenth-century mausoleum. The black-lacquered Osaki Hachiman shrine is a designated National Treasure.

Shimabara The castle records the tragic Christian rising of 1638 (*see p. 81*).

Shimoda At Ryosen-ji temple Perry (*see p. 117*) negotiated Japan's first modern treaty. Townsend Harris, the first permanent American diplomat in Japan, resided in Gyokusen-ji temple, which contains mementoes of him and the graves of some of Perry's sailors.

Shiraoi This former Ainu village is now a living museum devoted to illustrating Ainu lifestyles, rituals and handicrafts.

Shizuoka The Kunozan Toshogu shrine built in 1617 by shogun Hidetada commands a fine view of Suruga Bay and is designated an Important Cultural Property.

Nearby Toro is the site of a 2,000-year-old village uncovered in 1943 and under excavation ever since.

Shuzenji The ninth-century temple is especially associated with the Minamoto (*see p. 50*).

Takada This resort, one of the snowiest cities in Niigata Prefecture, is the birth-place of Japanese skiing, introduced by an Austrian army officer in 1911.

Takamatsu This port on Shikoku island features the beautiful Ritsurin Park, laid out 350 years ago on the site of a villa owned by the Matsudaira clan. Nearby Yashima was the scene of a famous confrontation in the Heike wars (*see p. 50*).

Takayama This remote old castle-town, famed for its carpenters, is known as 'little Kyoto' because in one two-mile esplanade (Higa-shiyama Teramachi) it offers the visitor no less than five shrines and thirteen temples. There are also two preserved Edo-period merchant houses open to visitors. It also has the unique Takayama Jinya (Historic Government House), the 'mini-palace' and headquarters of the local administration of the Kanamori clan; it was first built in 1615 and reconstructed in 1816.

The Hida Minzoku-Mura Folklore Village preserves thirty examples of the traditional farm houses and buildings of the area.

The Hida Kokubun-ji temple was originally founded by Emperor Shomu (*see p. 23*) in 746 but the oldest surviving part now dates from the sixteenth century; next to the 3-storied pagoda (1821) stands a gingko tree reputed to be 1,200 years old.

The Shoren-ji temple, overlooking the town, was moved to its present site in 1960; its Main Hall (1504) is said to have been made from a single cedar.

There are also specialist museums devoted to lacquer-ware, *inro*, traditional toys and the local 'lion dance'.

Toba This port is famed for the 'Wedded Rocks', a pair of islets linked by a sacred rope. Mikimoto Pearl Island celebrates the dogged career of Mikimoto Kokichi (1858–1954) who succeeded in 1892 in perfecting a technique for inducing oysters to create artificial pearls.

Tokyo Paul Waley's *Tokyo Now and Then: An Explorer's Guide* (Weatherhill 1984) is a large and learned guidebook, good on the historical background.

Jean Pearce's *Footloose in Tokyo* (Weatherhill 1990) is a compact introduction based on the 29 stops of the circular Yamanote subway line. To a first-time visitor the sheer size of the capital can be overwhelming. Orientation can be assisted by appreciating the special character and major features of particular districts:

Marunouchi: the central business area to the west of the main station, itself an imposing Meiji-period red-brick structure of historic interest as one of the few buildings to survive both the 1923 earthquake and the 1945 bombing; the Industrial Bank of Japan (1974 by Togo Murano) is an elegant contrast to the mundane office-blocks around it.

Hibiya: Tokyo's 'Broadway', featuring many theatres; also a major park.

Yurakucho, Roppongi, Akasaka are amusement areas.

Ginza: exclusive shopping and the Kabuki-za theatre (*see p. 108*); the moated Imperial Palace (reconstructed 1968) is nearby; the Tsukiji Central Wholesale Market (fish, meat, vegetables) is to the south.

Kasumigaseki: government area dominated by ministries and the National Diet Building.

Ueno: centred on the city's biggest park (planned by Le Corbusier) which contains numerous museums, including the National Museum of Western Art (also designed by Le Corbusier) ; another, the Shitamachi, recreates a typical street scene of the area before the 1923 earthquake; there is also a suitably massive statue of Saigo Takamori (*see p. 123*).

Asakusa: a maze of small streets focusing on the Asakusa-Kannon (Senso-ji) temple.

Shinjuku: Japan's largest station, handling 3,600,000 passengers a day; a dozen skyscrapers up to sixty storeys high (spectacular view from Sumitomo HQ building's 51st-floor observation deck); huge underground shopping arcade.

Shibuya, Harajuku, Aoyama: trendy shopping; the Meiji shrine (reconstructed 1958) (*see p. 145*), the headquarters of NHK (Japan's BBC) and the Japan Folkcrafts Museum, housing the work of Soetsu Yanagi (*see p. 150*) are nearby.

Important parks and gardens in the capital include Hama Rikyu and Shinjuku Gyoen, both of which belonged to the Imperial family; the East Garden of the Imperial Palace, laid out 300 years ago around the original donjon of Edo castle (*see p. 84*); Kiyosumi garden, laid out in 1878 by Baron Iwasaki, founder of the Mitsubishi business empire (*see p. 130*); the Koishikawa Korakuen, laid out by the Tokugawa shoguns in the seventeenth century; Rikugien, an eighteenth-century walled garden; and Yoyogi park, which houses Kenzo Tange's spectacular 1964 Olympic stadium.

The Tokyo National Museum contains the best collection of Japanese art in the world. Adjacent stands a separate gallery of treasures from Horyuji (*see p. 23*). There are specialised museums devoted to swords, paper, salt and tobacco and a folk crafts collection housed in the former home of Yanagi Soetsu (*see p. 105*).

Other significant historic sites include:

Sengaku-ji temple: devoted to the memory of the 47 Ronin (*see p. 105*).

Yasukuni ('Peaceful Country') shrine: although only dating from 1869 this is a classic example of Shinto architecture; it commemorates the war dead and is famed for its cherry trees.

Zojo-ji temple: the red laquer gates date from 1605; the rare black Buddha inside once belonged to Tokugawa Ieyasu (*see p. 73*).

At Tokyo's Disneyland (1983) 'Tomorrowland' includes a 'Meet the World' audio-visual feature chronicling Japan's friendlier contacts with foreign countries throughout history. **Yamaguchi** Sesshu (*see p. 67*) laid out a garden here in the fifteenth century. In 1952 a Xavier Memorial Cathedral was built here in honour of the missionary saint.

Yokohama A fishing village until the 1850s and now the nation's second most populous city. The Club, Japan's second modern hotel, was opened in 1869. There are a number of Meiji-period buildings, a lively Chinatown (Chukagai) and specialist museums devoted to dolls, silk and the foreign community.

The 1930s liner *Hikawa Maru* is permanently moored in the harbour.

The Sankeien gardens, laid out by a Meiji-period silk merchant, contain a tea-house and a villa which once belonged to the Tokugawa.

The Yamate-machi area was the Westerners' favoured residential district and known to them as 'the Bluff': some of their houses, schools and

churches survive. In the International
Cemetery lie the bodies of Edmund
Morell (d. 1871), engineer of the
Tokyo–Yokohama railway *(see p. 129)* and Charles Wirgman (d. 1891),
artist-correspondent for the *Illustrated London News* and founder of the
satirical *Japan Punch*.

Glossary

Bakufu 'tent government' – administration of a shogun
Bonsai 'tray planting' – art of growing miniature trees
Bunraku puppet drama
Burakumin 'village people' – traditional outcast group
Bushi warrior
Bushido warrior's moral code
Byobu folding screens
Chanoyu 'hot water for tea' – tea ceremony
Chonin city people
Daimyo 'great name' – provincial feudal lord
Emakimono scroll to be unrolled horizontally
Eta impolite traditional term for *burakumin*
Fudai 'inner' lords, trusted adherents of the Tokugawa regime
Fumie Christian image made to be ritually despised to prove non- allegiance
   to the faith
Furusato home village
Fusuma sliding doors
Gagaku 'elegant music' – ceremonial music of the imperial court
Gaijin 'outside person' – a foreigner
Geisha 'accomplished person' – traditional female entertainer
Genro elder statesman
Go Kenin minor samurai bureaucrat
Haiku traditional verse-form of 17 syllables
Hamon crystalline pattern on a sword-blade serving as the maker's 'signature'
Han feudal domain of Edo period
Haniwa 'rings of clay' – tomb figurines of 4th–7th centuries
Harakiri 'belly-slitting' – vulgar term for *seppuku*
Hatamoto 'bannerman' – middle-ranking samurai
Hinin 'non-human' – outcasts of the Edo period
Ikebana art of traditional flower-arranging
Inro 'seal basket' – small, often highly decorated, box

Joruri   chanted narrative
Kabuki   Edo-period popular drama
Kakemono   vertical hanging scroll
Kakiemon   a type of glazed, enamelled porcelain
Kami   Shinto deity
Kamikaze   'divine wind' – typhoons which wrecked thirteenth-century
   Mongol invasion fleets; suicide pilots of World War II
Kana   phonetic scripts
Kanji   Chinese characters
Kendo   'way of the sword' – fencing
Koan   riddle used to assist Zen meditation
Kodo-ha   'Imperial Way' military faction
Kofun   4th–7th century burial mound
Koi   type of pedigree carp
Koku   measure of rice needed to feed an adult for a year
Kokugaku   'national learning' focused on ancient myths and poetry
Kokusaika   internationalisation
Kokutai   national 'essence' or 'structure' invoked as the basis of social solidarity
   during the militarist period
Kugai   pollution
Kuge   court nobles
Kyogen   'mad words' – comic interlude in *Noh* drama
Mingei   folk-crafts
Mugi Cha   barley tea
Naginata   halberd-type weapon, often used by women
Namban   'southern barbarian' – term used to describe Westerners in the
   sixteenth century; also screens depicting Westerners
Nembutsu   invocation of the name of Buddha
Netsuke   intricately carved toggle
Nihonga   painting in traditional Japanese style
Nihonjinron   writings about Japanese identity
Nirvana   Buddhist state of non-being
Noh   masked dance-drama
Obi   broad sash worn with kimono
Oiran   courtesans
Rangaku   'Dutch learning' – western studies
Renga   linked verse-form popularised in Muromachi period
Ronin   masterless samurai
Ryokan   traditional inn
Sakoku   'closed country' policy
Samurai   'one who serves' – a feudal retainer
Sankin kotai   'alternate attendance' at shogun's court required of *daimyo*
Satori   enlightenment in Zen Buddhism

Senryu   humorous short verse-form
Seppuku   ritual suicide by self-disembowelment
Shikken   regent
Shinjinrui   'new human race'; trend-conscious young adults
Shogun   'great general' – military dictator
Shunto   industrial relations 'spring offensive'
Soroban   traditional Japanese abacus
Sutra   text of Buddhist scripture
Tanka   31-syllable verse-form
Tatami   straw matting used as floor-covering
Tenno   'heavenly sovereign' – the Emperor
Tozama   'outer' *daimyo*, excluded from power in Edo period
Ukiyo-e   pictures of the 'floating world'
Yamabushi   wandering holy man
Yatoi   foreign employee
Yoga   painting in the western style
Yugen   term used to describe the beauty, mystery and profundity of *Noh* drama
Yukata   light cotton kimono-type robe
Zaibatsu   financial-industrial conglomerate of pre-war period
Zazen   deep meditation

Index

A TRAVELLER'S HISTORY OF GREECE

Timothy Boatswain and Colin Nicolson

The many facets of Greece are presented in this unique book.

In *A Traveller's History of Greece*, the reader is provided with an authoritative general history of Greece from its earlier beginnings down to the present day. It covers in a clear and comprehensive manner the classical past, the conflict with Persia, the conquest by the Romans, the Byzantine era and the occupation by the Turks; the struggle for Independence and the turbulence of recent years, right up to current events.

This history will help the visitor make sense of modern Greece against the background of its diverse heritage. A Gazetteer, cross-referenced with the main text highlights the importance of sites, towns and ancient battlefields. A Chronology details the significant dates and a brief survey of the artistic styles of each period is given. Illustrated with maps and line drawings *A Traveller's History of Greece* is an invaluable companion for your holiday.

A TRAVELLER'S HISTORY OF ITALY

Valerio Lintner

"Ideal before-you-go reading" **The Daily Telegraph**

In *A Traveller's History of Italy* the author analyses the development of the Italian people from pre-historic times right through to the imaginative, resourceful and fiercely independent Italians we know today.

All of the major periods of Italian history are dealt with, including the Etruscans, the Romans, the communes and the city states which spawned the glories of the Renaissance. In more modern times, Unification and the development and degeneration of the Liberal state into Fascism are covered, as well as the rise of Italy to the position it currently enjoys as a leading member of the European Community.

The Gazetteer, which is cross-referenced to the main text, highlights sites, towns, churches and cathedrals of historical importance for the visitor.

A TRAVELLER'S HISTORY OF SPAIN

SECOND EDITION
Juan Lalaguna

"General yet detailed . . . giving an insight into historical background. Very readable . . . many people would profit from putting contemporary Europe into context in this way and A-Level students will find these excellent for background study"

Books in Schools

Spain's vibrant and colourful past is as exciting to discover as is taking a fresh look at the tumultuous upheavals of the twentieth century. *A Traveller's History of Spain* will unlock the secrets of the country, its people and culture for the interested traveller.

Juan Lalaguna takes you on a journey from the earliest settlements on the Iberian peninsula, through the influences of the Romans, the Goths and the Muslims, the traumas of expansion and the end of Empire, the surge for national identity – right up to the current dilemmas that face post-Franco Spain.

A Traveller's History of Spain is an essential companion for your trip to Spain.

A TRAVELLER'S HISTORY OF TURKEY

Richard Stoneman

A Traveller's History of Turkey offers a full and accurate portrait of the region from Prehistory right up to the present day. Particular emphasis is given to those aspects of history which have left their mark in the sites and monuments that are still visible today.

Modern Turkey is the creation of the present century, but at least seven ancient civilisations had their homes in the region. Turkey also formed a significant part of several empires – those of Persia, Rome and Byzantium, before becoming the centre of the opulent Ottoman Empire. All of these great cultures have left their marks on the landscape, architecture and art of Turkey – a place of bewildering facets where East meets West with a flourish.

Richard Stoneman's concise and readable account covers everything including the legendary Flood of Noah, the early civilisation of Çatal Hüyük seven thousand years before Christ, the treasures of Troy, Alexander the Great, the Romans, Selcuks, Byzantines and the Golden Age of the Sultans to the twentieth century's great changes wrought by Kemal Atatürk and the strong position Turkey now holds in the world community.

A TRAVELLER'S HISTORY OF SCOTLAND

Andrew Fisher

A Traveller's History of Scotland begins with Scotland's first people and their culture, which remained uncrushed by the Roman invasions. Before the Vikings in 900 it was a land of romantic kingdoms and saints, gradually overtaken by more pragmatic struggles for power between the great families of Bruce, Balliol and Stewart. Centuries of strife led up to the turbulent years of Mary Queen of Scots, the Calvinistic legacy of Knox, and the bitterness of final defeat.

The dreams of the Jacobites are contrasted with the cruel reality of the end of the Stuarts and the Act of Union with England. Scotland now saw an age of building, industry and despoliation of their land. The result was much emigration and an obsession fostered by Walter Scott and Burns with the nation's past which glorified the legends of the Highlander and the Clans. In this century, a loss of identity and a drift to the south has been followed by a new surge of national pride with higher aspirations for the future.

A Traveller's History of Scotland explains the roots of Scottish history and is an excellent handbook for visitors.

A TRAVELLER'S HISTORY OF IRELAND

Peter Neville

The many thousands of visitors to Ireland are drawn by the landscape, the people and the underlying atmosphere created by its rich heritage.

The story of *A Traveller's History of Ireland* opens with mysterious early Celtic Ireland, where no Roman stood, through St Patrick's mission and the legendary High King Brian Boru. The Normans came in the twelfth century and this period also marks the beginnings of the difficult and tragic Anglo–Irish relationship. Reading the book helps one understand the complexities of the current political situation.

Its appendices include an A–Z Gazetteer, a Chronology of Major Events, an list of Kings and Queens, Prime Ministers and Presidents, Famous Battles, a full Bibliography and Index. There are Historical Maps and line drawings to accompany the text.

A TRAVELLER'S HISTORY OF FRANCE
SECOND EDITION

Robert Cole

"Undoubtedly the best way to prepare for a trip to France is to bone up on some history. The Traveller's History of France by Robert Cole is concise and gives the essential facts in a very readable form" **The Independent on Sunday**

"Hundreds of thousands of travellers, visit France each year. The glories of the French countryside, the essential harmony of much of French architecture, the wealth of historical remains and associations, the enormous variety of experience that France offers, act as a perennial and irresistible attraction. For these visitors this lively and useful guide provides the essential clues to an understanding of France's past, and present, in entertaining and sometimes surprising detail"
From the Preface by the Series Editor, Denis Judd.

In *A Traveller's History of France* the reader is provided with a comprehensive and yet very enjoyable, general history of France, from earliest times to the present day.

An extensive Gazetteer which is cross-referenced with the main text pinpoints the historical importance of sites and towns. Illustrated with maps and line drawings *A Traveller's History of France* will add to the enjoyment of every holidaymaker who likes to do more than lie on a beach.

A TRAVELLER'S HISTORY OF RUSSIA and the USSR

Peter Neville

A Traveller's History of Russia gives a comprehensive survey of that country's past from the earliest times to the era of perestroika and glasnost. The reader first learns about prehistoric Russia and its nomadic invaders, then the story of the city state of Kiev is traced up to the crucial year of 1237 when the Mongol invasion took place. the rise of Muscovy with its colourful panoply of rulers from Ivan Moneybags to Ivan the Terrible, the despotism of the Romanovs and the Russian Revolution are dealt with in depth. The book concludes with an account of the rise of the Soviet state, its world role and current metamorphosis.

There is an A–Z Gazetteer for the visitor which is cross-referenced to the main text and highlights sites, towns and places of historical importance.

Illustrated throughout with maps and line drawings. *A Traveller's History of Russia and the USSR* encapsulates the nation's past and present and is a unique cultural and historical guidebook to that intriguing land.

A TRAVELLER'S HISTORY OF ENGLAND

Christopher Daniell

"This compact volume delivers a solid, comprehensive and entertaining overview of England's history . . . a delightful source." **Library Journal**

Illustrated throughout with maps and line drawings, *A Traveller's History of England* offers an insight into the country's past and present and is an invaluable companion for all those who want to know more about a nation whose impact upon the rest of the world has been profound.

All the major periods of English history are dealt with, including the Roman occupation, and the invasions of the Anglo-Saxons, Vikings and Normans, and the power struggles of the medieval kings. The Reformation, the Renaissance and the Civil War are discussed, as well as the consequences of the Industrial Revolution and urbanism, and the establishment of an Empire which encompassed a quarter of the human race. In this century the Empire has been transformed into the Commonwealth, two victorious, but costly, World Wars have been fought, the Welfare State was established, and membership of the European Economic Community was finally achieved.

A TRAVELLER'S HISTORY OF LONDON

Richard Tames

A full and comprehensive historical background to the capital's past which covers the period from London's first beginnings, right up to the present day – from Londinium and Lundenwic to Docklands' development. London has always been an international city and visitors from all over the world have recorded their impressions and these views have been drawn on extensively throughout this book.

At different points in London's 2000-year history, it has been praised for its elegance and civility and damned for its riots, rudeness, fogs and squalor. Visitors and London's own residents will enjoy discovering more about the city from this fascinating book.

There are special sections on the Cathedrals, Royal Palaces, Parks and Gardens, Railway Termini, The Underground, Bridges, Cemeteries, Museums and Galleries, The London Year as well as a full Chronology of Major Events, Maps and Index.